D1000137

DISCARD

COMMUNITY COLLEGE LIBRARY

00104 9612

Mr. Tubbs' Civil War

Charles Tubbs.
From the collections of Schaffer Library, Union College.

Mr. Tubbs' Civil War

Nat Brandt

OAKTON COMMUNITY COLLEGE
DES PLAINES CAMPUS
1600 EAST GOLF ROAD
DES PLAINES, IL 60016

SYU

Syracuse University Press

Copyright © 1996 Nat Brandt
All Rights Reserved

First Edition 1996

96 97 98 99 00 01   6 5 4 3 2 1

Unless otherwise noted, photographs courtesy of Peter C. Andrews.

The paper used in this publication meets the minimum requirements of American National Standard for Information Sciences—Permanence of Paper for Printed Library Materials, ANSI Z39. 48-1984. ∞

Library of Congress Cataloging-in-Publication Data
Brandt, Nat.
Mr. Tubbs' Civil War / Nat Brandt. — 1st ed.
p.   cm.
Includes bibliographical references (p.   ) and index.
ISBN 0-8156-0391-6 (alk. paper)
1. United States—History—Civil War, 1861–1865—Personal
narratives.   2. Tubbs, Charles, 1843–1913—Correspondence.
E464.B73   1996
973.7'81—dc20   96-21719

Manufactured in the United States of America

To Joan and Peter Andrews

A journalist by profession, Nat Brandt has been a newswriter for CBS News, a reporter on a number of newspapers, an editor on the *New York Times,* managing editor of *American Heritage,* and editor-in-chief of *Publishers Weekly.* Since 1980, Mr. Brandt has been a free-lance writer, chiefly in the area of American history. He is the author of *The Man Who Tried to Burn New York,* winner of the 1987 Douglas Southall Freeman History Award. *The Town That Started the Civil War,* a Book-of-the-Month Club and History Book Club selection; *The Congressman Who Got Away with Murder; Con Brio: Four Russians Called the Budapest String Quartet; Massacre at Shansi;* and *Harlem at War: The Black Experience in WWII.*

Little knew we then the anguish
So soon to shroud our smiling Land
Little thought those friends must languish
Beneath grim war's red dripping hand
Their blood be poured, Oh such libation,
A willing ransom for the nation.

—Leonard Leverne Kimball[1]

Contents

1863

1864

1865

Illustrations

Acknowledgments

This book would not have been possible without the cooperation of Peter Conners Andrews, whose grandfather—John Tuttle Andrews—is the author of three of the letters in the collection on which the book is based. I am grateful for his encouragement and the enthusiasm he shared with me in researching the background of Charles Tubbs and the letter writers.

I am indebted also to Betty Allen, Assistant Archivist, Union College, Schenectady, New York; Laurie McFadden, Director of Special Collections, Alfred University, Alfred, New York; James D. Folts, Head, Research Services, New York State Archives, Albany; and Louise Arnold-Friend, Reference Historian, Historical Reference Branch, U.S. Army Military History Institute, Carlisle Barracks, Pennsylvania. Scott P. Gitchell, Director of Research, Tioga County Historical Society, Wellsboro, Pennsylvania, not only was helpful in the research dealing with Wellsboro, Osceola, and the county, but also generously vetted the parts of the book dealing with them and the Tubbs family. Miriam B. Kahn of MBK Consulting, Columbus, Ohio, performed an invaluable role in helping to research the military careers and lives of the letter writers.

As usual, my wife Yanna was instrumental in turning my manuscript into a readable book. Her constant—and efficacious—admonition is, "Remember, you're telling a story."

Introduction

Charles Tubbs experienced the Civil War vicariously. He never volunteered nor was drafted in the Union military forces. But many of his friends went to war, and it was through them that the day-to-day experience of the war came alive for him in the most personal way. Throughout the war, Tubbs received more than 175 letters from his friends, ordinary young men, all products of rural New York and Pennsylvania. Their viewpoint was that of a farmer-, a student-, a teacher-turned-soldier. From what they wrote, and in a way that no newspaper account or official dispatch could describe, Tubbs was able to taste the turmoil of battle, the camaraderie of camp life, and the loneliness of the soldier far from his home.

A descendant of a pioneer Yankee family, Charles grew up in Osceola, Pennsylvania, where the extensive Tubbs family were among the prominent members of that small village. The first Tubbs had moved to Osceola in the Cowanesque Valley after the Revolutionary War.[1] Charles was born on July 11, 1843, to James and Anna Gleason Tubbs. His father was a successful farmer, his mother a descendant of a Massachusetts man who moved to the valley in 1809. A brother, Henry, was born a year and a half later.

Charles was thirteen when he entered Union Academy, a private school situated at Academy Corners in neighboring Deerfield Township. He was a precocious student—a member of its literary society, the Amphictron, and, at sixteen, taught some classes at Union Academy in the nearby little village of Mill Creek. Because of the shortage of trained teachers, it was not unusual for talented students such as Tubbs to obtain teaching positions. Just two years later, when the Civil War broke out and he was three months shy of being eighteen, he briefly replaced a professor at Wellsboro Academy who resigned to join the army. At the time, the *Tioga County Agitator* stated that young Charles was "a gentleman every way qualified for the post."[2]

Charles subsequently entered Alfred University, where his literary leanings, scholastic achievements, and political aspirations quickly led him to his election as president of the Orophilian Lyceum, a prestigious discussion and debating society. All his friends from Alfred who later wrote him about their war experiences were "Brother Oros."

Alfred traced its beginnings to 1836, when it was founded as a religiously oriented private school, and was second only to Oberlin College in Ohio in admitting both male and female students. Like Oberlin, it had been founded by God-fearing, morally strict individuals—in Alfred's case, Seventh Day Baptists—and again like Oberlin, it was purposely isolated from the many distractions of everyday urban life.[3] The school was situated along the gentle slope of a wooded hill above a meandering creek "amid a people of integrity, and of industrious and unobtrusive habits." It was two miles from the nearest Erie Railway depot in the rural Southern Tier section of New York State— actually only some fifty miles of winding backwoods roads from the Tubbs' home in Osceola across the border in Pennsylvania. Even after the school became first a preparatory institute called Alfred Academy in 1839 and then a university in 1857, its strictures remained rigid. There were prohibitions against "Unpermitted association of ladies and gentlemen," "Use of tobacco or intoxicating drinks," "Games of chance, profane or obscene language," and "All disorder and impropriety of conduct."[4] All of which evidently suited the handsome young Charles Tubbs, for he was a martinet and a rigid perfectionist. As one of his friends, John Andrews, wrote, "I am done with excuses for I know full well how you regard them."[5]

Tubbs thrived in the atmosphere and enjoyed the distinction of speaking at commencement exercises in both 1862 and 1863; his topics were "Manifest Destiny" and "Love of Country," respectively. Upon graduation in the latter year, Tubbs matriculated at Union College, in Schenectady, New York, majoring in the classics and participating in the Philomathean literary society. He was graduated with honors during the height of the war in July 1864 and entered law school in Ann Arbor at what was then called Michigan University.

At first glance, it is curious that Tubbs himself never volunteered in what everyone in the North called the War of the Rebellion. There is no question that he was dedicated to the Union cause. Statements that his friends made in their letters to him clearly acknowledge Tubbs' patriotism. "In all our associations, our walks and talks, our thoughts and discussions," wrote Leonard Kimball, "we ever prized *Liberty* above all other treasures. The very winds of Heaven taught the lessons of *Liberty*. These im[m]utable precepts, so early inculcated, now urge me on." Kimball thanked Tubbs for his "manly expressions of devotion to our com[m]on cause."[6]

Tubbs, however, chose to continue his education rather than enlist. There is no evidence that he was a pacifist or in any way incapacitated and ineligible for the draft. Nor is there any evidence that, if drafted, he paid another man to serve in his place—a not unusual practice. Did he doubt his ability to cope with the hardships of a military life? Was he afraid? He never confided what if any reservations or fears he had about military life. However, what is clear is that Tubbs had a passionate interest in learning and teaching as well as a burning political ambition, and for whatever reason, he was unprepared and unwilling to interrupt his education.

Of all his friends, only Tubbs' roommate at Alfred, Orrin Stebbins, questioned his decision not to volunteer. Stebbins was so enraged by the attack on Fort Sumter in April 1861 that he declared, "I live for the Stars and Stripes, *and for them I am ready to die!!!*" He was ready to enlist, Stebbins wrote Tubbs four days after Fort Sumter surrendered, "Will you? We *must* fight; it is no *time for cowards!*"[7] A month later, after enlisting, Stebbins again wrote, "It is my duty, and it is *your* duty to help raise the Stars & Stripes from the dust, and fight beneath its fold until it once more floats."[8]

The emphases were Stebbins', but after hearing from Tubbs, he had a change of heart. He applauded Tubbs' decision to stay at Alfred. What Stebbins now wrote clarifies Tubbs' reason for not enlisting. "I can only Say," Stebbins declared, "go on, you are in the right path, even in these dark and Stormy days. Your life will be worth more in the Senate chamber than on the battle field. On the battle field one crack of a rifle might lay you low and the world would be no wiser for you having be[en] in it, but where you are you are doing Such that will be rept. when the ivy entwines that old Institution."[9]

Similarly, other friends cheered him on. One, David Armstrong, who recalled eating "birch bark" with Tubbs when they were children,[10] said, "I am glad to learn that you are still climbing the hill of secince [sic] and may Continue on and fin[al]ly reach the top."[11]

Like Stebbins, two other Alfred classmates believed it was important that Tubbs continue his schooling. One, William Prentice, was so upset that another friend had fled to Michigan to avoid a draft call that he had "half a mind to write to the Provost Marshall at St Claire to have him ar[r]ested."[12] But Prentice took a different view of Tubbs. He said he thought Tubbs would make "a very good soldier, though I had much rather you would not go with the Army."[13] Prentice insisted, "After we soldiers have done all we *can* the country will not be saved but the struggle will be transfer[r]ed to a new field." "*Then* will come your turn to labor & I should be poorly satisfied with you, ashamed to own you as my friend, if with all . . . your opportunities I thought you were not preparing yourself for the contest."[14]

In a similar vein, John Orr said he believed the "cultivation of the mind" was "the noblest work of man Education prepares him for usefulness. . . . In no previous Age has our Country needed men of such powerful intellect as now." Orr said he believed Tubbs to be a *"true man,* & as such you wield an influence that will tell in the restoration of peace & quiet to our beloved country."[15] Orr was positive that Tubbs would become "one of life[']s *real actors*[.] I know that you are aiming high[.] God speed your efforts[.]"[16]

Andrews, Kimball, Stebbins, Armstrong, Prentice, and Orr were among seventeen friends who throughout their service in the Civil War wrote to Tubbs. As one of them put it, "A good correspondent is a thing to boast of[.]"[17] The men served in various regiments of Union armies representing New York State, Ohio, and Pennsylvania. They participated in some of the most famous battles of the war—among them, Shiloh, Antietam, and Gettysburg. They took part in fighting that included the sieges of Charleston, Fredericksburg, Richmond, Nashville, and Mobile. They were in both Red River campaigns. They protected Washington, guarded Cape Hatteras Lighthouse, and fought outside Atlanta.

Often the soldier's "desk" was his own lap or a rough board. He wrote sheltered in tents battered by wind and rain, by candlelight and by moonlight, with, in the distance, a bugler playing tattoo and the call for lights out or the whistle of a mail boat making him rush to a conclusion. "Did you ever write in a dark closet with half a dozen uneasy fellows jog[g]ing your elbows?" wrote one.[18] "I am writing on the ground all curled up," wrote another.[19] Still another complained, "My hands are so cold now that I can scarcely hold my pen."[20] It is no wonder, then, that the penmanship of Tubbs' soldier friends was sometimes almost impossible to read or, fortunately in rare cases, totally unintelligible.

Almost invariably, a letter writer would begin his letter with a thank-you for receiving a letter from Tubbs or an excuse for not answering one of his letters sooner. Almost invariably as well, the soldier ended his letter with an apology for any mistakes it contained and, almost without exception, with a plea for Tubbs to "write soon" again in reply. The apology was obviously expressed because the letter writer feared that Tubbs, the perfectionist, would easily spot the grammatical and spelling errors. As for the request for a response, it is clear that to a homesick soldier far away from home, Tubbs' letters were an important contact with normal life. "You remember how the bird that sang at the gates cheered the prisoner of Chillon," wrote William Prentice, alluding to a sonnet by Bryon. "Your letters have a similar effect upon me in my present occupation."[21] Asa Spencer said he'd been asked—

no, commanded "from home" by "General Order No 1"—to limit his correspondence only to letters to his family and wife, "But when I come to consider my friend Charles Tubbs . . . I think I am justifiable in this instance of obeying only in part."[22]

Whatever they thought or did and wherever they served, the seventeen young men, in writing Tubbs, voiced their patriotism, described the dreadful scenes of combat, complained about their commanders, yearned for family and friends. Some of them also wondered whether they would survive the war and return home.

This is their story.

The Letter Writers

John Tuttle Andrews, Captain (breveted), Company D, 179th Regiment New York Volunteer Infantry

David Armstrong, Private, Company F, 49th Regiment Ohio Volunteers

Mordecai Casson, Jr., Sergeant, Company C, 2nd Veteran Cavalry, New York Volunteers

William Thomas Humphrey, M.D., Surgeon, 42 Regiment of the line-13th Pennsylvania Reserves (Bucktails)

Harlan Page Kimball, Private, Company I, 103rd Regiment New York Volunteer Infantry

Leonard Leverne Kimball, Private, Company E, 34th Regiment New York Volunteer Infantry

Orville Samuel Kimball, Orderly Sergeant, Company I, 103rd Regiment New York Volunteer Infantry

Henry Reynolds Maxson, Sergeant, Company C, 85th Regiment New York Volunteer Infantry

John Orr, Captain Company F, 107th Regiment New York Volunteer Infantry

William R. Prentice, Captain, Company H, 161st Regiment New York Volunteer Infantry

George Pratt Scudder, 1st Lieutenant, Company F, 45th Regiment Pennsylvania Volunteers

William Edward Self, Private, Company A, 42nd Regiment of the line-13th Pennsylvania Reserves (Bucktails)

Asa Spencer, Private, Company B, 136th Regiment Pennsylvania Volunteers

Orrin Mortimer Stebbins, 1st Sergeant, Company A, 42nd Regiment of the line-13th Pennsylvania Reserves (Bucktails)

Samuel Stevens, Private, Company A, 42nd Regiment of the line-13th Pennsylvania Reserves (Bucktails)

Allen A. Van Orsdale, 2nd Sergeant, Company A, 42nd Regiment of the line-13th Pennsylvania Reserves (Bucktails)

Philip Taylor Vanzile, Private, Battery E, 1st Light Artillery Ohio Volunteers

Author's Note

Some of the letter writers were better educated than others, but even those who had gone to Alfred University were prone to make mistakes. Many of the seventeen shared certain writing habits—of not starting a sentence with a capital letter, of not adding punctuation such as a comma, or of not bothering to end a sentence with a period. In order to save space on precious stationery, which was scarce, more often than not they also failed to indicate paragraphs.

In the letters quoted throughout this book I have followed the style, spelling, and punctuation of the individual letter writer unless the meaning was unclear. In a few cases, I have eliminated a word that was mistakenly repeated, and, for the sake of clarity, I have added, in brackets, a character, a word, a phrase, or punctuation that in haste the author of the letter obviously had intended but omitted. I have also taken the liberty of indenting what would ordinarily be paragraphed, so that material that is quoted is easier on the reader's eye.

Mr. Tubbs' Civil War

Prologue

This a brief sketch, though it may be uninteresting to you, will yet serve to show the kind of life we lead. Itself a splendid Panorama, Green wavy grass, quiet lakes, dark lethsome Bayous bordered with Live Oaks, whose green leaves struggle in rain to look cheerful through their somber burden of moss. Bands of armed men with bristling bayonets waving banners and triumphant music, now moving in peaceful streams, & with regular tread over green fields, where herds of cattle & horses graze unfrighted[,] and anon rushing in apparently confused masses through the thunder of guns[,] smoke of battle, to strew those sam[e] quiet fields with slaughtered men, & lighting incendiery fires in once quiet beautiful Homes seeming as if man was turned loose to strew the universe with wrecks emblematical of his own unbridled passions & ruined goodness. All this we see & hear & feel, unmindful all the time of our assimulation to these tumultous scenes through which we are passing[.] Yet I feel their influence & dread their effect upon my future life.
—William R. Prentice, Bayou Teche, La.[1]

[H]ere I am away, far from friends in a distant land and near the lines of our Country's enemies to do all in our power to crush the vilest and most detestable conclave of national robbers known in The annals of man[.] But I can exclaim of them as Tell of the winds 'Blow on[,] This is The land of Liberty'! and being such I may add she will live.
—Allen A. Van Orsdale, near Darnestown, Md.[2]

The firing all day was constant, sounding like the popping of corn on a very large scale, and closed just after dark with a terrible crackling of musketry and the slow booming of cannon. Old soldiers when they heard it said a charge was being made. It lasted only a few minutes, and then all firing ceased . . . Passing a hospital at the Head quarters of the 5th Corps I saw a pile of legs, arms, hands and feet, and quite a number of bodies lying by a newly dug hole—the "final resting place". It was a hard looking sight, and I hurried on.
—John T. Andrews, near Pegram House, Va.[3]

1

It is discouraging both to soldiers & our friends at home to protract this war so long[.] Do not think I am becoming unpatriotic for I am not. My motto is to continue this war until this rebellion is crushed out: it was for this that I came here & to day I feel proud to know that I am here to assist in redeeming our honor as a <u>nation</u>: to preserve our Government as left us by our forefathers & our glorious old national flag from the ruthless hands of a set of tyrants & traitors.

—John Orr, near Stafford, Va.[4]

I saw sights that made my heart ache: one fellow from Regt—Sergean[t] Ward from Hornellsville with his leg off b[e]llow the knee. He was doing well & he seemed content, another with a leg off above the knee . . . another with an arm off at the shoulder, still another with a bullet wound in the breast & many others I dare say were there who had suffered the same whom I did not see. All seemed cheerfull[,] feeling proud no doubt of the sacrifice they had made[.] As I left these poor fellows I felt more content & encouraged to know that I am where I can share with them the danger of battle & all the trials of the soldiers life[.] I feel very patriotic to night[,] Charles.

—John Orr, near Stafford Court House, Va.[5]

Last Sunday I went with the first funeral procession from this Company. The body was that of a member of the 77' N.Y. Regt who left their sick with our Surgeon. The squad marched with guns reversed, the butt up, under the left arm, marching in slow time to a solemn tune. When arrived at the grave, at the Soldier's Home, we rest on arms while the coffin is lowered in the grave. To rest on arms the muzzle of the gun is placed on the toe of the left foot[,] both hands rest upon the butt[.] Then three rounds are fired over the grave and we march away. Such is the burial of a soldier[.]

—Henry R. Maxson, Camp Warren, D.C.[6]

I do not much expect it that we will ever meet again but if we never do you may know that your old room mate lies sleepin on the battle field.

—Orrin M. Stebbins, Camp Curtin, Pa.[7]

1861

· CHAPTER 1 ·

The Call to Arms

Friend Tubbs . . . There is no use of disguising facts[.]
We have a great work before us[.] It will cost life,
blood & treasure[.] But we shall take it, at all
hazards[.]
　　　　　　　　　　　　　—*Dr. William T. Humphrey*[1]

T here was nothing special about Osceola, except perhaps how and why it acquired its name. In 1851, several years before Osceola broke off and declared its independence from the town of Elkland, a post office was established in the village. It had to have a name, and a debate ensued over what to call it. One settler, a Tubbs relation, had once published some "poetic effusions" in a regional newspaper using the dateline "Pindarville." Other settlers started jocularly referring to the area as Pindarville and now wanted it as the name of the post office. Someone else suggested "Bridgeport," possibly because the state erected a bridge spanning the Cowanesque River in 1849; the new bridge eliminated the need either to contend with the slender foot span that previously crossed the river or to pay the sixpence the ferryman charged for a ride in his dugout. But another resident suggested the name Osceola. Osceola was a renegade Creek Indian who had become a leader of a band of rebellious Seminoles in Florida, outwitting federal troops until he was tricked and captured. In the manner of the day, a public meeting was held and the decision put to a vote. Perhaps because the majority of voters were, almost to a man, abolitionists and Republicans, and the Seminoles had sheltered runaway slaves, the name Osceola won. Years later, when the area residents broke off and declared their independence from the town of Elkland, Osceola became the official name of their new community as well.

Osceola was like so many other sleepy, backwater towns in north-central Pennsylvania. A horse-drawn wagon on its dusty dirt main street took only a matter of minutes to pass by the smattering of rough-

5

hewn wooden homes, general store–cum–post office, and cemetery. Other, more narrow roads fed off its main artery in the direction of a tannery, a blacksmith shop, a grist mill, a sawmill, a sash-and-blind factory, an apple nursery, and the numerous farms in the vicinity. On one dirt byway, Tubbs Road, the white clapboard home of Charles Tubbs' family stood.

The town, occupying some seventy-five hundred acres, was bisected by a river that the Senecas of the Iroquois League had called Cowanesque—"Beautiful Squaw." The Indians knew its valley as a hunting ground. Bears, deer, elk, panthers, otter, wildcats, mink, martin, beaver, and wolves roamed the forest. The settlers who came after the turn of the eighteenth century devoted most of their energies to cutting, hewing, hauling, and sawing the bountiful white and Norway pine, oak, hemlock, and ash. They were also able to grow wheat, corn, oats, barley, potatoes, corn, sorghum, orchard fruits, and tobacco in the fertile valley's alluvial soil.

On the eve of the Civil War, the official population of Osceola stood at 450 men, women, and children. Actually, many more gave Osceola as their place of residence because the village, in the northernmost section of Tioga County, rested on the border with New York State. In that hilly region of the Alleghanies, the boundary between the two states was so difficult to determine that a number of New York residents thought they lived in Osceola.

The community was close-knit, familial, hospitable. One of Charles Tubbs' friends who taught in Osceola before enlisting in the army, expressed it succinctly. He wrote Tubbs nostalgically from Tennessee, "I would give a heap to be in O———[.]"[2]

Despite the fact that most residents of Osceola were antislavery, they tended to ignore the ominous events propelling the nation toward war. By early April 1861, seven states had seceded from the United States and set up their own Confederate States of America with Jefferson Davis as president. The situation threatened both Fort Sumter, off Charleston, South Carolina, and Fort Pickens at Pensacola, Florida, both within Confederate territory. The townspeople, Charles Tubbs later recalled, "believed all the warnings to be Southern bluster and bravado, which would pass away without result, as such idle vaporings had in the past."[3]

One reason that the citizens of Osceola did not pay attention to the warning signs was their isolation. Osceola had no rail link to the outside world. The nearest railroad stations, together with the closest telegraph offices, were twelve miles away—in Lawrenceville to the east, or over the border in Addison, New York. Unless a traveler or a teamster came through and stopped long enough to pass on the news, the town's citizens had to wait for the arrival of the daily stagecoach from Addison. Its crusty driver routinely carried in his mail pouch a day-and-a-half-old copy of the New York *Daily Tribune*.[4] The paper's arrival immediately prompted a gathering of most of the male population at Crandall's store, where the proprietor—or, if he was busy, one of the other men—read the newspaper aloud.

The news that Fort Sumter was fired upon on Friday, April 12, 1861, stunned Osceola's residents and caught them totally unprepared. More than half a century earlier, the state had required that a militia company be established, but the annual May training camp became "a farce" in the late 1840s and none had been held in the past twelve years. The men who were equally adept at wielding axes and guns had all but disappeared.[5]

However, said Tubbs, "the iron hail that rained on Sumter and the President's call for 75,000 men aroused our quiet hamlet." The students at Osceola High School chipped in to purchase the materials that the young women in town then fashioned into an American flag. The youths erected a twenty-foot-tall pole on the cupola of the schoolhouse and, "amid great cheering," the flag was raised. On a Tuesday eleven days after the outbreak of the war, students and residents held a rally in support of the Union, and that same week sixteen volunteers left Osceola in wagons for the rail station in Lawrenceville,[6] prepared to answer Lincoln's call for volunteers. They were to serve three months because most people, including the president, thought the "rebellion" would be quickly squelched.

Among the sixteen who rushed off to volunteer were three men who represented Charles Tubbs' eclectic, and democratic, choice of friends: William Thomas Humphrey, Samuel Stevens, and William Edward Self. The first was a doctor. The other two were barely literate locals; one was a carpenter, the other worked as either a handyman or a farmer.

The doctor, Humphrey, was the oldest of Charles' letter-writing friends to join the army. He was thirty-six years old when he enlisted, his beard already turning gray. Humphrey was a native of Bainbridge, Chenango County, in south-central New York. He left home at eighteen, working first on a farm, then teaching school in Hornellsville. The next year, Humphrey began the study of medicine in the office of two Bainbridge doctors, then entered Albany Medical College, graduating in 1848 at the age of twenty-three. That same year he married a Bainbridge woman his own age, Mary Kelsey, and the couple moved to Elkland. There, Humphrey built up a prosperous practice in the Cowanesque Valley and adjoining towns. The couple had three chil-

Dr. William Thomas Humphrey.

dren before moving to Osceola in 1857. Humphrey was one of five married soldier friends who correspondend with Tubbs.[7]

Stevens, who was also married, was evidently a cousin of Tubbs',[8] but they were polar opposites in many respects, particularly in morals and education. For one thing, Stevens was an alcoholic. For another, as his letters reveal, he had no talent for grammar, syntax, or spelling. Ironically, Stevens suffered the ignominious fate of having his last name misspelled on army records as "Stebbins" (which actually was the last name of another friend of Tubbs'). Thus no regimental roster mentions Stevens by his true name. Perhaps the mistake was caused by his speaking a regional dialect. His comrade-in-arms, William Self, once misspelled Stevens' name as "Scobens."[9]

Stevens was twenty-five years old when he enlisted. He was a carpenter by trade. On army records, he is described as being five feet nine inches tall and having dark eyes, dark hair, and a dark complexion.[10] Stevens suffered frequent bouts of illness because, Self said, "he likes to drink so much he has been sick nerly all the time and 9 tenths of the sick is caused by drinking."[11]

Though Self was also semiliterate, he turned out to be the most prolific of Tubbs' seventeen correspondents: he wrote twenty-eight letters to Tubbs. Self was about twenty-seven years old, had known Tubbs as a childhood friend, and relied on him for advice about setting aside some of his army pay in a bank. It appears that Self did not have much formal schooling. He worked as either a handyman or a farmer. One thing, though, is certain: he had amazing stamina and was accustomed, he said, to "hardship." He described himself as "Tough as a bear[.]"[12]

Self, Stevens, and Dr. Humphrey joined other volunteers, all from the Cowanesque Valley, at Lawrenceville, where they were organized into a company that the men decided to call the Anderson Life Guards, in honor of Major Robert Anderson, who had defended Sumter. They then proceeded south by rail to Camp Curtin, just outside Harrisburg.

The camp was located two miles north of the Pennsylvania capital on an extensive county fairground that was dominated by a racetrack and pavilion. It was linked directly to Washington by an adjoining rail line. The camp's main purpose was the induction of recruits; it would be the state's largest mobilization and training center throughout the war. But the state at first was ill-prepared for the huge numbers of volunteers who flooded the camp and found themselves under military discipline for the first time in their lives. Many resisted any attempts to enforce military authority, and the result was an unruly camp. "I have heard more nois[e] in the last 24 hours than you have heard in the last 5 years," a friend of Tubbs wrote in one of the first letters he received. "I saw one night this week over 30000 soldiers, and more than 10000 spectators in one mass. It was one scene of commotion."[13] Another noted that all the men in his company had "slight colds caused by mode of sleeping which is a blanket spread on the ground or straw and overcoats as pillows and a blanket as coverlid."[14]

Worse still were the sanitary conditions. At night the men urinated wherever they chose. What sinks there were were quickly filled and covered with only a thin layer of soil, as a result of which human excrement filtered aboveground.[15] "Our men suffered very much," complained an officer from Tioga County. "For three days it rained almost continuously, mixed with snow. More than one-half of our men were without blankets and some without tents; many were thinly dressed, expected to be clad with the national blue as soon as we reached Harrisburg."[16]

The living conditions were one thing, the disappointment another, for the Anderson Life Guards had received a rough jolt upon reaching Camp Curtin. Pennsylvania's quota was already full; their service was not needed. The state's governor, after whom the camp was named—Andrew G. Curtin—urged the men to remain in camp while he called the legislature into special session to authorize the raising of additional state regiments. But the process took an unusually long time. The legislature ultimately authorized the underwriting of fifteen regiments, to be called the Pennsylvania Reserve Corps, to defend the state. However, a month passed before the legislators finally voted, and meanwhile the volunteers had to bide their time under conditions that were completely unfit for the thousands upon thousands of men who had thronged into Camp Curtin. Many of them simply gave up and left.

William Self said that after a week in Camp Curtin "we began to get dirty and sick and no liklyhood of a change." Only thirty-five of the 101 men who started out from Lawrenceville were left after more than a month in the camp. As a unit, the Anderson Life Guards slowly dissolved:

[S]ome say that they are afraid of yellow fever and crockadiles and others that they [s]hall rather go home and live a peaceable life with their wifes than to go to war and be killed[,] anything for an exuse to go to be shoire. it was rather tough for all of us but I have been here six weaks to day and no cloths but those which I wore away[—]shirt and a pair of pance which lasted about three weaks . . . when I left Osceola it was warm weather and I thought that it would be warmer here arainy to[o] its being farther south[.] the first fiew days it snowed and rained so that it was very cold and we had such a large company and little room that we had to sleep two deep and some on the ground[,] I for one.[17]

On June 21, the men from Osceola who remained—including Self, Stevens, and Dr. Humphrey—were at last mustered into Company A of a rifle regiment known by several names. Originally it was called both the 1st Pennsylvania Rifles and Kane's Rifle Regiment, or simply Kane's Rifles, after its organizer and colonel, Thomas Kane. The regiment was made up primarily of lumbermen from northern Pennsylvania. Kane had led them to Harrisburg by water on rafts that the men had determinedly built themselves. The regiment boasted a number of sharpshooters who took to tucking the tail of a deer into their hats as a symbol of their markmanship. Soon the others in the regiment followed suit. The "Bucktails," as they quickly became known, were mustered into the U.S. Army on June 11, two months after the war began. To add to the confusion, the regiment, once formed, officially the 13th Pennsylvania Reserves, was also known as the 42nd Pennsylvania Volunteer Infantry or, more familiarly in the federal army, as the 42nd Regiment of the line.[18] A month after its induction, with little preparation or training, the men were engaged in skirmishes in Virginia.

When news of what was going on at Camp Curtin reached Osceola, a childhood friend of Tubbs', Leonard Leverne Kimball, decided—as did a number of other Pennsylvanians—to join a New York regiment instead. Leonard was the oldest of three Kimballs who corresponded with Tubbs; the other two were half-brothers. He was the son of Clark Kimball and his first wife, Clarissa Cilley. His father was a harness and saddle maker, one of the earliest settlers of Osceola and one of its first storeowners. He traced his paternal descent to Richard Kimball of Ipswich, England, who arrived in America in 1734. Leonard was born May 31, 1838, the fourth of Clark Kimball's children by his first wife. His mother died when Leonard was eleven days shy of his first birthday.[19]

When youngsters, Kimball and Tubbs attended school together. Kimball grew to average height—five-foot-seven—and had gray eyes and brown hair. Two weeks before his twenty-third birthday in May 1861, Kimball, who was sometimes called by his middle name Leverne, enlisted across the border in Addison. He was officially mustered into service in mid-June in Albany as a private in Company E, 34th Regiment New York Volunteer Infantry. He gave his occupation at the time as a farmer, but, according to his father, he was also studying law, apparently with an Osceola attorney.[20]

Soon after enlisting and being sent to Albany, Leonard wrote Tubbs. He also found camp life distracting and complained about "the noise and tumult that here reigns supreme." Kimball went on to describe "a routine of the day's events" for Tubbs' benefit:

> At 5 A.M. the gun fires for rising; half an hour is then alowed for washing, folding up bolster and blanket, &c. From 5 ½ till 7 A.M. company drills, Breakfast seldom comes before 8 ½ or 9 o'clock. From 10 A.M. untill noon drill, with the assurance of dinner by 3 P.M. From three we drill an hour and a half. At five in afternoon again assemble for dress parade. This concludes the "labors" of the day, which is inconsiderable to the dis[cr]iption that governs us. We are hemed in with a tight board fence on a few acres of hard clay ground; guards are stationed on evry side and it is said to be death for a guard to give up his musket to any . . .
> There are nearly twenty-five hundred more in these barracks, who natu-

Orrin Mortimer Stebbins.

raly restless and capricious resort to a variety of amusements. The most promi-
nent however are dancing, jumping, playing cards &c. &c. We often meet with
incidents, both ludicrous and instructive. Take one for example. Last Sabbath
one man was unfortunate enough to tire out with the care and labors of his
soldier life. A sort of a rash broke out, and (strange to say) he coughed. The
doctor came and said he needed rest, and ought to diet. This man was not
satisfactory. It looked like the Measles.!!!! The doctor "gave In" it might be.
Another query[:] was it not the Small pox? The doctor was obstinate. Couldn't
be. But the story was soon told, each gave his version of it. In short in half an
hour groups might be seen everywhere bewailing the calamity and comon fate of
all, cursing the doctor, and counseling each other not [to] go into the barracks
to sleep. Next morning the patient was up and a great "calm ensued."[21]

Kimball tried to dissuade Tubbs from thinking from "the general
tenor of this letter that I am sick of the enterprise."

I beg to correct you. I have been even better satisfied than I expected. It is true I often, very often, think of home and friends. With all their cherished associations, yet they act only as an incentive to action. The more dearly held, the more worthy their preservation.[22]

Kimball, who declared that he prized *"liberty* above all treasures," said the 34th New York was preparing to march "down to the land of Dixie."[23]

All during the spring of 1861, as friends of his rushed off to enlist, Orrin Mortimer Stebbins, a classmate of Tubbs' from Alfred University, was grappling with what to do about his future. "Steb," as he was called, was probably the most widely known and popular of Tubbs' friends. An articulate man, he dubbed himself "Crocket" or "Col. Crocket"—a reference to pioneer woodsman Davy Crockett—and often referred to Tubbs as "Dan" or "Dan. Webster," the Massachusets statesman and one-time Secretary of State.

Stebbins was born in June 1833 in Madison County, a section of upstate New York southwest of Syracuse. His father had died when he was an infant. His mother remarried a man from Middlebury, Pennsylvania, not far from Osceola. Stebbins grew up working on his stepfather's farm there. Stebbins, a fervent Temperance man, served twice as the town's constable. But he always harbored a desire to acquire an education, and by the fall of 1856, when he was twenty-three years old, he had saved enough money to enter Alfred. While students there, both he and Charles taught part-time at Union Academy in Deerfield, Pennsylvania, just before the war. By the time war broke out, Stebbins was running his own school, Westfield Select, about ten miles west of Osceola.[24]

Stebbins told Tubbs that there had been "some big debates" among the men in Westfield, one lasting until midnight. He said he did not know what to do "unless I go to war." His "blood," he continued, was "foaming":

We live in an age of rebellion. . . . I can only say that I live for the Stars and Stripes, and for them I am ready to die!!!. . . .[25]
[I]t is time for every man who love his country to take the field and fight like a hungry tiger, until those wild barbarians are drove back to the dens, or hang between earth and heaven, kicking at empty space.[26]

Stebbins and Tubbs shared the belief that the chief purpose of the war should be the abolishment of slavery: for them, it was the root

WESTFIELD SELECT SCHOOL.
WESTFIELD, TIOGA COUNTY, PA.

O. M. STEBBINS, Teacher.

THE SPRING TERM BEGINS FEB'Y 25th, 1861.
TUITION:
Primary Branches, - - - - - $2 50
Common English, - - - - - - 3 00
Higher Branches, - - - - - 3 50

Board and rooms in private families furnished at very low prices.
No pains will be spared to make this School equal to any in the county. Come
to Westfield, all you who spend your time and gold in the gay and thoughtless
throng, and prepare yourselves for the responsible duties of life.

Orrin Mortimer Stebbins' business card.

cause of the war. All Tubbs' other friends, indeed almost everyone
else—Abraham Lincoln included—saw the preservation of the Union
as the goal of the conflict. But to Stebbins, "this contest will be
one unequaled in the history of the *world,* the ball is rolling and will
not stop, until Slavery is wiped from the land or freedom is *crushed forever!*"[27]

*Old John brown Set this war in motion, and threw himself beneath . . .
as the first martyr, and it will never Stop until that dark Stane of African
Slavery is wiped out so dry.*[28]

Stebbins' attitude was fortified when he later enlisted and his unit
joined in the defense of Washington, where the possession of slaves
was still legal:

*I agree with you when you say that Slavery is the <u>fountain head</u> of this
great Stream that is sweeping like a torrent across this continent, and Staining
this fair land with Northern blood, and whitening these plains with bleeching
bones.*

*When I was a School boy with you, I hated Slavery, but I knew not how
to hate it then, for I knew not what it was. But as I look around me to day and
See beneath the Shades of the Capitol, where the master minds of America meet*

*to mold the destinations of 30,000,000, the weary Slave toil like an ox or an <u>ass</u>
with no more hopes of the future than the Mule that draws the cannon, <u>I learn
to hate it</u>! When I see a country that might be the <u>Eden</u> of America desolate and
forsaken, with the buildings old and fast decaying, the land worn out and
baran, no churches[,] no Schools, no pleasant vilages with Students and happy
hours where peace and pleasure dwells but only a long train of vices and immo-
rality, wickedness and retchedness[,] Sin and corruption, and a mingled con-
glamorated mixed up mess of the human family of all grades and colors from
Midnight darkness down [to] <u>gingerbread</u>[,] I hate it worse than I ever knew
how to hate it!!! . . .*

*And I say <u>more</u>. I would never sling my knapsack and Shoulder my gun
again if I thought it would perpetuate that <u>damning</u> traffic or lengthen the
night of bondage to one of the lowest and most degrading of the Ethepapian
<u>rose</u>.*

*I say more. I would bury the Steel that hangs by my side to-night if I did
not think that this war would be the great volcanic Shock that would tair up
every root and branch of that <u>cansor</u> of this Nation!*[29]

The only question Stebbins raised was whether Lincoln saw the
war in the same way:

*You once thought that he was inclined to favor the South or in other
words <u>not</u> meddle with Slavery, but are you convinced to day that he is the
man for the times? <u>Are you convinced that he has laid the foundation for the
emancipation of every Son of Ham</u> that to night groans beneath the galling
chanes of Slavery? Are you Satisfide that he is true to country and breaths no
pra[y]er for that <u>cursed</u> of all <u>cursed institutions</u>—<u>the foundation of all our
national trouble</u>? <u>I know you are but if you are not, I am.</u>*[30]

Racked by despair after the fall of Fort Sumter and then by the
continuing secession of one more southern state after another, Stebbins
finally decided to enlist. He traveled alone to Harrisburg by stagecoach
at his own expense. Because of the loss of volunteers engendered by
the lengthy stay in Camp Curtin, he was able to join Company A of the
Bucktails, the same company that Dr. Humphrey, Self, and Stevens
were in. He enlisted as a private.[31]

Joining with Stebbins was his close friend, Allen A. Van Orsdale,
who was also a friend of Tubbs' from Alfred. Though Van Orsdale was
four years Stebbins' junior—he was twenty-four years old while Stebbins was twenty-eight—the two became almost inseparable, sharing
tent quarters and at least once penning a joint letter to Tubbs. Van
Orsdale was born in Broome County, New York, but lived in Jasper,

not far from Addison. Just under five feet eight inches, he had blue eyes, blond hair, and a light complexion.[32]

Van Orsdale entered Alfred in 1859, interested like Tubbs, he said, in "the purs[u]its of science and peace."[33] Like Self, he was very critical of Stevens' drinking. Like Stevens, his name was misspelled in regimental records: Vanarsdale. And like Stebbins, Van Orsdale was a teacher and motivated by his love for the United States. "I exclaim *My Country I am thine to do or die*," he declared. But in poor health almost from the time he enlisted, Van Orsdale sought the "influence of distin- guished friends" to obtain a position as an orderly master clerk[34]—a position described by satirist Ambrose Bierce, who served in an Indi- ana regiment, as "covering a multitude of duties. An orderly may be a messenger, a clerk, an officer's servant—anything. He may perform services for which no provision is made in orders and army regula- tions. Their nature may depend upon his aptitude, upon favor, upon accident."[35] Van Orsdale found that the job, which carried with it the rank of second sergeant, was not as taxing as "active military life" but that it did demand "so much writing until all of the old accumulated orders and requisition[s] were brought up [to date] that I hardly had time to write to my relatives."[36]

Perhaps as a joke, Company A elected Van Orsdale its "justice of the peace."[37] All the Bucktails certainly needed some discipline. Off the battlefield, they were notorious for being unmanageable. Stebbins com- plained that he despised "the manner in which we live" as well as "the low profanity of the camp." But he had a problem with military author- ity, too. He also hated, he said, "to be a *Slave* under those just one notch above me." He would like it much better, he continued, "if a man could Stand on equal footing with thos[e] no better than himself. but his dress and position make the man, and not the mind."[38] The issue became a sore spot when the Bucktails were later encamped across from Washington and it rained all day and night

and as we had no tents, or houses, (except for those who wore st[r]aps upon their shoulders,) there we must stand, or wade in the "sacred soil" of old Vir- ginia, nearly knee deep, for twenty-four hours. . . . Late at night, as I passed the window of a warm and well lighted room, where a few officers sat smoking cigars, singing songs, and occasionally taking a little "o-be-joyful," I could not but contrast their condition with those who were standing in the ice and mud on that dark stormy night, to guard the "rock of liberty."[39]

A month later, the men finally received oilcloth blankets that were supposedly waterproof. The blankets were intended to be fas- tened together in groups of three to provide cover for three men.[40] But the makeshift tents leaked and it was not unusual, Stebbins said, "if one wakes up in the night, and finds a little brook running on each side of him, and the water dropping in his face about as fast as sap drops from a maple tree."[41] At one point later, when Stebbins went out on picket duty before reveille, he passed through the Bucktails' camp and found more than half of the men "were actually lying [in] the water, some one, some two, and some six inches deep."[42]

Van Orsdale did not like military life at all—"'tis one of moral degradation. . . . an under officer or soldier is a *vassal*, you *must* bow, you *must* obey or die[.] there is no question 'Why do you so[.]' A good share of ones manhood or independence is restricted. If this were a common war I should say good bye soldiering."[43]

In the last week of June, the Bucktails left Camp Curtin, headed for the outskirts of the nation's capital. Stebbins by then had begun writing a journal of the experiences encountered by his fellow Osceola volunteers. He mailed them off to Wellsboro, the seat of Tioga County, where they were edited and reprinted in the *Tioga County Agitator*, a paper with strong abolitionist leanings. Using the pseudonym "Crocket," Stebbins described in detail the daily frustrations and successes of a soldier's life. The men had been issued blue blouses, blue cloth fatigue caps, and army shoes. They had also been issued some articles, including overcoats and undershirts, that they felt they would not need with summer ahead and would only add to what they had to lug about in their knapsacks. But what really upset them, Stebbins reported, was that they were issued old muskets from the Harpers Ferry arsenal bearing the date 1837 instead of the new "Minie rifles" they had been promised. The latter, which fired a cylindro-conoidal lead projectile, were more accurate, had a greater range, and could be reloaded more quickly than run-of-the-mill muzzleloaders. "Many of the boys absolutely refused to move one step until they had their rifles," Stebbins said. The men relented, however, after they were told that once the weapons they wanted could be procured they would indeed be a rifle regiment.

The 13th Pennsylvania left Camp Curtin by train in the dark hours about 3 A.M. on Saturday, June 22. Despite the early hour, "all along our route," Stebbins said, "thousands turned out from the hills and the valleys to meet us with everything calculated to cheer the hearts of weary and hungry soldiers." Before the week was out, the Bucktails' flag was flying "over Southern soil" at Camp Mason and Dixon, near Cumberland on the Maryland side of the Potomac River northwest of Washington—"on the line," Stebbins observed, "which divides freedom from despotism."[44]

· CHAPTER 2 ·

First Blood

*Friend Charles[,] Your kind letter Was recieved Some-
time ago but we got marching Orders in a day or two
and being on The move nerly all the time . . . I have
been out on a three days picket and Just came in so I
take this oppertunity to Write to you.*
—William E. Self[1]

$\mathbf{A}$s midsummer approached, the war was limited primarily to skirmishes in Missouri and Virginia. As yet, no major battle between the
North and the South had occurred.

As the two sides sparred and jockeyed for position, the 13th
Pennsylvania departed for Camp Mason and Dixon in Maryland. The
trip covered some one hundred and sixty miles by rail and fifty more
on foot over the Cumberland Mountains. The Bucktails made the
marching leg in two days, but it was not an easy trek. They sweated
profusely under the burden of the large knapsacks they carried on their
backs, the haversacks loaded with provisions dangling from their
sides, and their guns upon their shoulders. Compounding the problem
was the "hot S[o]uthern Sun pouring down upon us," said Stebbins,
"but I did it like a Roman."[2]

Once they were encamped, Stebbins and Dr. Humphrey went
into Cumberland, six miles away. Cumberland, Stebbins said, was
"one of the most dilipidated old towns" he had ever seen: "A man
would know if he was taken there in the night that Slavery had cursed
the ground around it." It was in Cumberland that Stebbins heard "the
first human bean say, *I am a Slave.* That sounded *harsh* on my ears."

Posted outside Cumberland was a unit of fancily uniformed Indiana Zouaves whom Stebbins and Dr. Humphrey stopped to visit. The
Zouaves had gotten into a skirmish with a band of rebels. Thirteen
Zouaves—"brave fellows"—had fought forty-seven of the enemy, killing twenty-three of them and losing only one man themselves. The

A Zouave adorns this envelope from David Armstrong.

encounter, Stebbins felt, proved that "we are in the *right*, and all we ask is to be loos[e] among *them*. We will scatter them like *Sheep*."

On the way back to their camp, Stebbins and Dr. Humphrey got a fright. They were passing by some woods when all of a sudden they heard a gun fire and a bullet "whised by our ears." The two men looked all around but could not see anyone. Was it a Confederate soldier? A southern sympathizer? Stebbins was upset. He was not carrying a weapon, and anyway, even if he had, it would have been one of the old muskets the 13th Pennsylvania had been issued. The men had still not received the rifles they were due.[3]

The stay at Camp Mason and Dixon was brief. Company A was soon on the march, heading this time to the Virginia border, chasing after rebel troops who had burned a railroad bridge. But they missed them by a half hour and remained untested in combat. "The Tioga boys are all well, and in good fighting condition," Stebbins happily reported back home in the *Agitator*. "I do not think there is a coward among them." And there was some joy experienced. The men had been paid: "all feel well, and *rich*." They now had money to buy delectables from the sutlers that followed the troops. "The next day every one had a pie in one hand and a quarter section of gingerbread in the other."[4] A week later, near Romney, Virginia, he could still report that "not one of our regiment has yet been killed or wounded."[5]

The 13th Pennsylvania Reserves was ordered back to Harrisburg, and then, after a brief stay at Camp Curtin, was sent again to protect Washington but by a different route—a dangerous one. They were to go through Baltimore and were told not to load their guns. The prospect was alarming. Shortly after the surrender of Fort Sumter to the Confederates in April, the Sixth Massachusetts was passing through the city on its way to Washington when a crowd of local residents began throwing stones at the soldiers. Shooting broke out between the civilians and the troops, and by the time order was restored, at least nine civilians and four soldiers were dead. Bullet holes that pierced the roof of one of the railroad depots where the Sixth Massachusetts had to change trains were still in evidence eight months later.[6]

To prevent a repetition of the incident, the Bucktails were ordered not to load their weapons. But the men ignored the order as they marched through the city. While their baggage cars were hauled by teams of horses between the Pennsylvania and Washington depots, which were two miles apart, the men walked the distance warily, shouldering their rifles and ready to fire.[7] Fortunately, no incident occurred. Stebbins, in fact, said he enjoyed "a fine chance to See the great S[o]uthern City" and was even able to grab five hours' shut-eye during the layover.[8]

Before the Bucktails reached Washington, the Union suffered a demoralizing defeat in the First Battle of Bull Run on July 21 outside Washington at Manassas, Virginia. The battle, the first great confrontation of the war, was witnessed by hundreds of sightseers, including congressmen, who had ventured out of Washington expecting to be treated to an entertaining spectacle. They were soon engulfed in the midst of a fleeing army as federal troops retreated in panic. The battle, an unexpected defeat, prompted Allen Van Orsdale to bemoan the "gigantic injury that affair inflicted on the cause of national unity and human liberty." He insisted, "We shall have no more Bull Run disasters . . . The great heart of the Nation is now firmly resolved to do or die[.]"[9]

Stebbins himself had the opportunity to visit the scene of the battle:

What a sight met our gaze, the whole country was one vast field of destruction—one barren desert, covered only with sham forts, rifle pits, barrels filled with sand, old wagons, broken down [train] engines and cars, chimneys and walls of burnt buildings, dead horses, piles of bursted cracker barrels, coffins . . . property of every kind and description that a panic stricken army would value less than life . . .

The ground where the last struggle was made is now covered with graves and white with bones. Many of the graves have been opened. The rebels buried

their own dead, and the bones of our men have since been interred by our
soldiers. . . .
    I learned from an old negro 70 years old who was not worth taking away,
that when old massa left . . . that he drove with him like a flock of sheep
between 75 and 100 slaves to some more secure spot.

Stebbins declared that Manassas was "not the Gibraltar of America but a grand humbug." Instead, he said, it was "a fine place for two
contending armies to meet and fight, and for one to run away. I do not
believe that there ever was a day since the battle of Bull Run when our
army, led by officers whose brain did not whirl with intoxication, could
not have taken it."[10]
    The Bucktails were sent to Harpers Ferry, where they were finally
issued rifles and Company A was brought up to strength—one hundred and one men.[11] But now that the soldiers finally had rifles, their
complaints focused on rations and their confinement to quarters. "[W]e
went one day after miles and a cracker or two apiece to eat," William
Self said. He was "Glad to Get that," he said, but "they wer[e] so hard
that they would almoste break a mans teeth."[12]
    Stebbins griped that "we are under the strictest kind of military
laws, and are not permitted to leave camp. This comes pretty hard for
the free rovers of old Tioga."[13] The "free rovers," an independent lot,
decided to only partly observe a national day of "humiliation, prayer
and fasting" that fall. A Tioga County minister, Rev. William Haskall of
Westfield, preached "a short, but eloquent and patriotic sermon" to the
men. The Bucktails decided, however, to forgo the eating restriction.
"[A]s we have to fast the most of the time," said Stebbins, "we con-
cluded to let others have that part of the exercise."[14]
    By the time Stebbins' remarks reached the *Agitator* in Wellsboro
and were reprinted, he was writing his next report from the 13th Penn-
syslvania's latest posting, on the Virginia side of the Potomac, some
twenty miles from Washington and a little over thirty miles from Manassas. It was "one of the most forlorn and forsaken countries I every
saw." What particularly struck the teacher-turned-soldier was that "for
miles, and miles, there was not a school house or a church to be seen."
Stebbins said that the Bucktails "have had no hard fighting yet, but
there are skirmishes nearly every day along the banks of the Potomac,
in which our men have in every case yet succeeded in keeping the
rebels from crossing."[15]
    That September, the Pennsylvanians were frustrated by their in-
action. Van Orsdale, for one, was upset that the Bucktails, assigned to
the Department of the Shenandoah, commanded by Gen. Nathaniel P.
Banks, had not taken the offensive. "There seems yet to be no move in

contemplation to take place immediately and appearances are that we are yet on the defensive . . . it is a burning shame for twenty millions of men to stand on the defensive to Eight millions, the miserable hirelings of an odious oligarcy full of such hellish designs."[16]

Instead, the Bucktails were champing at the bit, training endlessly and, at the same time, being kept in constant readiness to march at a moment's notice. Each men had three days' rations in his knapsack—two cooked and one raw—for there was always the threat—the hope, in their minds—of action. Stebbins wrote to the *Agitator* on the second Sunday of the month, not far from where the Chain Bridge spanning the Potomac linked Washington with Virginia, that "the loud peals of artillery are again sounding in the direction of the Chain Bridge, causing the hearts of thousands to throb quicker than usual, not with fear, for there is no mark of fear upon their noble brows; but with anxiety which they feel for the country they have enlisted to serve."[17]

Although the impatient Bucktails might not have realized it, they were being forged into a superior fighting force. Creative is the best word to describe the field tactics that Colonel Thomas Kane, a lumber, rail, and mining promoter, devised. Stebbins said that while the Bucktails were "ready to move at a moment's warning," they still spent about four hours a day "in the skirmish drill," with Kane as their teacher. The fighting maneuvers were being executed "at the sound of the bugle," an innovation:[18] the Bucktails employed a bugler rather than a drummer boy to relay their commander's orders.[19]

But an even more critical innovation in tactics was the premium Kane put on the individual soldier. Instead of moving forward in an exposed, and inevitably vulnerable, strung-out line of advancing men, the Bucktails were instructed to scatter under heavy fire, seeking whatever cover they could find—a tree, a rock, a fence, the ground itself. Any part of their line that was better protected than another was then responsible for pushing forward and engaging the enemy. Under cover of their fire, the more exposed portion of the line was expected to rush forward next. Moreover, it was each soldier's responsibility not only to take care of himself but also to use every chance to advance the line. And no shots were to be wasted. The Bucktails were taught to estimate the distance to a target and not to fire until an enemy was fairly in the sights of their rifles. Skilled marksmen, they practiced shooting long range, in distances ranging from two hundred to one thousand yards.

The 13th Pennsylvania Reserves developed into a trim fighting force, and that fall it was accorded a special honor. The regiment, reassigned to the Army of the Potomac, marched at the head of the entire army—"a post of honor and a responsible position," bragged Orrin

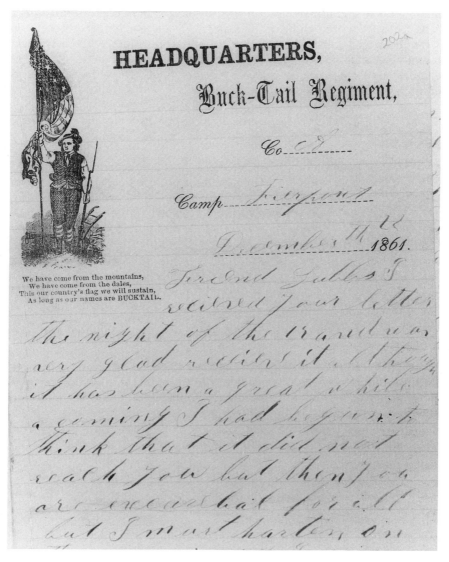

HEADQUARTERS,

Buck-Tail Regiment,

Co. _____ D _____

Camp _____ Fierpont _____

December 11th 1861.

We have come from the mountains,
We have come from the dales,
This our country's flag we will sustain,
As long as our names are BUCKTAIL.

Friend Gibbs I
recived your letter
the night of the 11 and was
very glad recived it. Althou
it has been a great while
a coming I had begun to
think that it did not
reach you but then you
are excused but for all
but I must hasten on

William E. Self employed stationery extolling the famed
Pennsylvania Bucktails.

Stebbins—at a grand review on the Virginia side of the Potomac near Falls Church, within sight of the Capitol.

Drumrolls roused the men at four that morning, while a waning moon was still visible. Thirty thousand spectators, some of whom climbed trees to catch a glimpse of the "well dressed, armed and equipped" army, witnessed the "grandeur."

Our bucktails, which were proudly cocked on nearly every hat from the Colonel down to the privates, attracted considerable attention.

Standing on the review platform as the Pennsylvanians marched by were President Lincoln, Major General George B. McClellan, Secretary of State William H. Seward, and Secretary of War Simon Cameron. As the Bucktails came abreast of them, Seward spoke out: "I will take off my hat to these boys." The others followed suit. "This was the first time McClellan, Old Abe, Seward and Cameron had ever pulled off their hats to the Bucktails," said Stebbins, who added:

McClellan looked young and full of youthful hope, while Old Abe looked aged and care worn and as I looked upon them, I could not but think that great[er] responsibility rested upon their shoulders than any king or queen, emperor or monarch of ancient or modern times had ever carried.[20]

The Bucktails finally got the chance to put their training in non-traditional tactics to use. As part of the Third Brigade, McCall's Division, they took part in a massive reconnaissance that centered on Dranesville, Virginia, in the last week of November.

Self's role began the very night that he received a letter from Charles Tubbs. He had no sooner read it when

we wer orderd to get our 40 rounds of catrages and days ration and [to be] read[y] for a Start at 4 Oclock. . . . as we Wer a passing along near there I saw some cavrlry which I told the boys that they wer the enemy but they did not believe it[.] but I [k]now it by the different collored horses and the way they ron and jumped the fences[.]

The Bucktails first confronted the Confederates face to face when they came upon a troop of fifty Louisiana Tigers busy cooking a meal. The Louisianians had bragged to some women in Dranesville that "they would like to meet those Buck tailes," said Self, "and they did to their sorrow." The Pennsylvanians "fired upon them and killed five of them[,] one being one of the Louisiana Tigers was shot through the back side of the head and came out his eye killing him instantly." Four times friends of the dead Confederate tried to pull his body to safety, but they were repulsed each time.

> [B]ut we had not gon far before we wer drawn in line of battle and shortly orderd to retreat which we did in good order about 100 or more rods[.] the artilery ahead they wer planted and ready for a charge in less than 5 minutes[.] soon the fight commenced[.]

The Pennsylvanians broke up the rebel charge, then went on the offensive themselves, driving the southerners from the field. William Self found the experience nerve-racking: "some of us," he said, "came near Getting shot" by both sides.

> [I]t lasted nearly 2 hours and fought Well and great was their loss[.] their loss is said to be nearly 300 hundred[.] our loss 4 or 5 but of our redgiment 3 of the 7 and a fiew of the 6 some considerable wounded but not dangerous[.] our Cornel was wounded in the head but not bad[;] he got so weak from the loss of blood and excitement that he had to be held on his horse[.] but it was a bloody seen to behold more so than eny thing we have seen[.] Yet our artilery don extry ordanry well[.] they killed 11 horses of the battery[,] blowed up their magarene[.]
>
> [I]t was a very bloody seen!—]oak trees the toughest I ever see was cut down and broomed up[,] the tops of pine trees wer cut off by them they so high that none took effect except one of the horses was shot in the leg . . . had it not been for the buck tailes the artilery would have ben taken[.] the boys Got a large amount of clothing Which they took of from them after the fight . . .[21]
>
> [T]hey are a rought looking lot[,] no uniform at all[.] they wer dressed like common laborers[.] their General was shot from his horse by a cannon ball[.] there wer 8 horses in t[h]ree rods square killed. I could count a dozen in the bursh that wer very thick just around me in one place but this was nothing to what it was in some places[.]
>
> [A]fter the fireing Was over we went around to serch the packets and to Get the clothes[.] One fellow Got over one 100 dollares[.] some got checks on South carolina Bank . . . I got a dayes ration of the secess bread[.][22]

For Stebbins, the fight lasted an hour that, he said, he would never forget:

> [I]t was one continual roar of artillery and musketry, without any inter-mission; and when our guns had silenced their battery, and their ranks broke, and men, terror stricken, began to flee before the Bucktails they had long wanted to face, our men rushed forward with one deafening cheer which echoed and re-echoed among the hills and groves, above the roar of artillery and the clash of arms."[23]

"[T]hat was the most fun that the bucktails has had in Sum time," Samuel Stevens observed.[24]

Stebbins, however, was appalled. Afterwards, he walked over the battlefield

and what a sight met my gaze! The ground was strewn with the dead and the dying; but I will not attempt to describe it, for you will only sicken at the scene. I saw trees that our cannon balls had cut down, over one foot in diameter—8 dead horses lay in one pile—broken wagons and mangled piles of humanity lay heaped together.[25]

Self survived the skirmish unscathed, but he and the others in Company A almost got shot by their own men when they returned to camp after dark and were fired on by Union sentries. No one, however, was hit.

Finally, after what had seemed like months of endless training, boring marches, and tedious waiting, the Bucktails had finally seen action and proved themselves.

· CHAPTER 3 ·

Rumors and Recruits

*I will close by wishing you a Happy New Year, hoping
that when another New Year rolls around, this rebellion will be wiped out forever, and all will be peace,
and . . . the hundreds of thousands who are now far
away from their joys, exposed to danger and death,
will be surrounded by the dear ones they have left behind, in their own pleasant homes.*
—*Orrin Stebbins*[1]

Ever since the First Battle of Bull Run in July, the seriousness of the
nation's division—the determination of the Confederacy, the unexpected great tolls of the dead and the wounded—made it clear that the
conflict would not be brief. Opposing forces soon faced each other
west of Virginia in Missouri and Kentucky, and south in the Carolinas.
A new state, West Virginia, was born, wrested from rebellious Virginia. The nation was truly at war. Even New York and the states of
New England, where not even a skirmish would ever take place, could
not escape the horror that accompanied the publication of the lists of
young men who were being killed and wounded. Ironically, in the
midst of the widening conflict that first October of the war, the nation
was united by the first transcontinental telegraph, which linked the
East with California.

Union soldiers, the Bucktails among them, had been elated when
George B. McClellan had replaced the aging Winfield Scott, a hero of
the War of 1812, as head of the army. "[T]hey all rejoice," Orrin Stebbins said, "that in McClellan they behold a man whose young and
active mind is capable of comprehending the magnitude of the work
before him . . . one who will soon heal up the wounds of our bleeding
country."[2] But the elation was short-lived. Within six months after the
Bucktails' involvement at Dranesville, the new commander of the Army
of the Potomac was the subject of a growing disenchantment.

27

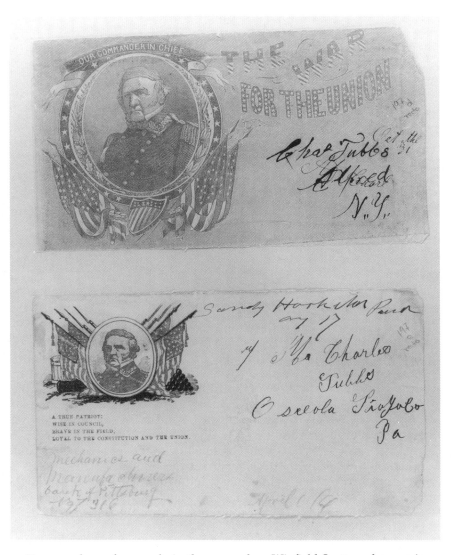

Two envelopes from early in the war, when Winfield Scott—who was in his mid-70s—was still General-in-Chief of the United States Army. He was succeeded in November 1861 by George B. McClellan.

Meanwhile, there was elation in the North that fall when a report spread that Charleston had fallen and Fort Sumter was recaptured. The joy changed quickly to disappointment when the report turned out to be false. From the outset when he heard the rumor, Stebbins was skeptical: "I don't think this is true. Yet I trust in God it may be." At the same time, he expressed vindictiveness:

I would like to write the Valedictory of S.C. over the hot embers of Charleston. I don't want one brick left upon another. I would like to see it as barren as it was when the wild <u>bulls</u> pawed its dry leaves a thousand years ago. Yes, I would be glad if an earthquake shock would sink it so deep beneath old Oceans waves that the little coral insects would never rear it to the top of the water. She has caused this nation trouble enough, and nothing but the cleansing fires of the Eternal can do her <u>Justice</u>.[3]

Pro and con, ill-founded reports such as the rumor about Charleston spread frequently throughout the North, often disseminated by newspapers. Within the first year of the war there were false reports that both Richmond and New Orleans had fallen[4]—that, indeed, as a friend wrote Tubbs, McClellan was dining in the Confederate capital.[5] Tubbs himself sometimes relayed or asked about a rumor he picked up. He heard, for instance, that there was a southern spy in the White House: none other than the president's wife, who was a Kentuckian. Gossipmongers made much of the fact that three of Mary Todd Lincoln's half-brothers were Confederate soldiers, a full brother of hers was a surgeon in the rebel army, and her two sisters had married secessionists.[6] Tubbs asked Stebbins about the report. His friend quickly disspelled it as a canard. There was not "one iota of Suspission," insisted Stebbins. "That was [a] grose lie."[7]

By the end of November, when the Bucktails fought at Dranesville, three more young men whom Tubbs knew enlisted, bringing to eight the number of his friends now in the service. Like the initial contingent from Osceola, one of the three, George Pratt Scudder, had gone to Harrisburg to enlist in late April.[8] But he and a group of young men from Wellsboro with whom he traveled were taken aback by the drastic change in the terms of enlistment. When they arrived at the state capital, they learned that volunteers were now being asked to sign up for three years, not three months. "If I thought we were truly needed so long in order to sustain the honor of our Country I you know would not hesitate to do it," Scudder said, "but I do not like to fight well enough to urge Myself on for that purpose."

Born in upstate New York in 1840, Scudder was one of eleven children. When he was eight years old, the family moved to Equinunk,

George Pratt Scudder.

Wayne County, on the Pennsylvania side of the Delaware River, where Scudder's father built a tannery. Eleven years later, the family moved again, this time to Middlebury Center, near Osceola, where Scudder worked on the family farm.

Scudder was twenty-one years old when he traveled to Harrisburg to enlist. Discouraged by the length of the term of enlistment, Scudder did not volunteer at first. He stayed on at Harrisburg and obtained a job as a messenger in a state agency through the influence of a brother-in-law—"not hard work but enough so to suit me and very nice." He expected, he said, to return home and "follow my harrow and follow my plow."[9] In fact, he purchased a farm in Tioga County.[10] But then within a matter of a few months, the once-reluctant Scudder changed his mind. Perhaps he was tempted by the offer of a post as second lieutenant with the 45th Regiment Pennsylvania Volunteers.

Whatever prompted his change of heart, once committed, Scudder turned into an enthusiastic and eager recruiter, working hard, he said, "to get our Company fill up to the Maximum." His unit, Company F, was made up of men from both Tioga and Wayne Counties. "That we may be victorious is all I ask," he declared.[11] Six months later, he was promoted to first lieutenant.

Scudder was a striking man: five-foot-eight, with black eyes, black hair, and a dark complexion. He was full-bearded and, until the war, robust but not overweight. After only a few months in the army, Scudder weighed 170 pounds, thirty-five pounds more than when he enlisted, the result, he said, of "potatoes and other rarities from the Sesesh farms."[12]

Scudder expected that the 45th Regiment would be sent to New Orleans. Instead, before the year ended, he found himself stationed on Fenwick Island, South Carolina. The voyage down the Atlantic Coast in an army transport was so pleasant, Scudder pondered the idea of "following the Sea after the War"—he was "sure," he said, that he "would make a tar[.]"[13]

Scudder sent nineteen letters to Charles Tubbs. He might have mailed others, but he burned a number of them because, he said, he did want to appear a "boaster." He did not like to brag about his combat experiences.[14]

The next to enlist, David Armstrong, was a childhood friend of Tubbs', but the two had not seen each other since the late 1850s, though they had apparently remained in contact over the years. Born in 1840, Armstrong grew up in Osceola, but at the outbreak of the Civil War was living in Fremont, Ohio, and worked as a carpenter and field laborer on neighborhood farms, haying, harvesting, and doing odd jobs as a handyman. He decided to enlist as he was completing the building of a barn. When he told his mother, she felt "pret[t]y bad." Armstrong tried to soothe her by saying he was only joking, but he took his father aside and informed him of his decision. He then went to his neighbors' house to say goodbye; their son was going to enlist, too, so the two young men set off together. They enrolled in the latter part of April and were eventually mustered into an Ohio regiment, the 49th Volunteers, in mid-August 1861.

Armstrong had hazel eyes and was clean-shaven except for a moustache. Otherwise, he resembled Scudder: he was five-foot-eight, and his hair and complexion were dark. And, like Scudder, he put on considerable weight in the army. Although a thin man when he enlisted—he weighed only 140 pounds—he gained as much as twenty pounds while in the service, and a photograph taken of him during the

David Armstrong.

war shows him as a full-faced young man. Semiliterate, Armstrong described himself as a "poor scholar" and regretted that he had not remained in school.[15]

The third new enlistee, Henry Reynolds Maxson, came from an extensive family in upstate New York whose name was a familiar fixture both at Alfred and in the army. Several faculty members and students at Alfred bore the name Maxson. And there were nine Maxsons alone, all apparently related, in the regiment in which Henry volunteered, the 85th New York.

Henry was born in Little Genesee, New York, in February 1839. At the age of nineteen he matriculated at Alfred. There, Charles Tubbs became his "Livy[,] Anabasis & Chemistry classmate as well as Brother Oro." Maxson is listed as having graduated from Alfred in 1862, but army records show that he had already volunteered in September 1861, when he joined Company C of the 85th as a sergeant. Maxson was twenty-two years old at the time, but a full beard and moustache tended to make him look older. He was just under five feet ten inches tall, had hazel eyes, brown hair, and a light complexion. Maxson gave his occupation as farmer, but wondered whether farming was his "true place."[16]

After training, the 85th New York was posted in Washington,

Henry R. Maxson.

across the river from where the Army of the Potomac had gone into winter quarters.

Across the river in Virginia with the Army of the Potomac that December, some of the first of Tubbs' friends to enlist paraded on a cold Sunday afternoon in another review featuring the 13th Pennsylvania Reserves. This time, the Bucktails' governor, Andrew Curtin, led the contingent of notables. Orrin Stebbins reported:

> He spoke in glowing terms of our first and last great fight—our coolness and our courage . . . He said he would have the word "Drainsville" inscribed

upon our banners. He reminded us of what we were six months ago. "Then,"
said he, "You were but raw recruits, but now you pass before me with a martial
tread, equal to any regular soldiers."[17]

The review took place at the Bucktails' encampment at Camp
Pierpont, where they and other units of the Army of the Potomac went
to great pains to make their quarters comfortable and into a shelter
against the coming winter. Stebbins visited the encampments of two
New York regiments:

They are located in a splendid grove, with their Streets as neat and clean
as a marble floor, with beautiful evergreen arches over every one, and with the
number of the regiments and letters of their company, hanging suspended at
the gate. A few rods farther on is located a regiment of cavalry . . . with
stables, 15 or 20 rods in length, or long enough to hold a thousand horses, built
out of poles, covered with green boughs and trimed in the grandest style, form-
ing one complete bower.[18]

The Pennsylvanians were more individualist in approach. "Bucktail City," Stebbins wrote in the *Agitator*, was not "like those whose
ruins now lie buried beneaths of the sands of Asia, or are entwined by
the ivy of Africa . . ."

Here every man is the architect of his own domicile, and this being the
case, it is not to be wondered at that we have as many models as we have
minds. Still the foundations are nearly all the same—built of round poles from
four to ten inches in diameter, and about seven feet by eight on the ground,
with a one little chimney and fireplace in one corner, great or small, according
to the size of the family, or taste of the mason. Our buildings are lighted by gas
and sky light. The gas we manufacture ourselves. The sky light we obtain by
stretching our tents over our huge foundations . . .
   Our city stands upon a pleasant hill near a little brook which bubbles by
. . . A busier set of men I never saw.—Some are sawing logs, some placing
them upon the foundation, some bringing stone, some mixing mortar, some
laying chimneys out of sod, and others chinking. Nothing but the merry songs
of the laborers and the ax of the pioneer can be heard.[19]

The men had been paid—privates earned $13 a month for the first
three years of the war[20]—"and some are a takeing it away from others
by card playing so some Will not have a cent in two weaks," Self reported to Tubbs:

[W]e amuse our selvs as well as though we wer at home[.] you ought to
be here and see the sport in the camp at night[.] we have a dance a moste evry

night[.] they doe not dream of what may take place evry day[.] they dident and swear as though they had a thousand Years to live[.][21]

Northerners were now wondering why the huge army McClellan had assembled in Virginia was idle. Why didn't McClellan seize the initiative and strike before the South could mobilize?

1862

· CHAPTER 4 ·

Casualties

Cosin Charles[,] my health is not very good at pres-
ent[.] it has ben good all Sumer till with in the last
two weeks but i think iwill cum out soon[.] it [is]
nothing but had cold[.]
—*Samuel Stevens*[1]

In February, two more friends of Charles Tubbs, the Kimball brothers, Orville and Harlan—half-brothers to Leonard Kimball—enlisted. Like Leonard, they chose to join a regiment across the border in New York State. But they evidently decided not to try to join Leonard's regiment, the 34th, because Orville did not "like" the unit. Anyway, although Orville and Harlan shared the same father as Leonard, and all three resided in Osceola, they were not close to him.[2]

The regiment that the two brothers joined, the 103rd, was a most unusual one. It was formed under the direction of a German baron and included a unit known as the German Rifles. And, except for Company I, in which the Kimballs served, all the other nine companies were almost exclusively German, even their officers. The men bore Austrian rifles until they were issued Springfield rifles in midsummer 1863. Because so many of the soldiers could not speak or understand English very well, communication was generally in their native tongue. Company C—the baron's "elite company," which bore the regiment's colors—was composed entirely of officers who had served in the Prussian Army. They were promised commissions in the U.S. Army, and when the commissions did not come through, they were miffed and abruptly left the service. As a result, the regiment went through the war with only nine companies.[3] Despite the remarkable character of the 103rd, neither Kimball brother ever mentioned a word to Tubbs about having any language difficulty whatsoever while serving in it.

Orville and Harlan were sons of Clark Kimball and his second wife, Hannah Whittemore. Like a number of Tubbs' friends, Orville

Orville Samuel Kimball.

taught public schools in the Osceola vicinity while still a student at Osceola High School. He left high school in February 1862 to enlist— against his father's wishes. Orville was nineteen years old at the time but gave his age as twenty-one because he did not have his father's consent. He worked on farms during the school recess in the summer and gave his occupation as a farmer when he enlisted.[4]

Orville appeared ungainly. His long face and neck made him look like a goose. His height—a fraction of an inch short of six feet—added to the illusion. Orville had blue eyes, dark hair, and a ruddy complexion. One of the most prolific of the letter writers, Orville wrote fifteen letters to Charles Tubbs and three to Charles' younger brother, Henry.[5]

Harlan Kimball, who was an intimate friend of Henry's, was the youngest of the letter writers to enlist.[6] He was six months shy of eighteen when he enrolled with Orville—evidently also without his father's consent. Harlan had attended a school in Osceola, Union Academy at nearby Academy Corners and, like Orville, was a student in Osceola High School when he joined up. Harlan also worked on farms during summer recess and upon enlisting gave his occupation as a farmer.

Harlan was slightly smaller than his brother—five-foot-eight-and-a-half—and though they shared the same parents, they were dissimilar in appearance. Harlan's eyes were hazel, his hair brown, and he had freckles sprinkled all over his face. Moreover, he was a thin, almost fragile youth, prone to sickness. Orville bemoaned the fact that although his brother was "a good soldier," his "rather slight constitution" was easily ravaged by "the inroads of disease, chronic diarrhoea and malarial poisoning."[7]

The new year, 1862, had been born in a cold, bitter winter. Men on both sides of the conflict huddled against freezing blasts reminiscent of Valley Forge. A number of them died, more from illness than bullets, for disease and infection claimed more lives than wounds did.

Somewhere between 600,000 and 700,000 men on both sides died in the Civil War, and for every man killed in battle, two men died from disease or inadequate care. Chronic diarrhea was the main cause of death in the Union armies. More than 1,700,000 cases of diarrhea were recorded by federal doctors during the war; 57,000 of them proved fatal. Contributing to the horrendous statistics was the fact that doctors failed to see diarrhea as a symptom of dysentery and considered both as separate diseases: they all believed loose bowels alone were diarrhea; they called the condition dysentery if blood was present. The doctors treated both ailments as the same sickness, and the medications they administered bordered on the medieval: calomel, strychnine, silver nitrate, belladonna, castor oil, turpentine, blackberry juice, opium, rainwater collected in tree stumps, and a concoction called "blue mass" that consisted of mercury, licorice powder, and rose water.

Most of the soldiers on both sides of the conflict were farm boys who had largely escaped a host of communicable diseases such as chicken pox, measles, and scarlet fever. Such diseases spread like epidemics in military camps, which were run without any regard to the basics of group living. Typically, soldiers in the field lacked pure water and proper latrines, were ignorant of hygienic standards, subsisted on poor food, were surrounded by vermin and insects, and were often exposed to the elements. Typhoid fever, diarrhea, dysentery, pneumonia, and malaria were common. Consumption was the main cause of discharges among white Union troops during the war, diarrhea and dysentery next.

Worse still for those wounded in battle was infection. Medical

Ephraim Elmer Ellsworth, who was killed after removing a Confederate flag from a tavern in Alexandria, Virginia, in May 1861, is commemorated on the stationery in this letter from Leonard Leverne Kimball.

science at the time of the Civil War was primitive, as were procedures about the care of the sick and wounded. Few doctors realized the connection between filth and infection. As a result, unsanitary conditions were common at field hospitals. Unwholesome conditions, too. William Self remarked after a series of severe rainstorms at Camp Pierpont in Virginia that "it is rather unhealthy weather for those sick and in the hospital lying on the cold and wet ground."[8]

At the beginning of the war, the U.S. Army had about one hundred physicians on duty. Only one doctor ordinarily accompanied a regiment, but the reality of the fighting soon led to the assignment of three physicians—a surgeon and two assistant surgeons—for each 1,000-man regiment. Although doctors who enlisted, such as Humphrey, were called surgeons or assistant surgeons, they were actually general practitioners, and few were familiar with the use of the one instrument critical in battle situations, the scalpel. Most of them gained their first experience in treating wounds as fighting raged within sight and sound. Humphrey, for one, was capable of treating common illnesses and diseases, but his skill under battlefield conditions was limited. Union surgeons performed almost thirty thousand amputations during the four years of warfare, but Humphrey handled only fifteen such cases—all dealing with arms, legs, or shoulders. He never dealt with wounds to vital organs except, evidently, as an assisting physician. The paucity of his own surgical cases is perhaps a reflection of his lack of ability, because during the war more than nine out of ten wounds came from bullets, and three of every four bullet wounds were in the limbs. That Humphrey conducted only fifteen such amputations is telling. Amazingly, however, only one of Humphrey's surgical patients died, of pyemia—the presence of pus in the blood. Chiefly because of infection, almost a third of all the amputations carried out by army surgeons resulted in death.[9]

Considering Humphrey's daily work environment, it is not surprising that in the winter of 1861–62 he came down with typhoid.[10] Nor is it surprising that, because of illness, before the year 1862 was out two other friends of Charles Tubbs' had left the army, and a third was on the verge of being discharged.

The year 1862 had barely begun when Leonard Kimball became too sick to continue as a soldier. Shortly after Orville and Harlan enlisted in February, Leonard was discharged on a "surgeon's certificate of disability."[11] Kimball, who argued against being sent home, wrote Tubbs that the doctor with the 34th New York "says I must not go any further, because of some lame, but I disagree with him there."[12] Leonard was mustered out more than four months before his regiment's term of service was completed.

What Kimball meant by his being "lame" had nothing to do with his ability to walk, as might be supposed. Maybe he should have used the word "incapacity," for he was going deaf. Leonard developed an ear infection while the 34th New York traipsed in severely cold and stormy fall weather from Camp Kalorama in Georgetown to Seneca Mills, Maryland. Unable to hear ordinary conversation, Leonard was declared unfit for duty.[13] His hearing difficulty never went away, but that did not deter him from twice later volunteering to serve.

At almost the same time as Leonard Kimball was being discharged, Allen Van Orsdale was ailing as well, possibly with malaria, though the diagnosis of his illness is unrecorded. Once before, when the Bucktails first left Camp Curtin, Van Orsdale had been left behind because he was sick. Now he was detached from duty to return home to recover, but he never made it beyond Washington. "He has been in a private house in Georgetown," Orrin Stebbins explained to Tubbs. "I saw him last Wednesday, he was alone in the 3d story of a house with no kind mother's hand to Sooth his fevered brow."[14]

Stebbins had been distraught without Van Orsdale's company. He was "lonely without him," he said:[15]

I will stand by that young man until the last drop of my best blood is spilt. If I was 1000 miles away in the midst of the rolling ocean upon the rock of Starvation I would divide with him my last morsel.[16]

Stebbins stayed by Van Orsdale's bedside until he had to report back for duty. Van Orsdale's father was coming to take him home, and Stebbins left his good friend thirty dollars to pay their way.[17]

Stebbins' mood changed to joy when Van Orsdale eventually returned to Company A, but his elation lasted only briefly. His friend's health, he wrote Tubbs, "is midling good[.]"[18] The sickly Bucktail's condition never got better. "His frail form was not enough for the hardships of the camp," said Stebbins, who finally realized that Van Orsdale would never be fit enough to continue as a soldier. Early in the spring, Stebbins joined other members of Company A in urging Van Orsdale to seek a medical discharge so that he could "retire to the peaceful vocations of a private life, before he had fully revenged the wrongs of his insulted country."[19]

Samuel Stevens became seriously ill, too: he was going blind. Stevens came down in July with what was described as incipient phthisis—a shrinking of the globe of the eye caused by cirrhosis of the liver, in his case obviously a result of drinking. He was hospitalized in February in Philadelphia but was apparently expected back with Company A: when he did not show up, he was reported as a deserter. At the time, however, Stevens was actually in Camp Convalescent in Alexandria, Virginia. Stevens finally returned to civilian life and died of the disease sometime after January 1863.[20]

The enlistment of the Kimball brothers in February had brought to eleven the number of Tubbs' friends who were on active duty. By the end of the first winter of the war, however, there were only eight left. But that summer, when classes at Alfred were out, three more schoolmates of Tubbs'—all again "Brother Oros" and all married men—enlisted.

The first to do so was John Orr, who joined Company F, 107th Regiment New York Volunteers, as a private. A native of Addison, New York, Orr was living in Tuscarora, in east-central Pennsylvania, when he enlisted in July 1862. At the time, he was twenty-six years old. A pious man, Orr had matriculated only a year earlier at Alfred and taught school in his free time. He was five-foot-ten and had blue eyes, brown hair, and a light complexion.

Orr was engaged to his wife, Melissa, for five years, and their marriage in her family home in Addison, nine months after his enlistment, when he was on furlough, was evidently prompted by her being pregnant. Nevertheless, Orr said that he was not sorry that he got married "even under the circumstances." "I have got a lively sort of a wife," he wrote Tubbs, "a trusting, devoted unselfish wife: one who is willing to make any sacrifice for my comfort." By then, he said, army food had made him the "fleshiest he ever was," though he suffered for some time from an infection caused by a botched smallpox vaccination. Orr said he would be the happiest of men if permitted to live and return home "because I shall more full[y] appreciate the blessings of peace & quiet."[21]

In the two years following his enlistment, Orr rose in rank from private to captain of his unit, Company F of the 107th. But another of Tubbs' friends from Alfred, William R. Prentice, won even speedier promotions.

Prentice also joined a New York regiment, in his case, the 161st. The innocuous pose of the full-bearded, stoop-shouldered twenty-six-year-old sergeant in a photograph that he sent to Charles Tubbs fails to do justice to one of the most successful of Tubbs' military friends. The photograph was taken shortly after Prentice enlisted as a sergeant in August 1862. Seven months later he was a lieutenant, and six months after that he was a captain.

Although born across the border in the village of Jasper, New York, which had a population almost quadruple that of Osceola, Pren-

William R. Prentice.

tice attended school in Osceola. He matriculated at Alfred in its preparatory course in 1856, graduating six years later, when he spoke at
commencement exercises on the topic "The American Flag." Prentice
married shortly after his graduation and before he joined the army; his
wife, Myra, studied painting in New York City for a time during his
three-year term of enlistment.

From the beginning of his service in the army, and throughout his
military career, Prentice suffered a variety of illnesses, but he was
never too incapicitated to serve. When he first joined the 161st, the
regiment was encamped at Elmira, where it remained until November
1862. By then Prentice was one of many of its members who had pneumonia. When the 161st traveled by train to New York City, he accompanied his unit, Company H, on a litter. Once in Manhattan, Prentice

was placed in a hospital, while the regiment camped on Long Island, awaiting a transport to sail to Louisiana. He was well enough to make the trip in December, and, in fact, his health improved during the long sea voyage. But when the 161st reached Baton Rouge, Prentice had to spend the first night ashore without shelter or even a campfire to huddle around for warmth. It was a cold night, and he suffered a relapse and spent two weeks in the regimental hospital.[22]

A close friend of Prentice's was the third new enlistee: Asa Spencer. Like Prentice, he also was a native of Jasper. The two had known each other since their preteen years and maintained their friendship throughout their schooling in Alfred. Spencer cherished their relationship, saying of Prentice: "A visit from him I considered a moral[,] intellectual and social feast."

A teacher by profession, Spencer was the village schoolmaster and had "wielded the birch" at Osceola almost continually from April 1856 to the spring of 1862. That August, while school was in summer recess and he was working as a harvest hand for a relation of Tubbs', he enlisted. He was then about twenty-four years old. Because of his teaching work in Osceola, and because he was also a graduate of Alfred, Spencer knew a number of Tubbs' friends from both places. In fact, he considered himself so much a part of the Osceola community that when the time came to enlist, it was to Osceola that he gave his allegiance.

Just as some of Tubbs' Pennsylvania friends joined New York regiments, Spencer did an about-face and, although born and raised in New York State, joined a Pennsylvania regiment. He and twelve local men enlisted in the 136th Pennsylvania, two companies of which were raised in Tioga County. Their enlistment term was for only nine months, and almost from the moment he enrolled Spencer suffered "considerable" from diarrhea, which became chronic. He confided to Tubbs that he had not told his wife, Betsey, because she would only worry.[23]

Before the year was out, Spencer was hospitalized. He had come down with a severe cold—possibly pneumonia—which left him with "the Canker soar mouth, throat, and stomach."[24]

So far, all of Tubbs' friends who had been discharged or were incapacitated were waylaid by illnesses—much more potent enemies, as it turned out, than bullets for his soldier friends.

· CHAPTER 5 ·

Friends and Enemies

Friend Tubbs. Sitting alone in my tent this evening, I
am reminded of the many plasant ones I have spent in
your society. I will confess to being a little <u>blue</u> to
night & that I would give a rum sum for the compan-
ionship of one single friend.
　　　　　　　　　　　　　　　—William R. Prentice[1]

Young soldiers, most of them away from home for the first time in
their lives, often grew homesick. Only after the war did doctors realize
that loneliness could lower resistance and cause soldiers to be highly
susceptible to the full, often fatal effects of any illness.[2]
　　Tubbs' friends were no exception. Their letters are full of expressions of longing for family and friends and for familiar sights and
sounds. After George Scudder ran into his brother Aaron, who had
enlisted in a different Pennsylvania regiment, he remarked to Tubbs,
"You better beleive I was no little pleased to see him the first time in 14
Months[,] A long time Since to be absent from Ones Mammie & Bro &
Sister I think so."[3]
　　Orville Kimball told Tubbs that he would "like to take a pleasant
walk through the fields and woods with a cool breeze or along the road
just after sunset[.] such scenes are fresh in my memory as if it was but
yesterday and I again live over the life of my boyhood day[s.]" One
night, asleep, he said,

my mind wandered back to my old home and I fancied myself at a party some-
where but I could not tell exactly where[,] surrounded by my old school mates
and friends[.] I had many a good chat with those whom I have always been
acquainted with[.] in the morning I woke and was almost surprised to find that
. . . I was still in North Carolina[.][4]

48

"I often think," Kimball wrote Tubbs, "of all those scenes of my earlier childhood and love to think of the many happy hours I have spent at your house on the long winter evenings[.]

[S]urely these were the happi[e]st days of my life those ear[l]y school boy days—[.] Often in Fancy's Vision *I have found myself in the midst of those same scenes and those old schoolmates and for a time I enjoyed them as of old, when the sound of the drum would wake me up* in Dixie[,] *then I saw it was a dream[.]"*[5]

"[N]aught but the cold hand of death can efface those early recollections," Kimball added.[6]

Back from picket duty one morning, Orrin Stebbins "took a Short nap" and also had a dream. "I awok[e] to write to the Same old friend who was with me in my dreams."[7] Stebbins sent his "love" to all the teachers at Alfred, "tell them the school in which I am engaged is full of toil and danger."[8] He would, he said, like to room with Tubbs "in that old Institution:

We would rehears[e] the Scenes of by gone days[,] days that were the proudest of our lives. How I would enjoy a morning walk by the Side of my old Friend Dan, *over those old* Alegany hills, *but tho' that privilege is denied me, my mind & heart is with you.*[9]

Tubbs' soldier friends also, not surprisingly, yearned for their wives, girlfriends, female companionship. When they wrote about women, it was never in a salacious or crude manner, but always with a kind of innocence. Often, the single men wrote about the same women: names such as Nell, Elizabeth, Jane, and Belle crop up in their letters. After all, they were all from the same small town, or had attended Alfred University together, and knew many of the same ladies. "[I]f I was at my own home I think I should like to See my Self a sitting by Some Madens Side and as long as she was willing," David Armstrong said. "I should like to See any body stop the fun[.]"[10]

Armstrong wondered whether Tubbs intended to marry "the Starr girl," who apparently was a student at Alfred. [Tubbs didn't.] As for himself, Armstrong, a hardworking laborer in his civilian life, was worried whether he would be able to find a wife with whom he could share his life. He had one possibility in mind, a "very fine daughter" of a friend of his who was a farmer in Tiffin, Ohio. She was "a bout 24 years old." He had once spent some time with her, time that had passed "so pleasantly that if ever I go that way you may be shure I will call and see her a gain[.]"[11] But Armstrong was not certain she would

Humorous cartoons adorn the stationery employed by Orville S. Kimball and William E. Self.

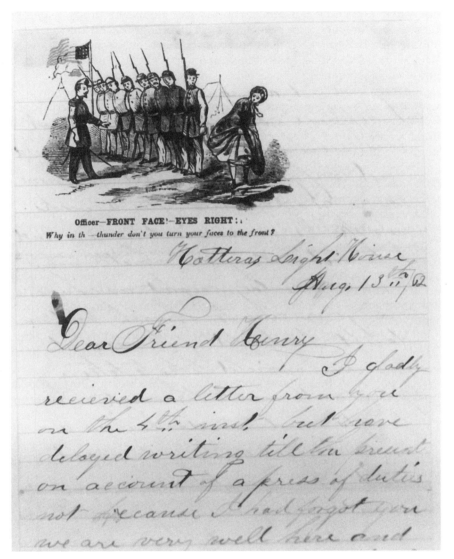

Officer—**FRONT FACE'—EYES RIGHT:**

Why in th—thunder don't you turn your faces to the front?

Hatteras Light House
Aug. 13th /62

Dear Friend Henry

I gladly
received a letter from you
on the 4th inst, but have
delayed writing till the present
on account of a press of duties
not *because* I had forgot you
we are very well here and

be available once he got out of the service. He asked Tubbs "weather there is or not some nice young Lady in that country left for me . . . I should like her to be neat[,] hansome and virtuous[,] also acquainted with work and willing to do the womans part as it should[,] one that you could recomend[.]"[12]

Perhaps George Scudder had the "Starr girl" in mind, or maybe it was another young woman they both knew, when he asked Tubbs whether he had kissed "that Girl, excuse me, (*Young Lady*[).] How you must have blushed, Ho!" Scudder said he knew Tubbs would not kiss her—"would not do such a *naty-ting!* If you did what will your Mother say when she find it out, or Your father[?]" Scudder confided that he had kissed the young lady in question, but he knew Tubbs "would not tell a story about it." As for himself, Scudder, who was then stationed on an island off the coast of South Carolina, said, "I have not see a White girl, Young Lady, or Woman since Nov. except at a distance." As a result, he was afraid that "when I go home I will fear them more than Gulliver did his wife after returning from his last voyage[.]" Scudder, who was appalled at reports about the many prostitutes who hovered around army camps, said that when he returned home he "would try and Stomach a kiss from a Mild nice good looking Young Lassee providing she had no paint on her cheek or lips."[13]

Like Scudder, William Self was concerned and wondering whether "the Girls will have much to doe with the Bucktails that live to Get back."[14]

Away from family and hometown friends, soldiers formed relationships that, they realized, might be ephemeral. David Armstrong spoke of

some of these noble boys . . . near and dear to him as a Brother[,] a school mate or play mate whom have spend meny a happy and peaceful hour together or have slept with him upon the ground or rails[,] poles or brush for nearly three years and suffering together at the same time[.] This is what will tye strangers together as brothers are tied together and fell them selves duty bound to love one another as brother[s] should love[.][15]

The bonding and loyalty of the men of Company A of the Bucktails prompted a rather unusual step to provide help for one another in a moment of need. They set up a fund to pay for decent medical care for wounded comrades and, in case of death, to provide money to send a soldier's remains home to his family for burial—"to sleep," Stebbins said, "in the scenes of childhood, where the loved ones can scatter flowers upon his tomb."[16]

The men broke the loneliness and tedium of camp life by devising their own amusements. To dispel the gloom, one *"dark, rainy* day," William Prentice took up his pen "to let my thoughts run away from the noise & confusion always attendent upon military camps, to rest for a while upon more quiet & congenial scenes." But the "laborious attempts" of the men of New York's 161st Regiment "to drown in fun & drollery, that constant *enui*," made it impossible:

In a "bunk" close by the desk at which I am privileged to write sit two soldiers, both fine specimens of the "man physical," who ar just now attracting the most of my attention. Together, they have mustered money enough to buy paper of tobacco, & one of them in mock auctioneer style is calling up the whole company to share in his great good fortune[.] They all smok round, & then as the stimulus begins to act upon their feelings, they break out in snatches of song, which when string togather, would constitute a medly worthy a mor dignified stage, & more pretending actors. "John Browns body lies a moulder-ing in the grave . . .["] "By the side of my Nellie dear[. . .]" While over them both they sing the undirge-lik song "God Bless our gin, gin forever. While stars as bright this blisful night we'l all get drunk togather."
"Vrum Ho! Bob. Ridley Ho!"
"Dont you hear me now."
"Jeff Davis built a wagon, & on it wrote his name."
"Then rally round the flag boys
"While we all take a ride"
& then, as the stimulus dies & their feelings assume a more reflective cast they sing
"Sleep, dearest sleep. I loved you as a brother."
"Kind friends around you weep.
"Ive kissed him for his mother."
—Softly this dies into
"Send them home tenderly."
Again the camp is quiet[,] soberer thoughts come over us all, & thus ebbs & flows the tide of a soldiers feelings, as the time slowly rolls round when he hopes to participate in more stiring scenes, & enter in earnest upon the work for which he has left home & friends the redemption of his country. Life in camp is really a very easy existence yet the true soldier feel[s] that it is slowly but surely undermining all his habits of industry & unfitting him for home society.[17]

When it came to dealing with the enemy, Tubbs' friends, like all the young Union men who fought the Civil War, depicted Confederate soldiers in terms of contempt—"damned rebs" and "traitors" were typ-ical appellations. To be sure, Confederate soldiers viewed "Yankee in-truders" in the same way. But in spite of fiery rhetoric, when they were not firing at each other, the men on both sides were quite content to treat one another in an amazingly friendly manner. It was not unusual—in fact, it was quite common—for opposing pickets, as they stood watch across a field or a stream, or from behind the shelter of rifle pits, to take a break from the killing of war and call a private truce of their own. George Scudder spent a Christmas Day on picket duty beside the Rapidan River north of Fredericksburg, Virginia, "watching the Rebs that they might not come over in force to Surprise us but still that did not keep them from coming over and paying us a friendly visit—that is one or two at a time. Neither did it keep some of our boys from going over to see them." Scudder went down himself to visit with the enemy sentinels "and the Rebels ditto—had a very plesant visit." Scudder said it might be surprising to hear "of the visiting of the guards of the two Armies but its so and I think it much better than shooting each other."[18]

After one furious battle, William Self was deployed with other Bucktails as skirmishers when night came, and "after a while the Rebels pickets finding we had posted our pickets for the night They began to talk with us." As Self stood guard,

finally a trade was proposed by us to exchange some coffy for some tobacco and one thing another[.] one of our boys went part way and the Reb the other 1/2[,] shook hands[,] talked a spell and returned . . .

[I]n the morning Their men came down on the river banks and began to talk as usual. We got a Richmond Daily Dispatch, had the accounts of the battle in it[.] this was the first papers We had had a chance to read since the fight. We went accrost With a boat and fetched some of them over[.] They would stay and talk till They got tired and went back.[19]

At one point, outside Petersburg, with pickets huddled in trenches less than sixty yards apart, Self said, "the Rebs Came out and Said That They would not fire if we would not[,] so we have not as there is no use of it pickets fireing at one another So Close as we are at them."

[W]e agreede that we would not fire on them and They the Same and if They had Orders to fire they were to tell us and we the same So That They Could Get into Their pits in time. The Same day They and our boys all got togather and had a long talk about the war and many other Things[.] They said They Wished it was over[.][20]

Such fraternization was expressly forbidden by both armies. As an officer, Scudder knew better than to participate in any seemingly innocent friendly exchange. Even though he thought that fraternizing was "much better than shooting each other," Scudder realized that "one might empart valuable informaton & be of serious injury."[21] But it was almost impossible outside the heat of battle to prevent soldiers on either side from taking an amicable attitude toward their enemy.

Many times, officers such as Scudder looked the other way when pickets conversed and swapped goods with southern troops. But on the eve of a major battle later in the war, when one of Tubbs' friends broke the rule against fraternizing, he ended up facing a court-martial.

· CHAPTER 6 ·

Generals

The questions are, Why were the rebels allowed to es-
cape at Manassas? Why did not the "grande armee" of
the Potomac push on Napoleonlike and crush them in
their retreat before they had time to fortify on the new
line of their defences? . . . Tubbs, "there is something
rotten in the State of Denmark"!!
                                    —*Allen A. Van Orsdale*[1]

The trouble with the Army of the Potomac, or virtually any other federal army, was lack of aggression, an inertia that Lincoln discovered he had to fight constantly. Otherwise, his armies would not do battle.

The year 1862 began dismally. Major General George B. McClellan, the General-in-Chief, was ill with what was diagnosed as typhoid fever. Lincoln, upset that the massive army McClellan had assembled had done nothing for five months, took advantage of his illness to take over military matters himself. His task was not made easy by a scandal—charges of corruption in the War Department—that led to the resignation of Simon Cameron. Edwin McMasters Stanton succeeded him as Secretary of War.

The few offensive moves that federal forces were making seemed, at first, halfhearted. Ambrose E. Burnside was on his way to North Carolina with an army and a fleet of almost one hundred vessels, and Ulysses S. Grant was headed into Kentucky from Illinois with another Union force. But Burnside's expedition was having difficulty getting transports and warships across the shallow bar into Pamlico Sound, and Grant's move was strictly a diversionary maneuver—before the end of January he and his men were back in Illinois.

However, on January 19, there was some decisive action. A Union force under Major General George H. Thomas succeeded at the Battle of Mill Springs in breaking the Confederate defense line that ran from the Cumberland Gap in Kentucky west to the Mississippi River. Then, a little more than two weeks later, Ulysses Grant's Army of the Tennessee, on the move again and aided by gunboats, forced Fort Henry on the Cumberland River to surrender. This fort, and ten miles farther, the more formidable Fort Donelson, were the major obstacles to Union advances in the South. Once Donelson fell to Grant on February 16, federal forces controlled a vital river artery bypassing the Mississippi.

Lincoln, meanwhile, tried to prod other generals—Henry Wager Halleck and Don Carlos Buell in the west—into action, but neither responded to the president's request to name a day when they would be ready to move. Frustrated, Lincoln on January 27 did what no other American president had ever done: he ordered the several federal armies to advance on the enemy, even setting the day the various forces were to set out, February 22—Washington's birthday. Four days later, the president issued another order, this one to force the recovering but still reluctant McClellan to open offensive operations in Virginia before February 22. The general, who resented the interference of Lincoln, had refused to tell a Cabinet meeting his plan of operations.

Despite the growing controversy that swirled around McClellan, the troops he commanded, no matter what regiment they were in, supported him nearly to the man. "The very Ground that McClellan . . . walk[s] upon is almost worshipped by the Soldiers," said George Scudder of the 45th Pennsylvania. The men appreciated the general's careful preparations because "Mack (McClellan is the Man) Though Slow but sure . . . what he accomplishes is with the least possible loss of life." Scudder was certain that "two thirds of the Whole Army" had confidence in him."[2]

McClellan seemed to inspire the troops wherever he went. John Orr of the 107th New York described the time the general and his aides rode by:

[H]e is a very fine looking man: as he passed our Brigade cheer after cheer arrose which he returned to each Co with a bow & pleasant smile which made at least a good impression on all giving them assurances of his sympathy & intrest in the welfare of all under his command.[3]

William Self of the 13th Pennsylvania was one of those who had "faith" in McClellan.[4] But the general's biggest supporter may have been another Bucktail, Orrin Stebbins. "MClellan is doing all that man can do," he wrote a highly critical Tubbs,[5] who in his letters to Stebbins mirrored the concern about the Army of the Potamac's apparent inactivity:

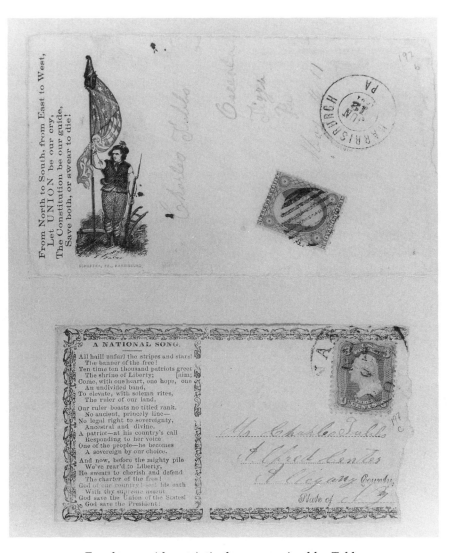

Envelopes with patriotic themes received by Tubbs
from William E. Self. Note the misspelling of McClellan's name.

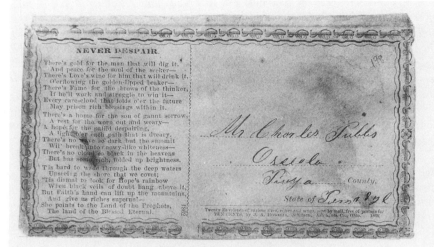

NEVER DESPAIR.

There's gold for the man that will dig it,
 And peace for the soul of the seeker—
There's Love's wine for him that will drink it,
 O'erflowing the golden-lipped beaker—
There's Fame for the brows of the thinker,
 If he'll work and struggle to win it—
Every care-cloud that folds o'er the future
 May prison rich blessings within it.

There's a home for the son of gaunt sorrow,
 A rest for the worn out and weary—
A hope for the palsied despairing,
 A light o'er each path that is dreary.
There's no wave so dark but the summit
 Wil' break into snowy-like whiteness—
There's no cloud so black in the heavens
 But has some rich, folded up brightness.

'Tis hard to wade through the deep waters
 Unseeing the shore that we covet;
'Tis dismal to look for Hope's rainbow
 When black veils of doubt hang above it,
But Faith's hand can lift up the mountains,
 And give us riches supernal—
She points to the Land of the Prophets,
 The land of the Blessed Eternal.

Twenty Envelopes of various Sketches and scraps, sent by mail, free of postage for TEN CENTS, by J. A. Howards, Jefferson, Ashtabula Co., Ohio.   1862

Mr Charles Tubbs

Osceola

Tioga County,

State of Penna &c

Major Gen. George B. McClelland.

Mr. Charles Tubbs
Alfred Center
Allegany Co. N.Y.

If you will visit the Potomac and then Say that we have done nothing after reviewing the forts, the entrenchments[,] the rifle pits, the breastworks, and framing embattlements which Stretch from Harpers Fery to Mount Vernon then I will give up. but you will say, this was all done last Fall. Admit it. Do you think we could move in the Winter? If you do, question . . . any man in whom you have confidence, and they will tell you that you might as well try to stop the thunderings of Niagara.

Why sir, I know that the North can form no correct idea of the fact. You could not move yourself without moving baggage trains ten times worse or cannons a hundred times . . .

Please look A[t] this side of the question: That when McClellan took command there were no forts to protect the Capitol[,] no boats on western waters, no Navy, No cannons of any account . . . in fact we had nothing but defeat and a disorganized army. But look to day? We are Strong and invincible . . . and all this has been accomplished by a Man in Whom the North has no confidence . . .

I only trust that time will prove to the North that McClellan is no ordinary Man but is Just the Man to bring Our Count[r]y Safe out of this dark ocean of battle and contention into the pure Sunlight of peace and freedom. He is buisy every moment of the time. He either Stands at the Wharf to give orders or is riding at lightning Speed from camp to camp or toiling over his Maps at Midnight . . .

I saw him to day as he dashed through our camp while his dark eys Scaned our tent, lifting his hat to every guard and private as he went to the City to Mingle his voice with Lincoln and Stanton.[6]

McClellan was one of the few generals to win praise from Tubbs' friends. Orville Kimball said the 103rd New York had "the fullest confidence" in Burnside.[7] David Armstrong of the 49th Ohio said there were "few Generals in this army I am willing to follow to Battle[,]" but two of them were Alexander McDowell McCook—one of the seventeen so-called Fighting McCooks of Ohio—and William Starke Rosecrans. Both, said Armstrong, "are not a fraid to fight."[8] William Self praised George Meade, saying that he never saw "Old Meeds" do "eny Thing but what he accomplished it nor does he ask a man to go eny farther in than himself. I have seen him where I Thought no man could ever live on a horse[.]"[9]

Far more generals drew the soldiers' ire. Their resentments were not unusual; soldiers faced with death in battle have traditionally questioned the wisdom of their commanders when even the best of plans go awry. But because their mail was not censored, Tubbs' friends were free to express their vitriolic opinions, which were far stronger than usual, run-of-the-mill, rank-and-file grumblings.

George Scudder thought he knew the reason the Army of the Potomac had not taken the offensive. It was "the most corrupt army ever in existence," he said, because there was "so much strife among the Gen'ls[.] Gen'l So and So is fearful that Gen'l So & So will be the rising star if he succeedes in an undertaking and consequently the other Gen'l So & So does all in his power to defeat the planes of the undertaking[.]"[10]

Scudder did not name names, but others of Tubbs' friends were not as reticent when it came to condemning specific commanders. William Self was critical of Edwin H. Stoughton, a West Point graduate who had risen from being colonel of a Vermont regiment to brigadier general in command of a brigade in the XXII Corps. Stoughton, who was captured in his bed by John Singleton Mosby's Raiders, was "no more fit for the posision than a dog," said Self. The trouble, he said, was "so meny incompetient officers."[11]

Self had even harsher words for two other generals. He said that Samuel Wylie Crawford, who at one time led the Pennsylvania Reserves, was "the worst General that ever Comm the Division and is not fit to live[.]"[12] Crawford, Self continued, was also "one of the meanest men in the whole army[,"] detailing men to work "like Common laboring men." Self said that "the men all Swear that they will Shoot him in the next battle." In fact, he added, Crawford had been shot at twice, "the last Time The ball Went Through his Whiskers but he could not find out Who it was."

Self had similar feelings about Irvin McDowell. Writing after the bloody Battle of Antietam, in which he was slightly wounded, Self said that "it would have been a good thing O Lord" if "a cannon ball took off" McDowell's head.[13] Self's resentment was echoed by Scudder, who said that there were "not 5 Reg'ts in this Grand Army that would go into a fight under McDowell again . . . All swear vengeance against him."[14]

David Armstrong felt the same way about Don Carlos Buell. Writing from what he called "Camp Lunatic" south of Nashville after chasing the Confederate forces of Braxton Bragg, Armstrong declared, "I am not in habbet of shoot[ing] northern soldiers Friend Charles but there is old Buell[.] I should like to be detailed to Shoot Old Buell."[15]

The Bucktails, always an independent lot, were adept not only at criticizing their commanders but also at taking matters into their own hands. During 1862, they were issued new weapons, breech-loading Sharps rifles—"the best Gun in use," said a gratified Self.[16] With a standard muzzle-loader, an experienced infantryman might be able to fire off three shots a minute, but with a Sharps rifle he could get off as many as eight shots. Moreover, the fastest way for a rifleman to load a muzzle-loader was to stand upright so that he could ram the bullet down the barrel—thereby becoming an easy target for an enemy sharp-shooter. He did not have to be exposed in that position with the Sharps rifle.

One day, after a number of engagements in Virginia, some of the Bucktails got fed up with being undermanned, particularly because the War Department had refused to allow their commander to return to Pennsylvania to recruit. The soldiers' resentment was fueled by the fact that, after a wait of eight months, they had been paid only half the amount due them. It was "dishartining Them," said Self. "You see it like riding a good horse til he can go no longer." So some of the men decided to quit:

This morning Co. E came out and stacking Their arms swearing that they wer [not] going to doe eny more till they got some pay and That They wer not going to fight untill we had some respect shown to us on the recruiting ques-tion[.] This is about the feeling in The Whole Division[;] they want amount to eny thing more under The circumstances and to day Captain Taylor Command-ing The Regt formerly Commanding H Co had a lot of big long guns while the rest of The Co have the Sharp Rifles[,] a very nice gun[,] the last in the seris[.] so he Takes The guns of E Co. and C Co. The former refused to the exchange and are marched off under Guard[.] What is to be done With them I doe not know[.] the lot has took them[.] . . .

I doe Say it is a shame for us to go into another fight as Small as we are[.] we used to have a Co. of 100 men and now all we draw rations for is 18 and if We Wer to go in now we could not makes more than 10[.] 8 and 10 is all We have for Duty and I dont like it my self although I go through them all safe but I may not always[.] There has been a good many Shot down [alongs]ide of me.[17]

Tubbs' friends wrote nasty comments about their commanders and articulated their inimical thoughts without worrying about being charged with insubordination. But uncensored letters that were read only by Tubbs were one thing; open breaches of army rules and regula-tions were another matter and could get the civilians-turned-soldiers into serious trouble.

A few months after the incident involving members of Company E of the Bucktails, Major General Samuel Peter Heintzelman, the com-mander of the XXII Corps, presented an American flag to one of the regiment's quartermaster officers, a captain by the name of Smith. Heintzelman said that the Bucktails could raise the flag if they could get enough men to erect a pole. Eagerly, according to William Self, virtually every Bucktail as well as men of the 1st Pennsylvania Reserves volunteered to do the job. But they had not reckoned with the reaction of William Sinclair, a colonel with another Pennsylvania regiment, the 6th, who had been promoted to general of the brigade in which the Bucktails served:

[I]t was a Splendid pole 125 ft high and a flag 40 feet long and 20 wide[.] after this was all over we proposed Three cheers for the flag and for Capt Smith Then some of them that raised the flag[.]

[W]e then returned to camp proud to think we had suceeded in raising so well but we had not been in [camp] long before I herd Some of the 1st hoellowing ["]fall in BuckTailes[,] Sin.Clair is cutting down the flag[."] this SinClair is our Brigadier General and is opposed to every Thing that we doe[.] So in we went for to sustain the flag but . . . by the time we had gone there he had his Sixth Regt there to cut it down[.] this is the Regt he used to have command of[.] They come up with Their guns while we had none but I tole the boys that we had beter take our guns along but they said no[,] They hardly Thought he would be mean enough for that to Cut down such a splendid flag[.]

[B]ut we got over there among them and as he [Sinclair] came up leading the charge against us he says to some of the boys to fall in[,] that he was going to arrest them[.] then we began to holloa at him and to stone him saying ["]get out of here you son of a bitch[."] The Stone wer at him so thick that he could not Stand them so that he went back accost the rail Road and the stone took him in the back and I understan that he had his $300 sword broke with a stone[.] he arrested about 30 of our Regt[.]

Sinclair then ordered a surprise roll call. Fortunately, however, Self returned to the Bucktails' campsite before his name was called and escaped being arrested. But he was angry. He got his rifle and was prepared to return to where the flagpole lay on the ground, but no one else in his company wanted to turn the confrontation into outright mutiny. "I did not go," Self rued, "but if I had I should have Shot the man that put the ax to the pole or should have tried to doe so[.]"

Self was certain that it would "go hard" with Sinclair for cutting down the flag. "[H]e is to[o] mean to live and if he ever leads this Brigade into action he will never come out alive I clerly think[.]"[18]

Although he was a first lieutenant and should have voiced his complaints in private, George Scudder openly challenged his superiors. Both he and the captain of Company F of the 45th Pennsylvania were publicly critical of the treatment their regiment received. Scudder did not amplify on the nature of the complaints to Tubbs, saying only, "There is a little dissatisfaction among some of the Officers (Our own tent included) because they think that Our Companies are not treated alike or as they ought to be[.]" But whatever he and the captain said was insubordinate enough to get them arrested. Their colonel, who "must have thought we were fools," released the two men the next day, Scudder said, "without charge or jury," much to his chagrin. He wanted to air the complaints. "Our release," Scudder explained, "should have been done by a board of officers assembled to examine into the matter."[19]

David Armstrong wrote to Tubbs in a rage about the conditions at "Camp Lunatic" outside Nashville. For one thing, he said, the slaves the 49th Ohio had freed in Tennessee "have their beds to sleep in and their reglar meals and when it rains they can go in shelter but the poor soldiers has not even a pillow to lay his head on and on the march we had no tents to sleep under[.]"[20]

Armstrong also complained about how difficult it was for a lowly infantryman like himself to get leave to go home. Officers were clearly favored. "[S]oldiers that had pigeon tirds on their Shoulders enlisted in a different kind of service for they are the ones that can get a furlough to go home." Armstrong said he had not even requested a leave "because I dont try to do a thing that I dont have any faith in and when I can muster faith a nough to try to get a furlough I will[—]that is faith that I can get one."[21]

Before the winter of 1861–62 ended, Dr. Humphrey recovered and was back with the Bucktails. By then, most of Tubbs' soldier friends were diverted from their grumblings by the promise of battle. Northern forces were beginning at last to stir into action. The Pennsylvanians, among others, were excited. "[A]t about Eleven O Clock," William Self said, "the air echoed with Musick and Soon cheer after cheer went up through the aire." The Bucktails were on the march. "[W]e had Forty Rounds of ammunition and Three day Raitions and our knaps a Weighing Sixty lbs . . . We Expected to Meet the Enemy in Battles aray."[22]

· CHAPTER 7 ·

On the Offensive at Last

[Y]ou wanted to know weather I had Seen Gen
Grant[.] . . . I know a little a bout his Generelship[.]
on Friday and Saturday there was skirmishing in front
of [his] pickets and in Stead of doubleing the pickets as
he ought to have don he drawed them in with a few
roads of the Camp and he unconcerned lay and Slept
and the first thing he know on Sunday morning the
balls come a flying in the tents[.]
                                    —David Armstrong[1]

Before the winter of 1862 was out, Lincoln's prodding began to pay
off. The war settled into the brisk, hard fighting typical of the next
three years of conflict.

In the second week of February, Ambrose Burnside captured Roanoke Island, North Carolina, giving the Union control of Pamlico Sound
and a crucial base for operations against southern forces in that state.
His victory was soon followed by the capture of the city of New Berne.
The battle for Roanoke had been a minor one—Burnside's 7,500 men
against fewer than 2,000 Confederates—but when the news reached
the federal forces in Virginia, the outcome was celebrated as a major
victory. William Self said that "there was cheering all over This army of
the Potomac," and to the accompaniment of the band of a Wisconsin
regiment, the celebration went on almost the entire night.[2]

At almost the same time, a Union army under Don Carlos Buell
met in spirit the president's call for action on Washington's birthday.
Spurred by Grant's taking of Forts Henry and Donelson earlier in February, on the 25th of the month, Buell's force, which included the 49th
Ohio, occupied Nashville. "[W]e have had som hard marching to get
heare," said David Armstrong,

The battle between the *Monitor* and the *Merrimac*
is commemorated on this envelope.

*we have waded rivers and creeks[,] we have went over hills and through valeys
and we have traveled on stones and good roads and we have waded mud bout
lap deep and we have laid out in the storms and cold weather, we have laid on
the bare ground and we have cut brush to lay on to kee[p] out of the mud . . .
and to get heare we marched in the day time and in the night.*[3]

To a southerner, the future must have now seemed ominous.
Federal forces controlled northern Virginia, others on the Peninsula
threatened Norfolk and the capital of the Confederacy, Richmond. To
the south, Union armies were menacing Savannah and Charleston; still
others were imperiling New Orleans and Mobile on the Gulf Coast. On
March 9, a Sunday, a memorable battle—the dawn of the modern era
of naval warfare—was fought between the ironclads *Monitor* and *Merrimac* in the gateway to the James River in Virginia, Hampton Roads.
The fight ended in a draw but was a tactical victory for the Union's
Monitor. The *Merrimac*, hampered by engine trouble and her heavy
draft, was confined to Hampton Roads and no longer a danger to federal ships. In addition, Confederate-held Norfolk was no longer secure.
The clash between the ironclads was no sooner over than Lincoln
relieved McClellan as General-in-Chief of all Union forces but left him
in command of the Army of the Potomac. For the time being, the presi-

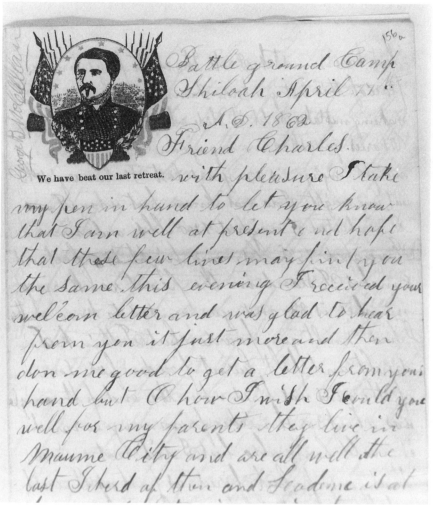

David Armstrong wrote from Shiloh on stationery featuring
the controversial George B. McClellan.

dent decided, there would be no General-in-Chief. All commanding
generals would report directly to the Secretary of War.

The stage was now set for almost constant warfare. Two battles
that soon followed, one in Tennessee, the other in Virginia, involved
two of Tubbs' friends—his childhood pal, David Armstrong, and one
of his "Brother Oros" from Alfred, Henry Maxson.

As winter turned to spring, the South tried to seize the initiative. A Confederate army under Albert Sidney Johnston headed toward Pittsburg Landing on the Tennessee River. Its target: to catch Grant's unsuspecting army by surprise.

Just behind the federal lines stood a small church, Shiloh Meeting House. Early on the Sabbath morning of April 6, the Confederates attacked.

The 49th Ohio, attached to Alexander McCook's division of Buell's army, was on its way to join Grant's forces. On the march from Nashville for the past three weeks, it was still a day away from Grant's position when, David Armstrong said,

we herd heavy Cannonnadeing[.] we left our wagons[,] knapsacks and over Coats behind and we went on for fight and we marched that day and night and the next morning we got in a boat and rode ten miles on the Tenn. river and the fighting was then 2 miles then from us and we got up of the boat and loaded our guns[.] in a Short meter we was at the boat whare the dead men lay and the spot whare to cause them to lay[.]

The 49th Ohio entered the battle about eleven in the morning of the second day of the fighting, April 7, serving as the left anchor of the division's Sixth Brigade. Twice in the next five hours the men performed the hazardous movement of changing front under heavy fire. Armstrong, who carried the regimental colors into the action, said, "[W]e fought till in the after noon and about 3 o clock and the rebels ran a way and then we could rest a little while[.]"

The men of 49th Ohio returned to the place where they had left their knapsacks, but most of their blankets were gone, filched by other soldiers. "[I]t was impossible to find a dry place to lay," said Armstrong, "but we laid down and it rained and when I a woke the water was a runing under me a bout 2 inches deep and I got up and sat by a stump under a blanket with another soldier[.] this was my nights rest and we did not get our tents till 6 or 7 day[s]."[4]

[T]he 49th Reg Stood up to the rack as well as any one could while the rebels just pored in the old Cannon balls[,] shell and shot[.] but what do you think went toward them[?] the generals say they never herd such Noble fireing in their lives[.] weather it is so or not I can not tell but I give them the best I had in the Shop[.][5]

The outcome was a standoff of sorts. Grant's forces, aided by the troops of Buell and Lew Wallace, held their ground. But their number of killed, wounded, and missing totaled more than thirteen thousand men. The Confederates lost fewer men, fewer than eleven thousand in all, but among them was their commander, Johnston.

By April, another Confederate army, this one under Stonewall Jackson, was in the Shenandoah Valley, forcing the Union to pull troops from the Army of the Potomac. But despite Jackson's maneuvers, the rest of McClellan's huge army, some one hundred thousand men, finally moved, edging toward Richmond in a five-month-long operation known as the Peninsular Campaign. On April 5, McClellan's forces began besieging Yorktown. Henry Maxson was with the 85th New York outside the city when a mysterious order came for the regiment to fall in before its usual time for dress parade:

> We knew it was not for that, but what it was for we knew not. Soon we started towards our picket lines [.] then I thought we were to be a reserve for a reconnoissance, but as we entered the woods near our outer pickets we were drawn up in battle line[.] then I learned we were to make the reconoissance ourselves.
>
> Forward we went in battle line passing our pickets who hoped we would not come back as a reg't did a few days before[.] Onward we went till once near the Warwick creek when pop goes a gun[,] crack crack gun caps[,] and we knew we were on _their_ pickets[.] onward we go till close to the creek or a widening of it when thicker and faster came the bullets[.]
>
> We learned but little of their works though driving in their pickets and hearing the long roll beaten in quite a no. of their camps[;] we got back to our camp all safe[,] one man having a ball lodged in the stock of his gun.

A few days later, on May 4, the Confederate forces evacuated Yorktown, retreating toward Williamsburg and leaving in their wake a road planted with landmines. The 85th started in pursuit:

> The Rebels were up to some tricks[,] planted shells in the road so fixed that when anyone stepped on one it burst. Only one burst on our road and that ahead of our Reg't killing one and wounding several.
>
> We passed many strong forts or would have been strong if our forces had held them in commanding positions but forsaken camps were left as if their occupants were in a hurry to get away only having time to spoil most of their tents by cutting them and venting their spite by writing some slang for us to read. We passed many fine plantations some with fine houses and large fields of

wheat quite well grown showing that they were preparing for a long stay and wished enough to eat[.]

Monday[,] the day of the battle near Williamsburgh[,] it rained all day[.] We were several miles back but could hear the musketry very plain and toward night were drawn up in line for any emergency and stayed up till midnight[.] Tuesday wet and weary we came on reaching a portion of the battle field at night and camping near it[.]

On the following day, Maxson strolled over the field where many of the dead were still lying, unburied. "The sight was enough[.] I cared not to run as many did all over the wood . . . where the severest part of the battle was fought[.]"

The 85th passed through Williamsburg, whose womenfolk, Maxson said, "looked very sour." He saw, he said, many captured Confederate soldiers:

As we passed some of the prisoners one of the guards said some one of the prisoners wanted him to ask if there would ever be an end to the Yankee army going through. I reckon he wished there would be an end of the Yankee army long before there was. We passed William and Mary's College[,] a fine edefice now used as a hospital. (This was where Washington was educated I believe.) This village is an ancient looking place[.] The houses are on an ancient style. We stopped Saturday night where we are now to wait for our provision train to come up[.]

Maxson supposed that the army would continue toward Richmond, but "The movement of so large an army is necessarily slow yet I doubt not the result is sure[;] we must conquer and that soon[.]"[6]

Three weeks later, as the campaign dragged on, the 85th New York had advanced only some thirty miles toward Richmond. The regiment was attached to a division of the IV Corps led by Brigadier General Silas Casey. A veteran of Indian fighting and the Mexican War, Casey was the author of a two-volume work on infantry tactics that was adopted by the U.S. Army in 1862 and widely used as well by Confederate officers. Casey's division crossed the Chickahominy River within eight miles of Richmond, reaching the Williamsburg Stage Road near the town of Seven Pines. There, confronted by a superior Confederate force, the IV Corps halted on Thursday, May 29, and dug in:

Just in front of our camp not ten rods distant was commenced a redoubt or small fort and on either side rifle pits as well as forming an abbattis in front toward our picket lines[.] So extended were our picket lines and so ardorous our labor that three companies from our Reg't and I think as many from every Reg't in the division were on picket and fatigue duties . . .

Saturday dawned quietly upon us[,] now soon to be a day of carnage.

Company C was just finishing dinner when, Maxson said,

we were aroused by the whizzing of a shell over our camp soon followed by another. The order came [to] fall in and we grasped our cartridge boxes and rifles[,] leaving everything else just as it happened we were soon in line.

Our Reg't took position in the rifle pits to the left of the redoubt, our Brigade . . . to our left, the first and second to the right and in front.

Maxson knew the Confederates were coming because the sound of the Union pickets firing against the advancing southerners had noticeably increased.

Our Batteries opened on them doing good work as did the infantry[,] their support, but the enemy came steadily on as fast as their ranks were opened they were filled by others and our advance battery was only saved by a gallant bayonet charge under Gen Casey's own supervision.

Those in front giving way gave us a chance to try our rifles and good service they did as was shown by the piles of the dead before us[;] at least two crack Rebel Reg'ts came up but went back terribly thinned in ranks. We held our place till our battery of brass guns was deserted and every Reg't of ours had fallen back.

Casey's division fought for three and a half hours, finally retiring before the overwhelming Confederate force. But, Maxson angrily reported, the division was "stigmatized" for what an official report called "falling back Unaccountably and disunitedly." All the other divisions in the corps except Casey's were commended for behaving "manfully." Irate, Maxson insisted, "I am conscious of doing my whole duty and believe most of the Division did theirs."[7]

CHAPTER 8

"The South"

*He [who] doubts the diere & scourging effects of slav-
ery ought to visit the South[,] tken it is as [a] whole it
is 50 years behind the North both in intellectual and
Agricultural improvements.*

—John Orr[1]

Most of Charles Tubbs' friends spoke about the southerners they encountered in a general way. They labeled them traitors or rebels but refrained, for the most part, from castigating them further. If anything, their lack of comment testifies to the fact that they found them to be much like themselves. A few of Tubbs' friends, however, were dumbfounded by the behavior of certain southerners and did not hesitate to detail their criticisms.

One day in mid-April 1862, while stationed in Virginia, Orrin Stebbins and his good friend from Alfred University, Allen Van Orsdale, took a walk around the countryside near Manassas, following the First Battle of Bull Run. After a few hours, they came upon a farmhouse with little log huts scattered around it. The house belonged to a doctor; the huts were for his slaves. Seeing the two Union soldiers, the doctor came out and invited them to join him for dinner. At the table, as the men dined on a meager meal of cold meat and hoecakes, the doctor's wife talked "about the country, the war, and of course about the slaves, for their whole life seems bound up in them." In the course of the conversation, the woman said, "The face of the land looks good, but in fact it is poor, and will only produce enough to keep the stock, which is the only thing profitable in this state, and that, at the present time, was of no value to any one."

We being rather green and inquisitive Yankees, of course must know what kind of stock was the most profitable, and asked if it was horses, sheep, or cattle. "Oh, no," she said, twisting her pretty little mouth in a dozen shapes, "it is neither of those. I have reference to the young slaves." We could not help laughing at the peculiar stress laid on the "stock," when used by a sensitive and modest southern lady, and especially when applied to human beings.— What a mockery of modesty when viewed through northern civilization.[2]

The following month, Stebbins was stationed for a time beside the Rappahannock River near Fredericksburg, whose main street, he wrote Tubbs, "reminds me very much of the main street in Wellsboro, but it is not as wide, or well shaded." Outside the town, on a green bluff, stood an unfinished stone monument that was ten feet high and surrounded by pillars. It was a memorial to George Washington's mother. The teacher in Stebbins was scandalized because the monument had been "very badly defaced, and abused in a shameful manner."

The rebels have broken off the edges and corners, for tokens to take home, cut their names upon [it] with knives, and have even been barbarous enough to use it for a target, until it is blackened with powder and lead.[3]

Despite what he felt about Fredericksburg—"the best looking city I have yet seen in the South"—Stebbins saw an infantryman on guard duty in the town step on the spring of a "torpedo" that set off a keg of powder, killing the man instantly. But what was worse, he said, was that "as his comrades were taking his mangled form by a house where a woman (not a lady) was standing in the door, she slapped her hands and shouted glory, and said she wished the whole Yankee nation was in the same fix."

Stebbins was so enraged that he thought that Fredericksburg "ought to be buried deeper beneath shot and shell, in less than twenty-four hours, than the walls of Palmyra are, to-day, buried beneath the sands of the desert!"[4]

An otherwise mild-mannered man, Asa Spencer was so troubled by the activities of southern spies and saboteurs that he became livid when confronted with the results of their sabotage. His regiment, the 136th Pennsylvania, was outside Frederick, Maryland, not far from where a saboteur had blown up a Baltimore & Ohio Railroad bridge. The "vile rebel" had been caught afterwards and hanged, the Osceola schoolmaster wrote Tubbs:

They buried him a little below the bridge with his hands projecting out of the ground. If it is right to bury a man in this position for his crimes I think they have done it with bad taste. For if it is right they should have buried him with his head downwards and heels sticking out showing his downward tendency.[5]

As pious as he was, John Orr expressed little charity of feeling for the southerners he met in both Virginia and Tennessee. It was, for one thing, a matter of morals: they were all untrustworthy. When confronted, he said, they all said they were Union sympathizers—and he knew they did not mean a word of it. To illustrate his point, Orr related to Tubbs an incident when he was in Virginia. One Saturday, he was in charge of picket duty for the 107th New York, with orders to arrest any suspicious person who tried to pass through the federal line:

About noon an old fellow (a citizen) living outside the line, came out to cut wood close to the pickets: the Corporal arrested him[.] It was just as we were releiving the outpost; as I came up with the Releif the Cor[poral] pointed out the prisoner. I told him I would attend to him as soon as we could send out the Sentinels. Before sending out the Sentinels we have them load their peices[.] I gave the order to load & and I guess the old fellow thought his time had come, for he began to tremble & shake like a leaf, saying ["*]sir—I meant-no-harm.[*"*] I kept him until the Field Officer of the Day came along. His wife soon came out to look for her husband & we had a pair of Seceshion inhabitants whether true or loyal I do not know. They of course said they were Union but they all say this[.] We finally released them, telling them not to be caught near our lines again.*

But "thus it is," Orr added, "that much valuable information is smuggled through our lines."[6]

In Tennessee, Orr also found that most of the citizens called themselves Union sympathizers. But here he went further, remarking on what he believed was their lack of both character and education. "[T]hey are a deceitful set of ignoramuses & there is but little dependence to be put in them," he told Tubbs. The South's citizens were "a very ignorant set & mostly rebels." Its society, Orr continued, "is composed of a far more ignorant indolent degraded set." He was especially appalled by some of the habits that southerners displayed:

Here children have been permitted to grow up uneducated, women chew tobacco[,] eat snuff with a stick. By the way did you ever hear of a fashionable practice here among the ladies called dipping? You see a lady with a stick in her mouth which looks very much like a penholder[,] *one end of this broomed up & dipped into a bottle of snuff then placed in the mouth, there sucked & chewed and if you waited awhile you would see a squirt which for accuracy of aim could not be beat by a . . . Sharp shooter. This I have seen[.] Do such filthy disgusting practices prevail in the North[?] Some may like the style but I wish to be excused.*[7]

Orr said that there was "a time coming[,] Tubbs[,] when this South-ern country will be settled by civilized people[.] What can we expect of a people whose God is *tobacco* & *niggers*: tobacco to eat & *niggers* to caress & fondle. In some sections[,] even here where the negro is bru-talized to the lowest extreme[,] he seems to have a more 'general knowledge' than many of the whites[.]"[8]

The Kimball brothers, Orville and Harlan, reacted similarly to the southerners with whom they came into contact in North Carolina. At the time of the Battle of Shiloh in Tennessee, they were with the 103rd New York outside the city of New Berne, North Carolina, some forty miles inland from Pamlico Sound, in the vicinity of the battleground that Ambrose Burnside's army had fought over and won—where, Or-ville said, "Rebel relics" of the fighting, knapsacks, "are not scarce."

But foodstuffs were at a premium compared to the prices that the northerners were accustomed to paying. For one thing, Orville noted that there were no crops in the vicinity. Residents took advantage of shortages and charged prices that were dear for butter, potatoes, cider, and oranges. Even partly rotten apples, he complained, cost three cents each. Moreover, the locals were asking five cents for three sheets of stationery and fifty cents for a pack of envelopes. "[A]t this rate," Or-ville said, "it wel not pay to buy many things[.]"[9]

Late in May, the Kimballs' unit, Company I of the 103rd, was transferred to Cape Hatteras, where work was still going on to repair the 140-foot-high lighthouse that Confederate troops had tried to de-stroy before evacuating the island. The brothers' view of the citizens there was particularly damning.

Harlan said they had to be on the alert for the "pranks" of the "wreckers," who "for several nights set up false lights on the shore to draw vessels on to the breakers."[10] Orville said that after one vessel loaded with molasses and sugar ran aground, its contents were soon available and could be bought "for almost anything." The islanders, who were cunning, had a reputation, he added, of even going so far "as to kill the poor sailors after they were wrecked."[11]

Orville thought the residents of the island, about six hundred in number, were "strange looking people." He said he had not seen "one intelligent man here yet," that "they seem to have no taste for learn-ing" and a "very limited kno[w]ledge of figures[.]" Because few books were available and no newspaper at all, Orville was prompted to think that the islanders were "half civilized." He readily admitted, "I detest the whole set of them." True, they treated federal soldiers cordially, he granted, but "each one runs down his neighbor[,] calling them seces-sionists almost invariably[.] to hear each one talk separately you would think he was the only Union man on the Island."

Both Orville and Harlan had mixed feelings about being stationed on the island. Their accommodations were certainly better than what they were accustomed to in the service. The brothers were sharing a room in "a large white house with Cook[,] rooms[,] dining room[.]," Harlan wrote Charles Tubbs' brother Henry. "[A]ll we have to do is set down to the table and eat after the fashion you do at home[.]" In addition to the abundance of army rations they now enjoyed, he said, "there are a plenty of chances to [ex]change for eggs[,] milk[,] chickens &C which are to us a luxury. Molasses can be bought for 20 cts a gallon[,] milk the same[.] Eggs 12 cts a dozzen."

But the climate was another matter. "I pity the guard that is pacing to and fro down in the field yonder[,]" Harlan said in the midst of a hot summer day. On the other hand, he continued, "Altho this burning sun may tell against this place there are things which tell in her favor. One is there is always one of the most refreshing breezes here I have ever seen . . . Pennsylvania can never boast of as fine evng as I have seen. Were it possible I would rather sleep day time and drill night."[12]

Orville was not much taken at all with Cape Hatteras. "[T]he flees and mosquitoes which are plenty all over the south at this season of the year are most tormenting in their attentions here," he said, and "should I chance to leave my window open I might as well bid farewell to sleep for that night[.]" Moreover, there were all kinds of reptiles—water moccasins, rattlers, and black snakes. But what he found "severely" troubling were the wood ticks. "[T]hey seem to breed in the sand and should one happen to sit down he know his fate[.] often if they are not brushed off they immediately fix themselves firmly without any conscientious scruples as to whether they have any such rights or not[.]" In addition,

> [N]aught is heard save the sullen roar of the Ocean waves as they rushing like torent break harmless on the sand here[.] we do not hear the warbling of birds as at home[.] there are birds here but they do not seem to sing . . . nothing is as cheerful here.

Orville's main problem was boredom. "We have nothing to do," he said. The men had little guard duty and no drilling whatsoever because their captain, first lieutenant, and two sergeants took sick. So to while away the time, the soldiers swam in the sea and walked along the beach, gathering seashells, or otherwise "lay in our rooms and amuse ourselves as best we can all day long." Orville was worried that his rifle would lie "unused as I fear it will till the close of the war."

Orville was also concerned about his younger brother's health, which had deteriorated in the southern climate. Harlan, he said, "is not so tough as he has been . . . he is and always has been subject to the chill fever and he once in a while has an attack of it but nothing to make sick so as to be confined to his bed."[13]

Harlan was worried, too, about the illness—in all likelihood, malaria—that plagued Company I. Writing the day after he turned eighteen in mid-August of 1862, he noted that five of its members, including its second lieutenant and orderly sergeant, were "lost" to the "fever," and fifteen more men were in the hospital. He himself was "not quite recovered yet."[14]

· CHAPTER 9 ·

Death in the Afternoon

I am as tough as a bull. My weight is about 170 lbs.
—Orrin Stebbins[1]

A few days into the summer of 1862, Orrin Stebbins stood guard with other Bucktails upon the bank of the narrow, shallow Chicka-hominy, within speaking distance of the Confederate pickets across the river and in plain sight of their artillery. The Army of the Potomac was now within five miles of Richmond. Every day there was skirmishing, and "scarcely an hour passes away," he said, "but what the cannons are thundering around us. Whenever a new ditch, earthwork, or fort is commenced, then the shells come howling over."

Stebbins had enlisted as a private, but now he was Company A's first sergeant, and as the men stood in formation a little later, awaiting orders,

our Major told us that he wanted us to remember three things, if we were so fortunate as to meet the enemy, viz. "Be quiet, be cool, and keep together, so long as we are united, we can never be conquered."[2]

On Friday, June 27, the third of a series of engagements known as the Seven Days' Battles took place—an engagement called variously the Battle of Gaines' Mill, the First Battle of Cold Harbor, or the Battle of the Chickahominy. The day began quietly for men of Company A of the 13th Pennsylvania Reserves. They were on picket duty opposite the town of Mechanicsville.[3] The Bucktails were relaxed, unperturbed. Sometime about one in the afternoon, Stebbins showed a photograph he had received in the mail to William Self and asked him if he knew who it was. Self indeed knew. It was a photo of their mutual friend Charles Tubbs. Suddenly, as the two men were speaking, Company A was ordered to return to camp immediately. Stebbins did not under-stand the reason for the urgency. "Steb," Self related, "says pshaw it is all foolishness[,] havent herd a gun or eny thing to come in for." But just at that moment a Confederate force commanded by Robert E. Lee attacked, and Company A reached camp barely in time. Pickets from Company K were captured before they could make it back, and two officers barely "saved their Skins" when their horses were shot from under them. A Confederate artillery battery came into sight and began firing "a steady rore like the ocean."

Steb and I wer together in the pits[.] we had Just finished and soon as our artilery opened on them out came a Brigade 40 yards off us on the double quick cheering and hooting[,] thinking to turn our Right but there was swamp 15 rods below as down they came to a small bridge to cross[.] they did not see us till they herd from us first[,] When we opened on them pileing ther killed and wounded top of one another[.] While a fiew rods to our left came out in front of our artilery[,] our battery pouring canester and grape into them mowing them down like grass by the 100[.] had there been the fighting the whole lenth of the line there would have been 20000 killed easy[.] there was 13000 as it was[.]

A spent ball or a piece of shell hit Self, but without force, leaving only a bad bruise.[4] Stebbins was also nearly hit. He was on his knees in the rifle pit when a bullet struck his cap and knocked it from his head. "[C]lose call Says he," Self reported, "picked it up as though nothing had happened." A sergeant named Millworth, who was next to Stebbins and Self in the rifle pit, was not so lucky. Foolishly, he was standing erect between the two crouching men. Self warned him to lie down in the pit, but the sergeant ignored him. He was struck by two bullets, one of which hit him in the head.[5]

Stebbins' blasé response when his cap was struck from his head belied deeper feelings. He was obsessed with dying. He ended several letters to Charles Tubbs with the maudlin "Yours until death," and in one letter he lamented that he had no family: "I have friends, but no wife and little ones to mourn my loss in case I fall in battle."[6]

Barely more than a month earlier, while the Bucktails were encamped at Fredericksburg, Stebbins went out of his way to visit a "beautiful" cemetery just outside the town. It was surrounded by a wall of brick, had a "huge" iron gate, and was shaded by "large and lovely weeping willows."

In this cemetery is about 150 newly made graves, where rebel soldiers are sleeping. There are 94 in one row, mostly from North Carolina. To this church-yard, the ladies of the city, and swarms of little girls, neatly dressed in white, come daily to trim the soldiers' graves, and scatter flowers upon their tombs.

As I stood and looked upon the low mounds around me, with the air fragrant with roses, and many of the graves white with pebbles and shells gathered from the ocean, I could not but contrast their long home with very many of our own brave soldiers, who have lain down their lives for their country . . . As I stood and gazed upon that silent history of the dead, the record of departed greatness, a feeling stole over me which language has no power to express.[7]

Stebbins' fatalism—his premonitions about death—even infected the reports he was sending to the *Tioga County Agitator*. Ordinarily, he mentioned his private thoughts only to Tubbs. His accounts to the *Agitator* were matter-of-fact, making note of the Bucktails' movements, camp life, and experiences for the benefit of the men's families back in Pennsylvania. But early that spring, on the first anniversary of his enlisting, he became personal, writing the weekly newspaper:

One year ago this bright May morning, I packed my valise, bade my parents and friends adieu, and with a hurried step started for the battle field . . . Never shall I forget my feelings as I passed from room to room, and gazed at the paintings upon the walls, and every familiar object, before the ratling stage bore me from the home I loved so well.[8]

Then, a week before the Battle of Gaines' Mill, Stebbins was disturbed to read the casualty reports coming back from four companies of Bucktails under their colonel, Thomas Kane, who had been temporarily detached from the rest of the regiment to fight in the Shenandoah Valley. His mood was somber:

No one but a soldier can tell the feelings of a soldier's heart, as they read the list of killed and wounded and there find the names of those they had learned to love, those who were as true as the steel they had learned to wield, those with whom they have marched, drilled, and fought side by side, either suffering upon a wounded soldier's bunk or sleeping in a warrior's grave. Yet it is cheering for us to know that they died at their post with their face to the foe, gallantly fighting for their country![9]

That night after the "close call," at Gaines' Mill on June 28, the Bucktails covered the rest of the division as it retreated. The men of Company A slept in the rifle pits, all the while listening to the groans of the wounded who still lay on the battleground.

The Confederates renewed their attack early the next morning. The fighting went on all day, until a New York regiment came to the Bucktails' assistance. As the relief force approached about sunset, Self said, "the rebels sent a shell and hit an orderly[,] cut him into in the middle[;] the upper part Went up among the tree tops while the other Stood on the feet part quivering as it was done so quick[.]"

On the third day, Monday, June 30, in a confused engagement at Charles City Crossroads, the 13th Pennsylvania and an artillery battery, although outnumbered, held another Confederate attack in check for nearly two and a half hours before being ordered to retreat across a swamp. Because of the noise of battle, Companies D and E did not hear the bugle call and were captured. But Stebbins and Self, with other members of Company A, had heard the command. They managed to cross the swamp and were running through an open field with the Confederates chasing them and "pouring" bullets at their backs when, all of a sudden, Stebbins fell. In their rush to escape capture, his companions in the company did not stop to help him.

Almost two weeks after the Bucktails' participation in the battle at Charles City Crossroads, a fatigued Dr. Humphrey, who had been meaning to write Tubbs for three months, picked up his pen while in camp near Harrison's Landing on the James River. His report, "a sketch of the late battles before Richmond," went into detail about the travails the 13th Pennsylvania had encountered:

> [A]s to results Our Regiment (the Buck Tails) at Roll Call number 142 men[.] Co E Commanded by Captain Niles was taken prisoners while leaving the Rifle pit on the morning of the 27th near Mechanicsville . . . 1/2 of Co (D) Also taken on the 3d days' fight. Only 10 Killed 30 Wounded & the rest Missing[.] So you see Our loss is comparatively Small of the Kiled & wounded.
>
> On the morning of the 27th Our Regt held the Enemy 2 hours until Our forces Could fall back 3 miles to the Gains House—Assisted with one battery of 6 pieces[.] Here was the greatest destruction of life . . . Our boys behind their entrenchments & Our battery Kept up a Constant fire which sent volley after volley into the enemies ranks As they marched out of the woods into An open space in dense columns at a distance of about 40 rods & as fast as the Enemy fell their ranks were immediately filled to meet the same fate[.]

Humphrey said he was not exaggerating in saying that ten thousand Confederates had been killed in the fighting:

> This point of the attack is where the Enemy Made the Attempt to cut Our lines[,] Outflank & Surround us. They finally with a largely Superior force Succeeded in getting around but it was when Our Division (Except the Bucktails) had fallen back 3 miles. Had we remained 5 minutes longer Our Regt would all have been captured. Co E being on the right were taken before leaving

the Camp[.] The rest of our boys barely escaped[.] The Rebel force at this point was not less than 20000[.]

It is known that this Success at this time in keeping the enemy in Check Saved Our Entire Army & prevented the flanking movement & also the breaking through our lines As Our forces were then enabled to concentrate & make a safe retreat to James River.

The reality, of course, was that Lee had saved Richmond. Humphrey insisted that to take the Confederate capital, the Army of the Potomac would need "at least" one hundred thousand more men:

The Enemy is strongly fortified About their Capitol & they consider this Point their only hope & are determined to hold it[.] Troops are well disciplined & have good Commanders[.] . . . But we shall take it, at all hazards[.]

The doctor reported that "Our boys" were in "good spirits" and rested, but that he personally was not:

3 days & nights I had no rest—but worked till I gave out several times[.] Eat but 3 hard crackers during the time I assisted the Brigade Surgeon & operated for all we could find of the wounded belonging to McCalls Division[.] Out of 12000 About 6000 are all who are left of Our Division[.]

Humphrey regretfully added that Stebbins was "among the Killed."[10]

Stebbins died in combat fourteen days after his twenty-ninth birthday. As far as Self knew, his body was never brought off the battlefield.[11]

Of the five friends of Charles Tubbs who had enlisted in the 13th Pennsylvania Reserves, one, Stebbins, was dead, killed in battle, and a second, Samuel Stevens, had died of the blinding disease he had contracted. Stebbins' close friend, Allen Van Orsdale, was home in upstate New York, discharged for medical reasons. Only two Bucktails with whom Tubbs corresponded remained—Dr. Humphrey and William Self—and Humphrey, just before the Seven Days' Battles, was hospitalized for several days, suffering from an ailment that he could never get rid of, chronic diarrhea.

Another friend of Tubbs' was seriously ill, too. Henry Maxson, who was serving with the 85th New York in Virginia, feared "the fever and ague."[12] He had lost his blankets during the fighting at Seven Pines and afterwards, trudging through the "Swamps of Virginia" and exposed to rains, he came down with what soldiers called "camp fever" and was hospitalized. He returned to his regiment in time for the Battle of Malvern Hill on July 1, but following it was again hospitalized. By the end of the summer, however, he had not recovered. Sick now with typhoid, bronchitis, and diarrhea, Maxson—Charles Tubbs' "Livy[,] Anabasis & Chemistry classmate as well as Brother Oro" at Alfred— was discharged from the 85th in early September and returned to his home in upstate New York.[13]

By the time of Maxson's discharge, the war was not even a year and a half old, and already the number of friends of Charles Tubbs who had enlisted and were still in the service had been dramatically reduced. Of the fourteen, only nine remained.

CHAPTER 10

Chance Encounters

[O]ne cannot see as much when in an engagement as
if he were standing in rear a spectator[.] He knows but
very little what is going on—except that before him—
unless he turnes & runs.

—*George Scudder*[1]

Anyone who has ever read *War and Peace* questions the reality of how often the lives of Tolstoy's characters intersect. They cross so many times that the novel's credibility is strained. But the truth is that such encounters happen every day, and it is no wonder that several of Tubbs' friends were involved in the same battles, sometimes unaware that they were facing the same dangers or, even more of a coincidence, that they crossed paths and suddenly, for a moment in the midst of war, saw an old, friendly face.

As summer turned into autumn in 1862, the fighting in Virginia and Maryland intensified. The battles fought—Second Bull Run, Maryland Heights, South Mountain, and Harpers Ferry—culminated in the bloodiest day of the war, the Battle of Antietam. Four of Charles Tubbs' friends saw action in one or more of the engagements, often fighting on the same battlefield without realizing that a friend was nearby.

"Bull Run is properly named," said William Self in a pun unusual for the little-educated private. Self's witticism was made after the 13th Pennsylvania, part of the III Corps commanded by Irvin McDowell, retreated from the battlefield on August 30 before a part of Robert E. Lee's Army of Northern Virginia commanded by James Longstreet. "The first day We give them fits but that McDowell is all the one to blame." (Self's assessment was briefly shared by higher authorities; McDowell was relieved of his command, though later exonerated.) The Bucktails fell back, demoralized:

We suffered for watter[,] rations[.] We wer without 5 days water[.] we could not get enough to drink[.] I drank watter that was so Thick I could hardly Swallow[.] the suffering was mor than that at Richmond[.] I thought we would never have another such as the Richmond fight.[2]

The Confederate attack and its implicit threat to Washington was so alarming that in the midst of the Second Battle of Bull Run, the 136th Pennsylvania, in which Asa Spencer had enlisted barely two weeks earlier, was rushed to the Capitol. There it helped to form a link in the cordon of defenses surrounding the city. Armed with axes, a detachment of the men set to work felling trees west and north of Washington so that federal artillery batteries would have a clear field of vision if the enemy advanced on the city.

A little more than two weeks later, as the fighting in Virginia continued, George Scudder led Company F of the 45th Pennsylvania Volunteers, part of the First Brigade, First Division, IX Corps, in an attack against Lee's army at South Mountain. Once at the base of the heights where the Confederates were positioned, the men sought protection behind a stone wall under a hill that shielded them from the enemy's grape and canister shot. They lay under cover, expecting the "Gray Backs" to advance, but when the Confederates did not, the First Brigade was ordered forward. The men immediately came under the fire of enemy cannon, but as they advanced, a Massachusetts battery passed them on the left, stopped, unlimbered, and returned the fire. Then other enemy cannon, only three hundred yards away, entered the artillery duel, targeting the Massachusetts battery and forcing its gunners "to leave ther guns and skedaddle under a heavy fire of shell & grape." Their panic, Scudder said, reminded his men of the First Battle of Bull Run, when green troops turned an orderly withdrawal into a rout: "an almos[t] Bull Run affair turned up" again, the young lieutenant informed Tubbs. The 45th Pennsylvania, though, did not budge.

Scudder said the men expected to be held in reserve, but "to our surprise" they were ordered forward ahead of three other units until they came to a wall and fence where they sought protection from "the most terrible fire of Grape[,] shell & Canenster from 6 batter[ies] of the enemy" that enfiladed them from the left and the right:

In this position it would not answer to l[a]y long so with a yell and a charge over wall and fence we went[,] Muskets & Minnie balls flying in proportion[,] down the hill and into a hollow under sheltr[.] We straigh[t]ened our lines and [went] forward again & for three times Within that time we had advanced nearly a half a mile[,] drove the enemy from back down the hill

Start[l]ing with fright Cavalry, Baggag trains & cassions which made an awful noise[.] Rg'ts began to brake and run but we soon rallied into position leading the 45th P.V. and the 46th N.Y. in advance of all on the Right of the hill[.] we were on the lay behind a stone wall bound not to leave until we should be obliged too but the Gray back did not advance that time[.]

Instead, the Union forces resumed their attack:

A line of skirmishers were thrown out and our Brigade with fixed bayonets advanced almost 50 yds up the hill and lay down again until about 4 P.M[,] The Grape & Cann[is]ter flying about us as thick as hail stones, When the Gray backs attacked our skirmish[er]s which were about 200 yds in advance[.] With bayonets still fixed the 45th charged forward facing a steady fire of musketry as we went[.] With what affect is not known but af[t]er the 3rd Chrge [silenced] three of their guns but the Division on our left were either to[o] slow or through neglect of their Commanders orders did not come up to support us in time and [as] we were just being flanked on the left we were ordered to fall back but waited to see if the division on the left would not help us[.]

The Union advance had not won much ground. Both sides exchanged heavy fire for two hours, until reinforcements came to the 45th Pennsylvania's support and "the Gray backs began to skeedaddle in all manner but few lived to get a[w]ay[.]" Scudder saw Confederate soldiers fall "by two[s] as they were running and the dead that lay in the road and behind the fences, in the fields & woods tell to[o] plain[l]y that but few got away."

An unofficial tally showed that the 45th Pennsylvania lost twenty-one killed and 115 wounded, seven of whom later died of their wounds. Of the thirty-eight men in Company F, one was killed and six wounded. Scudder was galled because "the reporters of the N.Y. Papers" identified the 45th as being a New York regiment in crediting it with the victory:

I will bet if Mr reporter had been with the 9th Army Corps he, unless a perfect rascall, would have written different than he did[.] Col [Thomas Welsh] I belive served one of them right when he asked him for a list of the Killed and wounded in our Rg't. "Sir[,"] said Col[,] "since I saw the account of the battles I have said I would kick the first reporter's———clear out of the Camp if they came in, not that I care anything for myself but When my boys do a grand work I like to see them have credit for it instead of others, So that their friends may know what they done and now[,] Sir[,] you cannot have the list (of Killed

&c) of my Reg't or Brigade and the Quicker you get outside my lines the better or you will see me fullfilling my saying[.]"[3]

William Self and the Bucktails also took part in the battle at South Mountain, though their attack was launched against a different enemy position. It was, said Self, "one of the neatest battles that has yet occured[.]" The 13th Pennsylvania had "a Whole Alabama Brigade" to contend with, he said. "There The Rebs wer on the mountains so steep that we had hard work to climb it and the Rebs could See us from where we wer Comming all day[.]"[4]

Five of Tubbs' friends were involved in the Battle of Antietam on September 17. And, as luck would have it, afterward three of them met by chance.

That bitter clash of arms was John Orr's baptism into warfare. Orr's regiment, the 107th New York, which had been encamped west of Washington guarding the Capitol, reached Sharpsburg on Antietam Creek after passing over a battleground where, for the first time, Orr said, "many of us saw in the wounded & dead that which gave us a more perfect realization of the horrors of war than we had ever experienced before." On the night of September 16, the 107th, part of the II Corps commanded by Nathaniel Banks, was ordered to fall in "very silently." Quickly, the men assembled and started to march. They had gone but a short distance when "the roar of cannon & bursting shell broke forth upon the stillness of the night air warning us of our near approach to the enemys line." While the 107th halted for the night, the firing continued at intervals and grew in intensity as dawn approached. Before the New Yorkers could prepare their breakfast, they were ordered forward:

[W]e soon came where the shot and shell fell much nearer than we liked to see them: the woods which the Rebels occupied on our front were shelled by our batteries until they were forced to leave[.] then our Regt advanced into a lane beyond the woods where we lay for some time flat on our faces exposed to a raking fire from one of the enemies batteries: we were soon ordered farther towards the right to support some batteries, the left of our Regt was placed in the rear of one and our right in front of another which occupied a rise of ground back of us: here we lay flat on our faces for over 2 hours exposed to the heating rays of the sun an the far more disagreeable roar of bursting shell and the suffacating smoke arising from the burning powder[.]

The Co which I am in is the second from the right and was directly in front of one of our batteries: while in this position a shell from the Battery in our rear burst wounding three in our Co and killing and wounding 4 others in the Co to our right[.] This excited our boys a little but they remained at their post: we soon fell back of this battery where we remained until all of the bat-teries of the enemy on our front were silenced[,] then we retired from the feild to obtain a little rest and refreshments which we needed very much for we were on the feild nearly 7 hr.

Our Gen soon came arround and extolled us for our coolness & firmness saying that battle was as severe as had occured during the war: while on the feild Gen Monsfield [Joseph K. F. Mansfield] was carried past us mortally wounded. Gen [Joseph] Hooker was also wounded near us. It was indeed a hard fought battle I need not say[;] we beat them badly driving them back from three to five miles the whole length of the line.

Orr had never witnessed such fighting or the aftermath of such bloodletting. The experience unnerved him:

To me the horrors of a battle feild were never before half realized: the deafening roar of bursting shells: the continual firing of small arms are nothing to shock the nerves or try the firmness of a mans spirit compared with the scene to be witnessed in the Hospitals found near the battlefeild[.] Suffering which no care can alleviate may be found here depicted so plainly on the faces of men wounded in all possible ways that it cannot fail to arrouse even the stoutest heart[.]

An entire day was wasted before the 107th started in pursuit of the retreating Confederate forces. Its route lay across the portion of the battlefield where the battle had raged the hardest. "[M]any of the ene-mies dead lay there unburied[,] presenting the most horrible scene I ever witnessed," said Orr, "but these are occurrences against which the soldier must steel his heart and check the sympathizing thoughts which come welling up in his bosom."[5]

Meanwhile, as the opposing armies drew apart and tended to their wounded and buried their dead, Asa Spencer had the surprise of his life. The 136th Pennsylvania had been detached from the defenses of Washington to bolster the federal forces in Maryland. Its troops were at the edge of a road leading from the battle scene when, in the midst of thousands of battle-weary federal infantrymen who clogged the road, Spencer bumped into three old friends from Osceola. Two of them were, like himself, corresponding with Charles Tubbs.

The Osceola schoolmaster first ran into Orville Kimball. Kimball, of the 103rd New York, had an attack of diarrhea after the fighting and raced off into the woods to relieve himself. When he had finished, he looked around and discovered that his regiment was gone. Kimball no sooner started to search for it when he ran into a relation of his mother's, William Eugene Cilley of the 86th New York, who was also lost. The two men slogged along a wooded lane, asking for the where-abouts of their regiments, when, out of the blue, Spencer recognized his friends from home. He was shocked by their appearance. Kimball, for one, "looked pretty hard" and both men, he reported to Tubbs, "were tired and hungry."

Spencer opened his haversack, which was full of crackers, and told Kimball and Cilley to "wade in." Pleased to see them eating, Spencer urged the men to go into a hospital to get warm, and he ac-companied them until Kimball stumbled on his regiment four miles away.[6]

No sooner had Spencer left the two men than he ran into another friend, William Self. The Bucktails had fought at Antietam, and Self had been struck in the thumb by grapeshot during the battle. The wound was the second minor one he received during the summer's campaign. It was not serious, and Self did not require hospitalization. But his unit, Company A of the 13th Pennsylvania, fared badly during the fighting and was now down to twenty men. The regiment itself, which had once numbered a thousand men, was drawing rations for 312 men and not all of them, Self noted, were effectives.

The two Pennsylvania regiments—Self's Bucktails and Spencer's 136th—camped near each other the night after the battle, and the men from Tioga County in both regiments took the occasion to share a con-genial visit. Self and Spencer—the semiliterate farmer and the school-master—shared anecdotes about their mutual friend, Charles Tubbs, who was then still at Alfred University. Self, now a veteran campaigner, "had to laugh," he said, at the new regiments that had arrived to fight the enemy, in particular the men in Spencer's 136th Pennsylvania:

> They wer complaining of Their rations when they come here[.] oh They said them crackers are so hard[.] They could [not] eat them and so it went with eny thing[.] They wondered Why they did not give them soft new bread[.] . . . Says I to them if You can get enough of them hard crackers and salt beef[,] or as some call it mule beef[,] says I, if You can get enough of That all the time you are in the servis You may be Thank full then[.]

> They Would Get me [to] tell of some of the battles I have been in[.] I tole them that we went into the battle of Bull Run with 2 days rations and they had to last us 7 days and When we wer skirmishing we would go through the cor[n] fields pickin off the ears and put them in our haversacks Then roast them When We got a chance . . .

> Then They came down to see our guns and oh they Thought if they could only get one of Them they could doe the buisness and They could[.] They are the Sharps Rifle britch loaders[.] I tell You they done the work at South Moun-tain and one Thing more which pleased me to here them tell when They came

here to camp and They wer clear tired out[.] I asked them how far they had marched[.] They Sayed they had been two days comming from Fredrick a distance of about 25 miles[,] and we marched 18 and had the South Mountain fight in 1 day[.]⁷

Self's humor escaped Spencer, who had yet to experience any combat. He found the march from Frederick to Sharpsburg a study in macabre contrasts. "Frederick City," he wrote Tubbs,

was situated in a washbowl or a basin with a circular chain of hills for its rim . . . As we passed up over the rim of the bowl I discovered that we were only exchanging one of less beauty for one of greater; the two rims being joined togather[.] On this we halted for dinner and sat down to a dish of sardeens . . . After dinner we took up our line of march through this 2nd basin. The way was lined more or less with wallnuts, butternuts, chestnuts, apples and other choice fruit together with green fields.

But then their route became

marked by the misiles of the two contending armies which passed through before us[.] The trees[,] fences on either side[,] unexploded shells[,] dead horses[,] mules and newly dug graves were plainly to be seen before and consequently we needed no guide.

The 136th camped for the night before resuming its march the next morning. Again, the contrast impressed Spencer:

A little before noon we came out into some of the prettiest country that I have seen in Maryland. Splendid groves on either side met the view. We encamped for dinner in a beautiful meadow where I had the privilge of enjoying two dishes of sardeens . . . This was by all odds the pleasantest camping that I have experienced since I have been in the service.

The countryside the 136th traveled through, Spencer said, "continued to be delightful until we got within three miles of Sharpsburg," when, as they approached Antietam Creek, the men "began to see the effects of the great Antietam battle." The 136th camped a mile from the cornfield where the most vicious fighting had occurred and in sight of where Hooker was wounded. "The barns," he wrote Tubbs, "are filled about here with the rebel wounded."[8]

In that one day of fighting at Antietam, the Army of the Potomac suffered more than 12,000 casualties, including over 2,000 men killed.

Confederate losses totaled nearly 14,000 men; of that total, 2,700 were killed and about 2,000 others missing. That not one of Tubbs' friends who participated in the battle suffered any serious injury is remarkable.

· CHAPTER 11 ·

Ringing Out the Old

*I am glad to tell you that I am well . . . and have
stood a heavy shower of lead and Iron and I had a
clost distance to shoot at the gray backs and this the
way the Old year went out and the new one came in
and it may be you would like to know how I spent
Christmas[.]*

—*David Armstrong*[1]

Before the year 1862 ended, two of Tubbs' friends fought in major
battles waged almost seven hundred miles apart in Virginia and Tennessee. Both were Confederate victories.

Before the first battle, Fredericksburg, there were major changes
in commands in the Army of the Potomac that affected the Bucktails.
For one thing, Ambrose Burnside succeeded George McClellan. For another, Captain Charles F. Taylor, the brother of the well-known traveler and author Bayard Taylor, now led the 13th Pennsylvania, and the
Bucktails were attached to the First Brigade of William Buel Thomas's
division, VI Corps.

William Self was not especially pleased about Burnside's promotion. He wrote Tubbs that he did not have "the faith in him that I have
in Mc clellan nor should I have for I neier have fought under him and I
have under Mack." Even during the earlier setbacks outside of Richmond, when the army was forced to retreat, he said, "evry think was
done up in order" under McClellan, and the army "never lost a waggon" though it faced the "Whole Rebel force."

On the other hand, Taylor's promotion from a company captain
to colonel of the 13th pleased Self. The young officer—Taylor was only
twenty-two years old—"is a very fine man," said Self, "one of the best
in the Regt[,] the Best I guess." Taylor's company had been one of the
four Bucktail companies detached temporarily to fight in the Shenan-

92

doah Valley earlier in the spring. "I herd," said Self, "that he had his u[n]iform nearly Spoilt with bulletts but did not hurt him."[2]

By the time Burnside crossed the icy Rappahannock to oppose Lee at Fredericksburg during the second week of December, Lee's entire army of nearly 79,000 men was in position to confront him. Burnside's force was greater—some 122,000 troops, most of whom took part in the attack. Burnside's plan was to get his huge army across the river by erecting pontoon bridges at three points. One of the spans was more than four hundred feet long.

The 13th Pennsylvania began to move as soon as it grew dark. To the Bucktails' amazement, as the regiment approached the crossing, a uniformed general was there, spade in hand:

[O]ld Burnside Was on the pontoon bridge Shoveling dirt so as to keep *the artilery and men from makeing a noise. When our Division came to cross he said they acted as though they did not fear man or the Devel[.] Soon as we crossed We had to be put on Guard along the river to protect The rest and The bridge[.]*

By the time the Bucktails got across the Rappahannock, more than thirty thousand federal troops had preceded them. The Pennsylvanians assumed that they would maintain their current position and were surprised when orders came to move ahead, where they would bear the brunt of the fighting:

[W]hen We came to cross our Regt amediately <u>went</u> to the front[,] all the *rest had stoped and we passed them. We deployed out as Skirmishers[,] advanced down the lines from Fredricksburg[.] here we came uppon thers[.]*

Face to face with the enemy, the 13th Pennsylvania halted for the night. As Self looked on, the Bucktail pickets and their Confederate counterparts chatted and traded coffee and tobacco. All the while, he said, he could hear "great noises" coming from the enemy camps— "chopping[,] the rattle of waggons." The Bucktails speculated whether the Confederates were retreating or just moving their baggage trains out of the way because of the impending fight:

[I]t proved to be the latter. morning came and as The fog cleared away, *The Rebel Cavelry on the left made an advance and came to a little to[o] close so we fired on them. here was the first gun fired[.] presantly I could see their [army] in the rear of Their Skirmishers getting in posision. The extend of their line could not be seen owing to its imense length. at the same time there was our army moveing up in our rear . . .*

[A]s I was gazeing uppon The Two armies moveing up and the bayenots glimering Think Say I I thought some of [us] Will lay low before night and as all These Thoughts ran through my mind Boom goes one of their large Guns to the right opposit of the town cross fireing on our Troups as they wer getting in posision[.] tore up the mud around us some.

Another regiment replaced the Bucktails, who were ordered to rejoin their brigade farther to the right. As the men started off, a Confederate battery opened fire:

There we wer runing around in search of our Brigade under a murderous artilery fire. but it did not hurt eny of us[.] we even fetched up then and had to Support 3 batteries[,] something that no one Regt never before did that I knew of.

Confederate sharpshooters were now firing on the Pennsylvanians from a railroad cut where they were hidden. Self, though, saw one of them rise and begin to run:

[S]ays I to The Orderly of our Co does you see him[.] yes he says[.] Well says [I] See if I dont stop him[.] so I up with my Sharps Rifle[,] elevated it for 200 yards[,] fired[,] down came the rebel[.] There They hollowed Abe has fetched him down[.] during The Time we wer laying there I think I killed or wounded 2 others[.]
[T]here we wer not much more than 800 yards from the rebels fortifications[,] our Battiers fireing all the time to get some reply from them but they held their fire so as to draw us on.

The Bucktails were now ordered to move forward into a hilly wooded area behind several other units.

So we up and Started but we had not gon more than 100 yards when they opened on us with Double charges of grape and Canester from their earth Works. Such a sight before was never was saw. the way men fell. we lost 1/2 of our Co. 204 killed wounde and miss in The Regt and we could not fire as we wer going up on account of our own men being in front of us.
[O]ne Shell came into our Co broke one mans leg[,] a new Recruit[.] This Was the first fight he Was ever in[.] he is now dead. he has a brother here in the Co[.] The same shell knocked down 2 or 3 and came near fetching me down[,] knocked me backwards[,] but we suceeded in driveing them[.] drove the guners from their guns but by This Time we had lost so many men That we could as not Take The Gunes away. a Rebel Adj General came out and says ["]come on my s[outhern] brave boys[,] Take This battery and the day is ours.["] but his

*brave boys we nerly all killed or Taken prisoners[.] he was taken and he said if
there had been one more Division had went in as ours did The day Would have
been ours.*[3]

Despite the courageous fighting of the Bucktails, the Army of the
Potomac was forced to fall back, defeated. "[O]f all the battles I have
been in," Self said, "I never saw the tuck took out of our Regt as Was
there before we had a chance to return the fire much. [I]t Was a slick
thing getting back over The river as we did."[4]

Burnside's forces suffered a total of more than 12,650 casualties,
including nearly 1,300 men killed, at the Battle of Fredericksburg. Confederate losses were less than half those figures. But there was little
rejoicing in the South. Even though it had suffered heavy losses, the
huge federal army was far from destroyed. In fact, Lee was criticized
for not pressing his advantage and destroying the North's forces when
he had the chance to. But Lee had no idea that his troops had inflicted
such heavy losses, and he expected the Union army to rally and attack
again.

Severe losses also plagued the federal force in Tennessee, but this time
the killer was not shot and shell. In the main, illness was striking down
the troops. By the last week of December, after a year of service, David
Armstrong's company in the 49th Ohio was virtually depleted. "[W]e
had nine men die and thirteen discharged," he informed Tubbs, "and
on this long march we have a good many more[.] som has died[,] som
has been taken prisoner and the worst of all there has [been] a number
desirted[.]" Company F, which numbered ninety-three men before the
campaign began, could muster only twenty-eight now. It was so un-
derstrength that Armstrong was serving as one of the company's two
cooks.

The long march Armstrong referred to was the trek through Tennessee and Kentucky "behind the heels" of an invading Confederate
army led by Braxton Bragg. The 49th, attached to the First Brigade,
Second Division, of the Army of the Cumberland, commanded by William Rosecrans, trooped from Nashville to Louisville to Frankfort, finally catching up with Bragg's forces at Lawrenceburg, Kentucky, where
the two sides skirmished.[5]

On Christmas Day, David Armstrong and what was left of Company F were encamped south of Murfreesboro. Rations were short, so
the men went out on a foraging expedition, scared up "the greese
backs," and had a brief fight. The 49th returned to camp with what
little provisions they had been able to find. The next day, with three

days' rations, blankets, and rubbers stuffed into their haversacks, they moved out against the enemy.

On December 30, the two armies fought at Stones River outside of Murfreesboro in a battle that lasted into the new year. "I guess you have seen the Old year shot Out," Armstrong quipped in a letter to Tubbs, "well[,] Charles[,] I have had a chance to help shoot it Out. I think I improved the thing."

I would not say that I Shot any body but I have took several good deliber[a]te aims at them a bout fifteen rods distance from them dirty greese backs. . . .

[T]his was one of the hard times that a soldier has and we was so short on rations that the fourth Brigade isued an ear of corn to the man[.] I think this is hard times when a soldier will run for an ear of corn as soon as hog dont you[?] but the reason of this is that the rebs Cavalry got in the rear and burnt our provision train of one hundred wagons.

The fighting did not go well for the 49th, chiefly, Armstrong said, because the division's commander, General Richard W. Johnson, was "a perfect ass and there is not a man in the division that has a bit of confidence in him nor do they like him."

Johnson was captured almost as soon as the fighting started; so, too, was their brigade colonel after two horses were shot from under him. The regiment's lieutenant colonel was shot dead, and its next in command, a major, was wounded. Under a severe crossfire, the 49th fell back:

[W]ell after we retreated back we made a stand and drove the rebs back and then we saw a hevy force coming up on our flank and we was so few in number we gave back again and then we gave them all they wanted and the fighting at this place was don a bout ten Oclock P.M. and our men made a charge and drove them out of their rifle pits and all was still that night and the next morning the rebs was gon.

Although the Confederates could claim they had won the battle, they lost so many men—some 11,800, or almost a third of their force— that the victory was a pyrrhic one. As a result, the South's invasion of Kentucky and Ohio was doomed. The Union army suffered even heavier casualties—nearly 13,000 men in all. The already thinly manned 49th lost twenty more men—two killed, eight wounded, and ten missing. But Armstrong still felt strongly about the Army of the Cumberland's commander:

Friend Charles[,] you may have herd the thing talked on why our General Rosecran did not do better heare[.] wonder ye not for he don as well as any man could and Sir there is a few Generals in this army I am willing to follow to Battle[.] let it be ever so [t]hat one is . . . General Rosecran[.][6]

The 13th Pennsylvania spent Christmas Day camped near Belle Plain, Virginia. William Self had in hand a letter from Charles Tubbs that came the day before "and was read with the Greatest of pleasure[.]" He was responding immediately, the Bucktail went on, even though he was not able to obtain a postage stamp. He apologized because he had to mark the envelope "Soldiers letter," which meant that Tubbs would have to pay the three cents due when he received it.

"What sort of a dinner doe you think I have to day for Christmas dinner[?]" Self asked facetiously. "[A] few fried crackers called Sluckum here and a little Coffee." In response to a question from Tubbs, he declared:

You wanted to know much I waied[.] I doe not know as I have had no chance to weight myself in a long time but I guess I am merly a 1/3 heavier now Then When you last saw me[.] I have got so that I can stand eny kind of fait and fire very Well.[7]

1863

· CHAPTER 12 ·

Emancipation

*I should like to see the negro free but whare
would I like to have him after he is free[?] . . . please
tell me whare you would like to have them placed[—]
amongst the whites or by them Selves[?]*
—David Armstrong[1]

Although they were abolitionists and believed that slavery was morally wrong, Charles Tubbs' soldier friends were often trapped in their own ambivalent feelings. They were frequently critical of the southerners they met, both white and black, but they leveled their strongest criticisms against the blacks they encountered. They often neither understood nor sympathized with the former slaves. Some struggled to reconcile their antislavery belief with what they perceived as reality. When they did praise blacks—as they did with respect to black soldiers for their fighting ability—they did so grudgingly. But as for the blacks they routinely encountered—field hands, in the main— they had contempt. It is deeply disturbing to read their blatant expressions of prejudice.

Tubbs' friends mocked the way blacks talked, made fun of the way they looked, held their noses at the way they smelled, complained about the manners they exhibited. In fact, his soldier friends showed little understanding of the slave experience. They did not realize that blacks behaved the way whites expected them to behave. Subservient and submissive, they acted like what we today call Uncle Toms. Nor did Tubbs' friends take into account the fact that the ones they met, the field hands, were illiterate because they were barred from learning to read and write, or that the blacks lacked certain manners because they rarely were ever involved, as house slaves and black craftsmen were, in social interaction with their masters and mistresses.

Perhaps part of the reason for the reaction of Tubbs' friends is the fact that no more than a handful of blacks, if even that many, ever

101

Two Union officers in Virginia with contrabands working as servants.
Author's collection.

lived in Tioga County. The only recorded one is a female slave that one
of the early pioneers in the Cowanesque Valley, Israel Bulkley, brought
with him when he settled in the Osceola area in the early 1800s. She
served him for a number of years, until a black man bought her freedom by working for Bulkley and took her away. Bulkley would have
had to free the woman eventually, anyway, because Pennsylvania in
1780 enacted a law providing for the gradual abolition of slavery by
1808.[2] Similarly, few if any blacks lived on the other side of the state
line in New York, where slavery was abolished in 1827.

While some of the soldiers, Orrin Stebbins in particular, articulated their passionate hatred of slavery in letters to Tubbs, the truth is
that once their regiments reached a state in which slavery existed, their
reaction to the blacks they met was mixed if not altogether negative.
Tubbs' friends invariably referred to them as "niggers," but that was
not unusual. The term was in common usage in the mid-nineteenth
century. But at the same time that Stebbins was cursing the "vile tread
of slavery" to readers of the *Tioga County Agitator* back home, he was
also speaking of "coons" working in a cornfield.[3]

Other friends voiced similar disparaging remarks or drew uncomplimentary analogies. In describing a temporary encampment in North Carolina, Harlan Kimball wrote Tubbs that it was "on a sandbed which the great Deser[t] of Africa in heat woul[d] no more compare than a little nigger (which are thicker here than hair on a dog) would to a dark night[.]"[4]

His older brother Orville, who expressed even stronger critical comments about blacks, spoke of meeting an old friend from Osceola who was in a different regiment. The man had not changed a bit since they had last seen one another except for one thing: "you can hear him curse the negro now and he would not when he came here[.] he has often wondered what made me so down on the negro and now he see it for himself."[5]

When stationed on Otter Island, South Carolina, early in 1862, George Scudder complained, in the midst of writing a letter to Tubbs, that he could not concentrate: "Darn the niggars[,] they makes so much nois Singing Massa Lincoln come for to free dem."[6] The only females he saw on the island were "black Wenches every hour in the day, and some times oftener. When they come around the Quarters begging victuals from the Cook I take a musket and level it at them and you had better beleive they scamper. *The black rats*—Give them a Chance and they would eat one out of a house & home and then they take your carcass and devour that."[7]

Scudder recounted with relish an incident about a "Contraband (female)" who "jumped & screamed with all vengeance" on being treated by an army doctor for a sore throat. A quartermaster's cook had played a prank on the woman, convincing her to tie a string around her head so as to "draw" up the sore throat and cure it. Scudder did not see the prank as cruel.

You would laugh to hear them go on about the times they are going to have & &C with Uncle Sam. "Some say he was down to Port Royal the other day." One Soldier asked him how he looked. "Couldent say sir. him tall I expose but gots lots of Money and a great sympatizer wid the Niggars[.]" . . .

But darn the Niggars[.] When you have seen as much of them as I have you will wish them in purgatory with all their Masters after them[.] Lie[,] steal and lousy is the name for them beside the sweet perfume they bring along with them as the[y] approach you[.] Many things they are not to blame for but cant help it[.] hope to have something done with them that will be human and let them take care of themselves.[8]

John Orr was in Maryland when, he said, "We got us a Secesh negra while at Leesburg & captured another the other day, but they are poor property[.] Confound the niggers[,] I dont want them arround me when I can avoid it, yet they are human & should not be treated as brutes. There are many in the Army. Many of them were employed by Cols & Generals[,] ride the best of horses: this makes our boys all out of patience, but poor nig is all right—Get-out-way dar[.]"⁹

Later, when in Virginia, Orr's company retained two *"boys"*— "colored chaps, both of them from rebeldom." One of the blacks had accompanied a Confederate regiment as a servant. "When we came across him," said Orr, "he was nearly starved & worn out, but he is as fat now as a brick." Orr asked a photographer to take some pictures of the two blacks sitting together with him and other officers of the 107th New York. "I wish I had one to send you," he wrote Tubbs. "They look very natural but comical just like all niggers are[.]"¹⁰

William Prentice was in Baton Rouge, Louisiana, when the new year, 1863, began. He said that contrabands "continue to flock in" to the 161st New York and that as many as eighteen hundred were being housed in tents and a former female seminary. "The men are kept at work upon the entrenchments during the day, while women, with from one to three young darkies in their arms, make daylight hideous by grinning at passers by through windows [and] doors of their tents & cracks in the fence. It would be worth a journey to this Rebelious state to see this sable crowd."¹¹

The response of Tubbs' friends to Lincoln's Emancipation Procla-mation, announced after the Battle of Antietam in the fall of 1862, is as astonishing as their remarks about blacks are disturbing. As of January 1, 1863, all slaves still in states in rebellion were automatically consid-ered free. The effect of the proclamation was crucial. The goal of the war suddenly changed from being the preservation of the Union to a crusade to free all slaves.

Some of Tubbs' friends, abolitionists though they might be, crit-icized the president's decision. "I did not think Uncle Abe would ever make the Slaves Free in such a time as this when he has no place for them," David Armstrong said. He insisted that he had "no objection" to freeing the slaves, "but," he quickly added, "I wish they would wait till this fuss is over." Moreover, Armstrong could not visualize living alongside blacks. He referred to those whom the 49th Ohio came into contact with as "a sauc[i]er set of people I never saw and for them to have their home in Ohio[,] Pennsylvania[,] New York[,] Indiana or any of these free states I Opposed." Armstrong said that since he expected to return to live in the North, he would not want "this mixing two Colores to geather[.] I do not beleave in [it.]"

Armstrong's solution was to resettle the former slaves out West where they would be "by them Selves[.] there is Terretory a plenty for them[.]" It would be "easier," he said, "to colonise the negros then to free them in time of peace."[12]

William Prentice said he had vowed "eternal hostility to *Slavery Everywhere*." He declared that it "has always fettered the feet of Progress. It has been the *Moloc[h]* to which genius has been sacrifised, & at last has plunged a *continent* in *Misery*."[13] But, at the same time, Prentice thought that the Emancipation Proclamation "was plainly unconstitutional except in the light of a war measure."[14]

The thought that blacks might sometime be given the right to vote and thus gain control of the South dismayed Orville Kimball: "[T]hey can not govern even themselves as a whole."[15]

Despite the many negative reactions that Tubbs' friends expressed, they were not blind to the accomplishments of blacks who joined the Union army. Major General Benjamin Franklin Butler raised a black regiment, the Louisiana Native Guards (Corps d'Afrique), in September 1862, the first of three black regiments that were mustered into service in the state that fall. Other efforts to raise black troops were vetoed by Lincoln until after the Emancipation Proclamation took effect. In all, before the end of the war, some 300,000 blacks served in 166 regiments, most of them as infantrymen. About 60 of those regiments were active in the field, though few saw action in more than one battle. About 2,750 black soldiers were killed or mortally wounded in the war, as were 143 of their officers, all of whom were always white.[16]

Those of Tubbs' friends who came into contact with black troops or fought beside them always seemed surprised at their capabilities. John Orr, for one, was amazed one day while the 107th New York was stationed at Wartrace Bridge, Tennessee. On the opposite side of a river was a contingent of the 1st U.S. Colored Troops. "It was quite a curiosity to see the nigger act the soldier," he said, "but they seemed to do it pretty well. Many of them make good soldiers; they are always on the alert & woe be to the person or thing which attempts to pass a negro sentinel after he calls out *halt*." Orr said that he was "glad to see them in the field," though, he added, "I rather not fight beside or among them." They suffered "a want of judgement" because they were trigger happy, he said.[17]

Orville Kimball noted that black soldiers recruited from among ex-slaves were so enraged by the way they had been treated that they were difficult to control. Like some white soldiers, they too sought revenge for deliberate acts of barbarism. For instance, later in the war, during the battle for Charleston, Kimball recounted an incident after the so-called Fort Pillow Massacre, when a Confederate cavalry division reputedly murdered all the black troops after the fort surrendered. Kimball said that at one point the 103rd New York captured two "rebs" and "it was almost impos[sible] to restrain the collored soldiers from running them through with the bayonet in remembrance of Fort Pillow &c[.]"[18]

Earlier, when Kimball was stationed on Folly Island, South Carolina, a black brigade arrived and took part in a review, as did an integrated Connecticut artillery battery nicknamed the "salt and pepper battery." "[T]hey marched very well and [I] was glad to see the black D——s doing some service," he said, but, he continued, "let them have their place alone and seperate[.]" The general commanding the district had authority from the War Department to raise as many black regiments as possible in South Carolina, Florida, Georgia, and Alabama, and Kimball hoped he would "draft all the 'niggers' in these states that are large enough to be soldiers and use the rest for serva[n]ts."[19]

The only blacks other than troopers who ever drew any praise from a friend of Tubbs' were a group of men and their families who were able to take over a small Confederate steamer carrying five cannons and ammunition and deliver her to the federal vessels blockading Charleston. "I say Bully for the Niggars," Scudder said. "Much valuable information will be received from these Contrabands and well should the Government reward them for their conduct[.] They deserve it."[20]

There is no indication of how Charles Tubbs felt about his friends' remarks. He himself was an abolitionist. Was he distressed by the wide gap between what his friends deplored about slavery and what they expressed about the blacks they met? Did it pain him and in any way affect his relationship with them?

Tubbs was mute on the subject. Not one of the letters his friends wrote to him mentions whether he either agreed or argued with what they said.

· CHAPTER 13 ·

Tourists and Politicians

*On the dome of the Capitol I could see at one view the
whole City, Georgetown, Fairfax Seminary and could
almost see Alexandria . . . and many other fancy
things which I have not yet mentioned.*

—*Asa Spencer*[1]

As the new year began, Asa Spencer was as far as a soldier could
be from a battlefield. He was the clerk in a hospital's baggage room,
responsible for taking care of the knapsacks of sick and wounded
soldiers.

The Osceola schoolmaster, who had enlisted for nine months' duty
with the 136th Pennsylvania, was the latest of Charles Tubbs' friends to
become seriously ill. Though he suffered continually with chronic diarrhea, he had not shirked from doing his "duty," he wrote Tubbs. But in
November 1862 at Warrenton, Virginia, he caught cold and felt so sore,
he said, "I could scarcely open my mouth to eat anything at all for a
while." While his regiment moved on to Rappahannock Station, Spencer
was excused from duty and stayed behind in an army hospital that
held some six hundred sick and wounded men. He recovered enough
to serve as a ward master there, and when the patients were transferred to Washington in December, Spencer went with them.

His new home, Columbian Hospital, was on "a beautiful table-
land" with a "fair view of nearly the whole City" of Washington. The
five-story building, situated on Meridian Hill west of Fourteenth Street
about two miles north of the White House, once housed a woman's
college. "Where then were heard the Merry Laught[er] of the School
Girl, now is heard the groans of the dying patriot," Spencer said.

"[F]or a soldier who had been in the habit of living on hard
crackers garrisoned by worms," Christmas dinner, prepared by the
hospital's cooks and a group of soliticious Washington women, was, he
said, a special treat: "onions, turnips, pototoes, apples, oranges, oyster

soup, mince pie, bread, cheese, cranberry sauce, Ale, and Roasted Turkey and some other fixings that have slipped my mind."

After Spencer fully regained his health, he was assigned to work as one of the waiters in the hospital's mess room, and then he "crawled up a little higher, or at least into a little better position"—that of clerk in the hospital's baggage room. The duty hours were light: from nine to eleven in the morning and from two to three in the afternoon. He had time, he said, to visit a friend from home, Dr. William Humphrey, who was then recuperating in Washington from a recurrence of diarrhea. The rest of the time, Spencer added, he read or wrote to, among others, Tubbs. Where was another old friend, William Prentice? he asked. "We were brought up together; attended school together; and were very intimate and confidential with each other . . . I think of him often and long for a good visit with him."[2]

Spencer's undemanding duties at Columbian Hospital left him so many free hours that he paid several visits to downtown Washington. It was like a dream come true, the war notwithstanding. Places he had read about, celebrated individuals he had heard about—there they were, right in front of his eyes. Spencer was having the time of his life.

One day, Spencer went up on the dome of the still-being-refinished Capitol to view the city and spent several hours at the Patent Office, where he saw George Washington's military coat on display as well as "all kinds of moddles that human genius has brought into shape."

On another day, Spencer visited the Supreme Court, the Senate, and the House of Representatives. Presiding over the Court was Chief Justice Roger B. Taney, the author of the Dred Scott Decision that denied blacks any rights under the Constitution. James Mandeville Carlisle, one of the most celebrated lawyers of the time, was arguing a case when Spencer entered the courtroom. A number of other notables were there, also: Attorney General Edward Bates, who had run against Lincoln for the presidency and, despite being named to a Cabinet post, opposed the admission of West Virginia as a state; former Attorney General Reverdy Johnson, who favored conciliation with the South; and Jeremiah Black, who had served James Buchanan as both attorney general and secretary of state.

The Senate was debating a finance measure when Spencer next went inside the Capitol and took a seat in the gallery. Willard Saulsbury, a Democrat of Delaware, was addressing it. Bored, Spencer walked across the building to the House wing, whose members were discussing whether to seat representatives from the liberated sections of Louisiana. There, among others, he was able to identify a number of the congressmen about whom he had read so often: Alfred Ely of New York, who was taken prisoner at the First Battle of Bull Run; John Fox

Potter of Wisconsin, who once challenged another congressman to a duel; two Indiana representatives, Schuyler Colfax and Albert Gallatin Porter; and two Unionists from Kentucky, John J. Crittenden and Charles A. Wickliffe. The latter had served in the War of 1812 and once been postmaster general under John Tyler.

On another day in the House chamber, a massive Union demonstration—a "very spirited and enthusiastic" meeting—was held. The rally was scheduled to begin at five in the afternoon. Spencer got there a half hour early to find the galleries filled to overflowing. Lincoln and his Cabinet sat below, facing Spencer, so he had a "fair view" of the president. A delegation of Ute chiefs from Colorado who were in Washington to confer with the commissioner of Indian affairs was in the audience, too. When, finally, the doors below opened and the rally committee came in, wearing red, white, and blue rosettes, Spencer "could think of no other comparison than that of honey bees swarming." The Marine Band struck up a rousing march. Then came speaker after speaker, among them future vice president Andrew Johnson; Charles F. Adams, son of John Quincy Adams and grandson of John Adams; and Rear Admiral Andrew Hull Foote, whose gunboats played an instrumental role in Grant's successes at Forts Henry and Donelson on the Cumberland River.

But Spencer's biggest thrill came on a Saturday in late February when the president held one of his public levees. Spencer visited the White House, toured the rooms—"The very cream of Society were prominading through the different apartments"—and then got to shake hands "with the father of the country."

Spencer, who apparently had never fired a gun in battle, was, meanwhile, fighting a different kind of war, as commander, as he put it flippantly, of the "Rat Department." He was "surrounded" in the baggage room at Columbian Hospital "by an army of 1000 large sized ratts which are perfectly quiet by day but raise hot by night."

There has been no general engagement yet; However I see frequently reconoisance parties; pickets out and can hear them very plain at work on their fortification. Day before yesterday we had a slight skirmish but after one charge the enemy retreated[.] No loss of life on either side. I think we are on the eve of a terrible battle which is to settle the rat question forever. I am bound to defend said property that is in my charge to the last; and if needs be Sell my life as dear as possible[.]"[3]

Spencer's remarks about his anticipated "terrible battle" with vermin—even his excitement about his sightseeing in Washington—seem, on the surface, to be in poor taste. Friends of his from Osceola who were in the army were sick or dying or dead as the result of a very real war. Spencer and the other soldiers who were corresponding with Charles Tubbs were basically farm folk, insulated all their lives from the outside world. That was true even of those educated at Alfred University, a school isolated in a region given over to farming and lumbering. Evidently, the first large city any of them ever saw was either Harrisburg—if they enlisted in a Pennsylvania regiment—or Albany— if they chose a New York one. The Civil War offered an opportunity they would not have otherwise experienced, and it was not unusual for them to want to share what they saw with Tubbs.

Orville Kimball reacted with the same awe that Spencer evinced on seeing the Capitol when the 103rd New York was briefly posted at Camp Richardson, south of Arlington, Virginia:

> *The hill of this fort has a commanding view of the City of Washington[,] Georgetown and vicinity and Potomac with its steamers and sail crowding up and down[.] This new and nearly finished dome of the capitol surmounted by the statue of the Goddess of Liberty is high above the surrounding buildings[.] The President[']s house, where so many of our illustrious men have had their abode[,] held their levees during the fashionable winter months[,] gathered together the noted of America in a social gathering, this and The Treasury building shows white among the green foliage[.] around near or down to the river Washington Monument unfinished stand[s,] the commencement of a noble column[,] one that would stand for ages to interest the eye of her visitors.*[4]

Both Kimball and Allen Van Orsdale got to see Harpers Ferry when their regiments passed through it early in the war. The city attracted special interest because of the famous raid on the arsenal there in 1859 led by the abolitionist zealot John Brown. Ten of Brown's twenty-one men were killed by U.S. Marines led by Robert E. Lee. Brown himself was hanged after being convicted of treason.

Van Orsdale, who, coming from upstate New York, was no stranger to striking vistas, was mainly entranced by the ambience, "Mountain scenery" that was "indeed grand."[5] Kimball, however, had much to say about the town itself. Almost all the buildings in Harpers Ferry were deserted when Kimball's regiment reached it. The 103rd took up quarters in one of the abandoned structures, a large flouring mill, and Kimball set out to do a little exploring on his own:

> *I ranged around town, the place before all other places that excites the curiosity of the whole people. The long, shattered walls and falling columns, the ruins on every side, of devastated buildings[,] deserted hearth-stones mark the guilt and passions of man in our own age, and which can not escape the*

ressurrection of the Historian. But there is another object of still greater intrest which[,] though exposed by the scathing flames, is being part chiped away by the thousand sons of the North who seek to lay a last tribute of respect to the memory Old John Brown—[.]

The Engine House, which you remember, the desperate Old man and his followers took for their Fortress when "hardly pressed," is a small sized build-ing with solid brick walls and heavy iron plated doors. It seems to be un-changed since then: the[re] are still the two port holes which the Old Fellow dug through the thick walls . . . & At one side a pile of bricks marks the place where Brown was taken up wounded and bleeding.

You know that I always admired his motives and sympathised with his cause, but regarded [h]is course of action not only inconsistent, but highly criminal[.] But when I compare his rebellion with the present and contrast the motives of each, I must confess that I view him in a more exalted position, and exclaim well done you faithful old "cuss[.]" I have nothing more censure.

All of the Gov. Buildings[,] the armory, a[r]senal[,] Machine shops, &c, have been destroyed by fire done mostly . . . last Spring, to prevent the enemy from getting them. Burnt muskets lie around by thousand[s,] all "resolved into their constituent parts," in the short space of an hour.

Kimball pried a chip of wood from the door of the engine house, "whittled" it down, and enclosed it in his letter to Tubbs.[6]

· CHAPTER 14 ·

Frustrations

> *Dear Charley . . . when a half sad, passive feeling*
> *steels over one, he sighs to be* alone, *or with* some-
> one *who can sympathize with him in his moods &*
> *sheer his depressed spirits. and I bethink me that while*
> *at Alfred your room was my resort at such times.*
> *—William Prentice*[1]

William Prentice was homesick again. Recently discharged from a hospital outside Baton Rouge, Louisiana, the young captain was nearly fourteen hundred miles from his home in upstate New York. On a lonely Friday, Prentice bemoaned his lack of friendships. He did not know anyone in his regiment, he wrote Charles Tubbs, "with whom I can be on *realy companionable* terms."

It was the second time that Prentice had been hospitalized for pneumonia.[2] He did not divulge to Tubbs the reason for his most recent hospital stay nor how serious his condition was, but for "a part of the time," he told him, "my prospects for recovery not seeming very flattering the blue would creep over me." He was, however, fully recovered by mid-January and feeling so relieved to be out of the hospital that, he said, "my animal spirits curl so high that positively I was *never* happier in my life."

Prentice discerned—but could not explain, he said—a startling change of heart in himself. Perhaps it was because of his loneliness now that he was out of hospital, or perhaps it was because of the coincidental boredom of camp life, but he said:

> [R]ight here is a thing which I do not understand. <u>Once</u> the thought of a <u>Battle</u> filled me with fear & horrid images of mangled bodies would immediately arise. But <u>now</u> that is all gone & a night alarm only serves to raise my spirits.[3]

112

His fellow soldiers in the 161st New York were just as restless as Prentice was to see action. They waited endlessly for the winter weather to let up. But the regiment was down to half strength and there was some question as to how effective it could be with only 478 men fit for service.

Confederate forces held Port Hudson, which they had heavily fortified and reinforced. From their strategic position high on the bluffs of the Mississippi, they controlled the river both north and south of Vicksburg.

The 161st was encamped nearby, part of a brigade in an army commanded by Nathaniel Banks. Banks was under orders to open up the Mississippi to federal forces—which meant taking Port Hudson. The general was reluctant to attack until at least the west bank of the river was under federal control. So he planned to advance north and link up with Ulysses Grant's army, which was approaching south from the area around Vicksburg.

There was already "quite a force" assembled at Baton Rouge by mid-January, Prentice wrote. In his own brigade, there were members of the 52nd Massachusetts and 13th Connecticut who, he remarked with some amazement, "are intelligent, but are *very small*." In addition, there were also five regiments of Louisiana recruits, two of which were black units—"Mostly River boatmen." So far, the brigade's duties, he said, had been "easy" compared to what other Union troops had undergone on the Peninsula in Virginia:

Still we have been obliged to lay ourselves down upon ground white with frost, for a nights rest, & I have when not so cold lain down in a heavy rain to get short bits of slumber given to the Picket on unexposed post. So tired that the firing of guns within a few rods did not awaken me, & then getting up finely soaked, to stand at my lonely post for 4 long hours. Yet even this I do not find unpleasant, & the danger one soon forgets entirely . . .

Twice since we came here, Yes 3 times, the "Long Roll" has sounded & we expected there was fun ahead. When boys so unwell that they could hardly be got out to Roll call would spring out, gun in hand, with a new light in their eyes, ready for the fray.

Only a few days ago there was an alarm. The 161st was formed & on a Double Quick for our positions in the Trenches in just five minutes. Our Reg. is not so perfect in drill as some others, nor does it put on as many airs; yet we do calculate that when "worst comes to worse[,]" that is in the "Tug of War comes," "When Greek meets with Greek," & all that sort of thing, that our Reg is to be equal to the best of the[m.]

Prentice had begun writing his letter to Tubbs on Friday, January 16. Because of foul weather and the press of duties, he did not get to complete his letter for two days. By Saturday morning, the ground had frozen as hard "as I have ever known it in N.Y. in Nov. & in the morning snow was visible upon the ground." When he finally picked up his pen again, on Sunday night, it was during a fierce rainstorm, the wind blowing "terribly[,] sucking our puny tent so that I can hardly write at all."

Last night there was much firing among the Pickets. Several were killed, but none from our Reg. News has come to day, tolerably well authenticated, that the Rebs are coming down from Port Hudson to pay us a visit & a battle is expected to morrow or next day at furthest. the order was issued to night that 100 rounds of cartridges be distributed to each men & everything indicates a contest soon.[4]

But Prentice's eagerness to do battle was not sated that winter. The "tolerably well authenticated" report of a Confederate attack against Banks' army turned out to be a rumor. And federal plans to move against Port Hudson from both the north and south became so bogged down by delays that the Red River Campaign, as Banks' movement was called, did not get underway until almost mid-April. By then, it was too late to coordinate with Grant, who turned his attention to capturing the Confederate stronghold at Vicksburg.

Meanwhile, up north in the Virginia Peninsula, George Scudder, with the 45th Pennsylvania, was as eager to do battle as Prentice was—and he was not only frustrated but angry as well.

In the latter part of January, a month after being defeated at the Battle of Fredericksburg, Ambrose Burnside's Army of the Potomac was still stuck some ten miles above the city. Burnside decided to begin a long-planned-for second effort to cross the Rappahannock River. The attempt became known as the Mud March.

Since the fighting at Fredericksburg, the weather had been excellent, but once Burnside's force began to move, the weather took a turn for the worse. A deluging rain that lasted the better part of two days turned the roads the army was passing over into quagmires. Bogged down in mud and slime, their ammunition trains and supply wagons completely mired, the wet and hungry soldiers could barely make any headway. After four days, their attempt to cross the Rappahannock was called off.

The Army of the Potomac turned back, dispirited. Disappointed as he was by the botched advance, Scudder was one of the few officers who still evidenced any confidence in Burnside. Scudder believed that Burnside was, above all, trustworthy. Writing to Tubbs as the rain pelted his tent, Scudder declared:

I can only say that events have placed Burnie in My confidence more than ever. Not that of the Fredricksburg disaster if such we may Call it—but because I think him qualified but more than all honest. It is an old maxim that an honest Man is hard to be found "especially in high officials" but if there be one I think Burnie is that one.

Scudder believed Burnside's chances for success were stymied by politicians, in particular so-called Peace Democrats who were seeking to end the war. "We have a great enemy in our front," he said, "but a worse one in our rear." Because of southern sympathizers in Congress, said the annoyed Scudder, Confederates on picket duty "boast of their success in the North.["]

The olive branch of peace extended by political scoundrels and rascals are doing more injury to our cause—Prolonging the war—More than all the defeats and disasters that has happened to our Armies and Navies[.] Were the people in the North as much united in their cause as the people of the South are in theirs ther's Rebellion would not last another six months and not a gun need be fired[.]

Scudder was especially disturbed by the schemes of Clement L. Vallandigham, an Ohio Democrat and anti-abolitionist who led the Copperheads, as the Peace Democrats in the North were called.[5] A vicious opponent of Lincoln, Vallandigham was active in the secretive Knights of the Golden Circle, which initiated or encouraged plots against the Republican administration.

Scudder, however, saved his greatest wrath for the man he once idolized, George McClellan. Scudder believed that the Army of the Potomac's favorite general had not "used his utmost energy to put an end to this rebellion when he was in Command of the Army but otherwise tried to prolong it! and succeeded in doing so on account of his connection." Scudder felt certain that the Peace Democrats would nominate McClellan as their presidential candidate in 1864:

He may be a great Martyr in the eyes of some people but a D-L poor one in my estimation[.] I would sooner help behead him than eulogize him if what I beleive is true and I get to see something more than I have seen yet—in his defence—to convince me that it is not true[.]

Scudder went to some length to explain that he could not help but change his "oppinions" toward McClellan. It was not a matter of being weakminded, or merely going along with "popular oppinyon," he said, for "the Grand Slaughter Penn is all for McClellan & God know[s] I have been with them along while." But the general belonged with those who "Should Meet with their just deserts[.]"

Hang by the neck between the Heaven & Earth until life is extinct. They should be found out as spe[e]dily as possible & their justice given them.[6]

· CHAPTER 15 ·

Defeat and Disappointment

*Friend Chas. I am at the Commissary of the Division.
I am there as a cook. . . . I am tolorable good at this
and if they want me to shoot rebs I can do that and
will not turn my hand over to any one at that game
for I have been tried different times.*
—*David Armstrong*[1]

After a furlough home to visit his wife, Melissa, John Orr returned
to Virginia to find that his regiment, the 107th New York, had just
participated in a major engagement: the Battle of Chancellorsville. The
battle, fought in the opening days of May, was another defeat for the
Army of the Potomac in spite of a change in commanders: Joseph
Hooker had replaced Ambrose Burnside. The Union lost nearly 17,000
men killed, wounded, and missing.

Fortunately, only two men in Orr's company were wounded, both
in the hand. Orr immediately went to visit the two soldiers in a tent
hospital. Later, he returned to Company F to resume his duties as its
second lieutenant and was deeply distressed by the condition of his
men. He wrote to Charles Tubbs that he "found the boys looking badly,
both officers & men . . . their countenances told a tale of hardship &
suffering such as only the soldier experiences." The regiment was in
such poor shape that it failed an inspection and the men were denied
leaves of absence. Orr was angry that the soldiers were "publicly dis-
graced" though "trying & will[ing] to do every duty."

The Army of the Potomac, Orr lamented, "has never acheived
any great success" and "lost many brave boys." His own regiment had
never had "a permanent well qualified leader." Chancellorsville, he
told Tubbs, "like nearly all the great battles of the war," had been
fought "without a complete premeditated plan of action."

Despite the defeat at Chancellorsville and the denial of furloughs
for the 107th, Orr insisted that the army was "*not* demoralized in the

117

least" and that his own men "still beleive that they can whip the rebels if given a chance."[2]

Asa Spencer's regiment, the 136th Pennsylvania, also fought at Chancellorsville, but the Osceola schoolmaster missed the battle, too, because he was working at Columbian Hospital in Washington. Coincidentally, the hospital was where many of the wounded from the battle were transported. Three weeks later, on May 29, when their nine-month term of enlistment ended, the men of the 136th were officially mustered out of the service. Spencer went home to his wife, Betsey, in Jasper, New York.

Meanwhile, some one hundred miles from Chancellorsville, a severely ill Harlan Kimball was on his way home. He had written his brother Orville in April from a hospital in Newport News, Virginia, that he was "getting some better but gains very slow." However, the eighteen-year-old Osceola youth apparently suffered a relapse and failed to respond to treatment for recurrent bouts of fever at the federal hospital in Newport News or later, after being transferred to another hospital in Hampton, Virginia. Harlan was officially discharged from the 103rd New York on June 7.[3]

With Spencer's and Harlan Kimball's departures from military service, there were now only eight of Charles Tubbs' friends still on active duty: John Orr, David Armstrong, Dr. William Humphrey, Orville Kimball, Henry Maxson, William Prentice, George Scudder, and William Self.

Of all of them, Armstrong was in an unusual quandary. He did not know whether to express disappointment or joy about his new status.

Armstrong was currently serving as cook for officers of Company F, 49th Ohio, though he made it clear to Tubbs that the choice was not his. "Since I have been in the survice I have always tried to obey my officers." Besides which, he continued, the officers wanted him to cook for them so much that they were chipping in to pay him a bonus for doing so. Including his pay as a private, he was now earning $25 a month.

Armstrong must have been an exceptionally good cook because his officers showered him with perks. He was named to an honor roll comprised of five men from each company of the 49th Ohio and, as a result, would be eligible for assignment to a scouting unit called the Light Battalion once a vacancy occurred. The battalion did not have to do picket duty. He also was awarded a permit to keep and ride a horse.[4]

But Armstrong admitted to Tubbs that, his new-found prestige aside, he felt out of touch with things. He attributed these feelings to the fact that it was "such a long distance to the army of the Potomac" from where he was stationed at Murfreesboro, Tennessee. The 49th Ohio was then part of the First Brigade of Rosecrans' Army of the Cumberland. Armstrong said he had no idea how the war was progressing—"the news that we get is a[l]ways been false"—but he did not believe that it would end before his enlistment term was up. He still had fifteen months to serve."[5]

The Ohio volunteers, in the meantime, were learning an unusual drill for advancing against the enemy. They formed in four ranks, one behind the other, with the idea of opening fire on command when within range of the enemy, advancing briskly all the while.[6] How effective the new "peculiar" drill would be no one, of course, could tell until the army again met an opposing Confederate force.

Following Chancellorsville, the Army of the Potomac and Lee's Army of Northern Virginia clashed anew at battles fought at Franklin's Crossing, Brandy Station, and Winchester, as Lee moved his troops toward the border with Pennsylvania. Then, in late June, he invaded Pennsylvania in the hope that a victory on northern soil would shift the federal pressure on both Vicksburg and Chattanooga, and, at the same time, encourage England to intervene on the Confederacy's behalf. At almost the same time, the Army of the Potomac once again got a new commander, George Gordon Meade. He took over command as elements of both opposing forces inadvertently stumbled toward each other. They met on July 1 at a crossroads in the little town of Gettysburg.

This time, John Orr was with the 107th as it headed into battle.

CHAPTER 16

Gettysburg: Two Views

[A]s soon as They Saw our Regt Charge down on
them They turned and run saying There Comes them
damed Bucktails and The Pa Reserve[.]
                                        —*William Self*[1]

Three friends of Charles Tubbs took part in the Battle of Gettysburg and saw the battle from different perspectives—Dr. William Humphrey from afar, William Self and John Orr in the very heart of the fighting. They provided Tubbs with a fascinating picture of one of the greatest clashes of arms during the war.

Alarmed by the incursion into Pennsylvania of Confederate forces less than fifty miles from Harrisburg, Governor Andrew Curtin issued an immediate call for sixty thousand men to repel the invaders. Eight men from Osceola responded, among them Leonard Kimball. He apparently was no longer troubled by the deafness that led to his discharge from the 34th New York almost sixteen months earlier. Kimball and the other Osceola volunteers were mustered into Company G of an emergency regiment and rushed to take up a defensive position at Shippensburg, northwest of Gettysburg.[2]

The man who had originally organized the Bucktails, Thomas Kane, was now a general and led a brigade. He had just recovered from pneumonia. He was racing by horse to Gettysburg to rejoin his brigade when suddenly he came face to face with a troop of Confederate cavalrymen from J. E. B. Stuart's corps. Kane, who was evidently in civilian clothes, used his wits. He adopted a southern accent and convinced the enemy horsemen that he was a friend. They let him go on his way.

The Bucktails, meanwhile, struggled to reach the scene of the battle. Marching almost one hundred miles in five days in the blazing summer heat with temperatures in the nineties played havoc with the men. By the time the fighting began at Gettysburg on Wednesday, July 1, the 13th Pennsylvania—part of the V Corps and now under the command of Major General George Sykes—was still across the border in Maryland. The Bucktails were down to fewer than 350 men fit for battle.[3] To keep up with the regiment, William Self said, Company A even marched at night.[4]

William Humphrey was there from the start. Waylaid again with diarrhea after the Second Battle of Bull Run, he had to be conveyed in an ambulance to an army hospital in Alexandria.[5] By the time he felt better, in the latter part of September 1862, he was asked to transfer to a new regiment organized in Pennsylvania that included three hundred men from Tioga County. Despite recurrent bouts with the illness that exhausted him, Humphrey agreed to join the regiment, the 149th Pennsylvania Volunteer Infantry, as its surgeon—that is, chief physician among the five doctors attached to the unit.[6] The 149th and another newly recruited Pennsylvania regiment, the 150th, called themselves Bucktails, too, or were called the Second Bucktails, but to the men of 13th Pennsylvania, the original Bucktails, the newcomers were "Bogus Bucktails."[7]

On the first day of the fighting, the 149th was posted to the north of Seminary Ridge and was one of the first federal units to engage the enemy. The fighting waged back and forth, the 149th attacking, then being attacked, attacking again, and finally being driven back, outnumbered by the Confederates.[8] The men fought at bayonet point but were unable to stop the southerners. Humphrey, meantime, had set up a temporary hospital in a local church. The men of the 149th fell back, regrouping at Seminary Ridge, with the result that the church was left unguarded and an enemy unit surrounded Humphrey's makeshift hospital.

The Confederates easily captured Humphrey and his patients and took control of the hospital. He lost his horse, saddle, medical stores, and surgical instruments. Humphrey remained with the wounded, caring for them as best he could, but when he had the chance, he climbed the steps to the belfry of the church and from a distance watched the battle grow in intensity as the two armies, North and South, maneuvered, attacked, and counterattacked.[9]

The Bucktails reached the scene of the battle on the second day of the fighting, Thursday, July 2. They entered the battle on the far left, or southernmost end, of the Union line on the slope of a hill called Little Round Top, where several Confederate divisions were attacking weak federal positions. An Ohio artillery battery to their left began to withdraw, but Charles Taylor, the young colonel of the 13th Pennsylvania, shouted to the gunners to stay: the Bucktails would protect them. Together with another Pennsylvania regiment, the Bucktails, bayonets fixed, charged down the hill and veered to the right through a boggy valley and toward a cluster of huge boulders called Devil's Den. "We came in on the double quick," said William Self:

> [A]t this time the Rebs wer driveing The Second Division from the ground and The Rebs wer up to the mouth of our Cannon and had we been three minutes later They would have had them . . . they did not try to fight &c wih [us] as we came on to them[.] They Throwed down There arms and run into our lines without asking[.]

Taylor led the charge, running and waving his sword. Reaching a low wall, he vaulted over it. The men who followed him captured the Confederates who remained behind the wall. While Taylor regrouped his men, a scouting party came upon a large group of Texans and Georgians in the nearby woods. Taylor, Self said, impetuously led his men forward, but he outran his men. Many of them fell behind, stumbling because of the rocky nature of the terrain:

> [H]ere he roshed ahead at The head of the Regt So fast That he and about half Dozen of officers and the Same of me[n] run into a Whole Brigade of Rebs and told them to surender[.] about 1/2 of them throwed down Their arms and Their officers a hollering to them to not Disgrace Themselvs to so fiew and They fired killing him almost instantly[.][10]

The Bucktails' daring action ended further Confederate advances in the Devil's Den–Little Round Top area.

John Orr with the 107th New York entered the battle on the same day that the Bucktails did, but on the opposite side, the right flank of the Union line of battle. Its "hardest fighting," though, came, he said, on the next day, Friday, July 3, when the Confederates assaulted the federal right:

> Our Regt (the 107) had but 2 men wounded But it was a mere streak of luck, for we occupied as important a position as any on the field. We were both a reserve and support for our batteries which fired over us. Friday afternoon when the rebels attacked our left centre their shell fell very close to us, but none were hit.[11]

William Humphrey was in the belfry of the church-hospital that Friday afternoon in the company of a Confederal major. Together they watched as, in a desperate attempt to turn the tide of battle, James Longstreet ordered George Pickett to form ten brigades. The Confederates charged the federal line across the road in front of Cemetery Ridge. The doctor saw the southerners thrown back in confusion. As

Humphrey cheered, the major swore. The next day, the battle over, Lee retreated. Union forces reoccupied the town of Gettysburg on Saturday, July 4, and liberated the doctor and the hospital.[12]

"Charles[,] that was a glorious vicitory for us, all that I regret was that the rebels wer permitted to recross the Potomac without a second fight," John Orr wrote:

Our Corps with the rest of the Army followed them, and had we pursued them as closely as we might have done, they could not have fortified but little and I am confident we might have destroyed one half of their remaining force[.][13]

As Lee's troops and their seventeen-mile-long wagon train burdened with casualties staggered southward, back in the direction of Virginia, the losses were counted up. Of the 75,000 Confederates engaged in the battle, 3,900 were dead, nearly 19,000 wounded, and 5,400 missing. Of the Union's 88,000 troops, about 3,200 were dead, some 14,500 were wounded, and more than 5,300 were missing.[14]

"[T]he end of this rebellion cannot be far distant," a jubilant Orr said:

You can hardly conceive[,] Charles[,] the good effect our many victories have on our soldiers. The discontent which has prevailed to so great an extent seemes to have almost disappeared: all men conten[t] & willing to continue the campaign. A continual success is what we need & it is just what we are having[.][15]

With Lee's forces falling back and the threat of invasion eliminated, the emergency Pennsylvania regiment in which Leonard Kimball volunteered was disbanded on August 7, less than five weeks after it was mustered into service. Kimball once again returned home to Osceola.[16]

There was another reason for northerners to cheer on Independence Day, 1863. After more than three months of skirmishes, battles, assaults, and siege, Ulysses Grant captured Vicksburg. Afterwards, William Prentice had occasion to visit the city:

I will only say that it is much larger than I expected & more substantially built. It is decidedly picturesque as there has been no attempt made at grading & the streets run up & down the hills, which look as though the tops of all the mountains in the universe had been clipped & tumbled down in this place. Some of the houses stand on places so steep as to be ascended by stairs. While the ground is supported by paleisades. The whole thing is now our Map of fortifications. A line of earth works near ten miles in length extend entirely around the town, while every commanding bluff is a small fort completely impregnable. In several places huge Columbiads stand lik bristling bulldogs in the very dooryards of the finest southern mansions. I am satisfied that with a sufficiency of provisions inside, these works could never have been taken.[17]

Prentice was jubilant when, less than a week after Vicksburg fell, Nathaniel Banks finally took Port Hudson. Prentice wrote Tubbs that after Gettysburg, the seizure of Port Hudson "may seem a small success & yet to *us* it is complete & *great*." Port Hudson, he continued,

has truly been called a Giberaltrar & has been the scene of many a short but severely contested fight & in Banks little army of 16000 men there is scarsely a company but has left one or more graves as remembrances of their struggles.

We found there 3000 effective men for a garrison & 2000 sick & wounded. The place was terribly torn by our shot.[18]

The Union now had control of the Mississippi River, in effect cutting the South in half and freeing Grant's forces for operations elsewhere. Taken together with the federal triumph at Gettysburg, the outlook for the Confederacy was bleak. Its death knell, many said, was sounded.

CHAPTER 17

Raising the Flag in the South

*The expedition was a most unfortunate one & reflects
badly upon <u>somebody</u>.*
                                    —*William Prentice*[1]

T he war in the South grew in intensity during the summer of 1863.
Three friends of Tubbs'—William Prentice in Louisiana, Orville Kimball
in North Carolina, and David Armstrong in Georgia—were in the thick
of it, and for two of them the fighting took a dangerous turn.

At the outset, Prentice could not have been happier. The 161st
New York was now in almost constant action. Once Port Hudson and
Vicksburg were under Union control, federal forces were able to begin
a sweep up the Mississippi, pushing as far north as Yazoo City, Mississippi. In the second week of July, a key two-day engagement was
fought on Bayou La Fourche, near Donaldsonville, Louisiana.

Donaldsonville was a flourishing town, the site of a small federal
fort built on a point in the river. At the end of June, a Confederate unit
attacked the garrison. At first the federals repulsed the southerners,
who fell back and then encamped about six miles down a bayou, within
threatening distance. Prentice was with the 161st New York when it led
the advance of a Union brigade ordered to take the enemy position.
After a severe skirmish, the federal troops drove in the Confederate
pickets. The New Yorkers halted for the night while the small battery
of four cannons that they carried with them began an artillery duel
with an enemy battery. The firing back and forth lasted until two
o'clock the following afternoon, when pickets of Prentice's company
suddenly spotted the Confederates advancing toward them:

*We were in line in a twinkling but shot & shell were pouring in a perfect
storm around us from 6 or 8 pieces of artilery which the Rebs brought to bear
upon us. Their advance was all the way through corn & cain fields, 10 & 12
feet high, so that we could do very little with our muskets for some time[;] at*

length our 4 6 pounders were obliged to fall back for want of ammunition. Then the slaughter began.

Trapped, all but one of their cannons abandoned, many men either dead or severely wounded, the survivors struggled to escape. But they found themselves outflanked on the left and the target of a "galling fire" from a battery behind a levee less than twenty yards away:

Here it was that we lost most heavily. But the men fought like tigers pulling back at the very slowest pace, still loading & firing occasionally we lay down behind some fence & gave them a steady volley once completely checking them, when the men rose up & giving a loud cheer asked to be allowed to charge, but that would have been madness so we continued falling back.

The federal brigade lost sixty men—a "considerable" loss, said Prentice, because it had fewer than three hundred men engaged in the skirmish. His own company's losses totaled two dead, three wounded, and one taken prisoner.[2]

Less than two weeks later, as part of the XIX Corps, Department of the Gulf, the 161st New York took part in a much more extensive expedition, this one designed to "raise the flag in Texas."[3] General Nathaniel Banks chose Sabine Pass, off the Gulf of Mexico, as the objective. He figured that his federal forces could then advance north to Beaumont and west, following a railroad line, to Houston. The result, Prentice said, was "the most desperate fight I ever witnessed."

At New Orleans, the 161st boarded the steamer *Gen. Banks.* She and a fleet of twenty-one other vessels set off for Sabine Pass, where a small Confederate fort stood guard at the mouth of the Sabine River. The expedition was under the command of Major General William Buel Franklin, a veteran of the fighting in Virginia who had been chastised for his role in the Union defeat at Fredericksburg. There was only one point where the federal troops could land, and then only in small boats, a few men at a time, and within such short range of the fort that, Prentice said, "every inch of it could be swept by grape & canister" from ten 32-pound guns.

The federal fleet took three days to reach Sabine Pass, arriving there about midnight on September 7 and anchoring off the fort. "So far so good," said Prentice. But secrecy had been breached and, alerted to the pending Union assault, during the night enemy troops rushed to the fort by train from Houston:

In the morning our Regt. & the 75th N.Y. were detailed to act as a storming party. Our boats were to be run up under cover of the Gun boats across the shallow chanel (we could not land westside, acct. of the swamps.) &

we were to land & storm the fort while the two Gunboats Clifton (Capt Crocker) & the Sachem (Capt. Johnson[)] ran past & give them a raking fire. The chanel is very difficult being narrow or rather there are two of them formed by a bar in the center. An[d] this the Clifton struck just as she got along side the batteries. The Sachem was more fortunate[,] getting merely by a shot entered her steam chest & all was over with her.

Nearly at the same moment the Clifton struck. She is only thinly coated with iron & at that short range the shot & can[ister,] grape made a clean sweep through her striking in the water beyond. She gave the batteries one terrible broadside but being perfectly helpless she was telegraphed to surrender & the signal officer on board ran up the white flag. Seeing this Cap. Crocker spiked every gun except the huge nine inch Pierot at the stern, reversed it, sent its terrible contents through his own machinery & then gave himself up. On board as sharp shooters were two Co.s. of the 75th N.Y. about half a dozen only escaped[,] from 30 to 35 killed & wounded.

On board the Sachem was Co D. from our Regt. commanded by Lieut Lindsey of my own Co. Many of his men were scalded by the steam[,] himself slightly. A corp[oral] Barber took a skiff with two of his Engineers & made their escape to one of the other boats: The two engineers were so badly scalded that they died the sam night.

Soon as the two boats surrendered two huge cotton [vessels] were seen coming round the bend of the river & so our whole fleet getting under way crossed the bar & made sail for the mouth of the Miss[issippi], which we reached on the 3d d[a]y. The men & horses on board suffered terribly for water[,] the men being reduced to half a pint per day, the horses going without[.]

Prentice felt certain that even if the federal gunboats had succeeded in running the batteries, "not a man of us" in the assault would have reached the batteries alive. The expedition, he continued, "*might have succeeded*" if secrecy could have been maintained. Prentice believed "somebody" was responsible and pointed his finger at Franklin.[4] He did not believe that the general had thought out the attack.

Banks was undeterred by Franklin's failure at Sabine Pass. He decided that fall to have his XIII Corps land near the mouth of the Rio Grande and work its way eastward. Banks was able to raise the Union flag in Brownsville and Corpus Christi, Texas, and take control of Matagorda Bay, but powerful fortifications at Galveston and at the mouth of the Brazos River blocked further advances. Banks appealed to Washington for more troops but was refused, so he returned to Louisiana and decided to try another campaign up the Red River.

Meanwhile, Orville Kimball was back in the Carolinas, encamped once again "on the shore of the Atlantic." Since his tour of duty on

Cape Hatteras a year ago, he had been "in various places and seen many a sick day when on the march from Antietam to Fredericsburg, have several times heard the whistle of the enemy's bullets to[o] near to be comfortable."[5] Skirmishes between battles were so frequent, Kimball said, that "we are not allowed to take off our accoutrements and if we sleep at all we are obliged to 'sleep on our rifles with one eye open' as the Col. says[.]"[6]

Now, in midsummer, he wrote Charles Tubbs that he was taking part in the siege of Forts Wagner and Johnson, two of the main defenses of Charleston Harbor. His own company was based on Folly Island, "among the palmettoes of South Carolina within sight of fort Sumpter where the American flag was first fired on in this great rebellion." Ever since, he said, the rebel flag has flown "defiantly" over the fort:

I can see it[,] a small piece of bunting[.] I would call it white as it appears to the naked eye[.] On the second day after we [arrived] here it was shot away and Yesterday I hear that it was Shot down three times[.]

Kimball's regiment, the 34th New York, was so close to the battery on Fort Wagner that its sharpshooters could get within thirty yards of it to fire at its garrison.

I learn that they are removing the guns from fort Sumpter in st[e]amboats[.] . . . this we cannot Prevent as the rebels have batteries and forts on both sides[.] we have a formidable line of intrenchments in front of Wagner and Johnson and will trouble them some to hold their possition and if Charleston is not ours by the 15 of September I shall miss my guess[.] the Rebels sent a flag of truce yesterday and wanted to remove their guns and ammunition from fort Wagner and Sumpter[.] this shows some encouragement to our brave men who have braved the dangers of this summer champaign[.]

Otherwise, Kimball said, he and the rest of Company I had little to complain about. He was "healthy tolerable," and enjoying meat and soup at dinner every evening.[7]

Orville's letter to Tubbs was dated August 24. Before he wrote again, sobering news came from his family in Pennsylvania: Harlan was dead. His brother had never been able to rebound from the deadly combination of chronic diarrhea and malaria.

Harlan died at home on September 8, twenty-six days after his nineteenth birthday. He was buried under a simple stone marker in Fairview Cemetery in Osceola.

By late summer, the Civil War was barely seventeen months old

and three of Tubbs' friends—Samuel Stevens, Orrin Stebbins, and now
Harlan Kimball—were dead.

Just before summer turned into fall that September, David Armstrong
was with the 49th Ohio when it played a crucial role in two days of
fighting at the Battle of Chickamauga.

The 49th was first posted on the extreme right of the fedeal line,
but before the fighting started, the regiment, part of the First Brigade,
Third Division, IV Corps, was shifted to the extreme left of the line,
where it joined the XIV Corps under Major General George Henry
Thomas. The regiment, with Armstrong bearing its colors into battle
again, attacked an enemy position in dense woods in midafternoon,
forcing the Confederates to run and capturing two guns. But enemy
reinforcements rushed to the aid of the Confederates and they counterattacked at dusk. The southern troops laid down a withering volley of
rifle fire, then, with a yell, rushed forward with fixed bayonets. The
49th reeled backward briefly, then rallied and repulsed the Confederates.

During the next day of the battle, the 49th was under constant,
severe fire but performed an extremely complex maneuver that managed to save the entire corps from being swept from the field. The
Confederates broke through the Union left and were encircling the center of the federal line. In a brilliant exploit, the entire 49th Ohio turned
about, faced to the rear, and poured a withering fire into the Confederate advance. Together with enfilading artillery fire from an Ohio battery, the 49th was able to turn the enemy back.[8]

Sometime during the heat of the fighting, Armstrong fell, hit by a
bullet. At first, the wound did not seem serious. He was hospitalized
for a time, but two months later he took part with the 49th in the Battle
of Missionary Ridge. There he merited the commendation of the regiment's commander, whose official report stated: "My color sergeant,
David Armstrong, was among the first on the ridge and proudly planted
the colors on the deserted works of the enemy."[9]

But after the battle at Missionary Ridge, Armstrong's wound started
troubling him, and he was hospitalized in Stevenson, Alabama. His
recovery was slow. In between two sick furloughs home in Ohio, before and after the turn of the year, Armstrong was again hospitalized.[10]

While these three friends of Tubbs' were engaged in the fighting in
the South during the summer of 1863, another of his friends from Alfred University, Mordecai Casson, Jr., enlisted. He was the fifteenth
volunteer with whom Tubbs corresponded.

Mordecai Casson, Jr.

Born in Otsego County, west of Albany, in 1839, Casson was living in Addison when the Civil War broke out. He was a month shy of his twenty-fourth birthday and still a student at Alfred University when he enrolled in July 1863, several weeks after the Battle of Gettysburg. He enlisted as a private in Company C, 2nd Veteran Cavalry, New York Volunteers, and soon rose in rank to corporal.

From the photograph that he sent to Tubbs, Casson looked ungainly, but that may have been because the uniform he wore did not fit him. Otherwise, he was an ordinary-appearing man, of average height—five-foot-seven—and had blue eyes, brown hair, and a light complexion. He sported both a beard and a moustache.[11]

Casson was in the minority in his regiment on the "negro question." His comrades-in-arms made fun of him for being an abolitionist.

"[T]hey are in favor of slavery," he wrote Tubbs, "& I have heard some of them go so far as to say that they did not think them human beings."[12]

For his part, Casson did not think much of many of his fellow recruits: "one of the Conscripts says he would give all he is or ever hopes to be if he was only out of the army." Men were enlisting simply for the large bounties: "patriotism seems to have become almost extinct."

The 2nd Veteran Cavalry went into training at Saratoga Springs. When it was ordered south to join in the defense of Washington, its horses were left behind. The regiment traveled by train via New York City and Philadelphia to reach the capital, encamping finally at Geisborough Point, on the southern shore of the eastern branch of the Potomac.

Geisborough Point was a major staging area for mounted troops, with a huge corral that housed as many as twenty thousand horses. Once there, the men of the 2nd Veteran Cavalry drew new mounts. At one point, Casson reported that fifty-five hundred of the horses broke loose during a gale and before they could be rounded up, almost three hundred of them drowned in the Potomac.

Casson, who was no stranger to the burdens that farm horses were expected to bear, was astonished at the weight of the "load for a common horse." Beside the rider:

> 1 bridle, 1 watering bridle, 1 halter[,] 1 saddle pair of sadde bags, 1 saddle blanket[,] 1 sursingle, pair of spong[,] currycomb & brush, picket jim lariat rope 4 ft long, nose bag[,] Carbine[,] Saber & Navy revolver with two catridge boxes & two cap boxes[.] These with over coat[,] two blankets & a change of clothes & sometimes a suply of forage constitutes a Cavelry mans equipments.[13]

Casson did not remain at Geisborough Point long. The 2nd Veteran Cavalry was soon transferred to the Department of the Gulf in Louisiana, where Casson met up with an old friend of his and Tubbs' from Alfred, William Prentice. The two soldiers were soon fighting for their lives.

CHAPTER 18

On All Fronts

*[H]ow changing is the life of a soldier[.] he cannot tell
at any time where he will be the next five minutes or
in what shape[.] always ready for any thing he lives
on uncertainties[,] knows nothing[,] cares nothing, a
mere tool.*

—Orville Kimball[1]

The Civil War was fought on three major fronts—in Virginia and
Maryland in the north, in Tennessee in the west, and in the Carolinas
and Louisiana in the south—and, as summer turned into autumn and
autumn into winter in 1863, Charles Tubbs was receiving accounts
from each theater of operations about the battles and skirmishes, the
soldiers' morale, and the personal worries troubling his friends who
were so far from home.

Of the fifteen correspondents who had enlisted since the beginning of the war, seven were still on active duty and writing Tubbs
whenever they could. William Humphrey and William Self were in Virginia; John Orr and George Scudder in Tennessee; Orville Kimball in
South Carolina; and William Prentice and Mordecai Casson in Louisiana.

In Virginia, Self had been through another battle with the Bucktails, this one at Bristoe Station, Virginia, in October, nearly three
months after Gettysburg, as the two opposing armies—the Army of
the Potomac and the Army of Northern Virginia—maneuvered south.
A corps of Lee's army commanded by A. P. Hill tried to outflank the
Union army and cut off its supplies, but it failed. The Confederates
then tried to capture the federal supply wagons but failed at that, too,
all the troops in the assaulting party being either killed or taken prisoner. The southern troops finally took up winter quarters on the northern bank of a narrow stream known as Broad Run, apparently not
anticipating any move on the part of the federal army.

But George Meade, who had been criticized for not following up on the victory at Gettysburg, this time took advantage of the Confederate complacency. In a surprise move, he sent elements of the Army of the Potomac across Broad Run. They captured two enemy brigades, six cannons, and a pontoon bridge. Self crossed the stream with the 13th Pennsylvania and wrote Tubbs from the Confederates' quarters:

> They had Theirs Whole army Camped here and wen to a good deal of trouble in fixing up for the Winter and now I tell You They left in a hurry[.] We found evry thing in The Camp You could Think of Twas thrown around and Cloths[.] there was one letter that was picked up that the fellow was Writing to his Sweet hart[.] he said That he had had no Time to Write along back and They have been fighting the Yankees and building Winter quarters but now That They wer done he would have nothing else to doe[.] . . .
>
> [W]hile he was writing This we Crossed the River below and They began to Run and great was the S[k]eedadle[.] an Old Farmer lives here said They snatched Their Things and ran about 5 miles before They stoped.[2]

For Orr, the months before the end of the year were occasionally pleasant ones but more often frustrating. His regiment had been engaged in picket duty along the Rapidan River, not far from Self and the Bucktails in Virginia, when it was ordered to Tennessee. The trip, by rail, took the 107th New York through Ohio and Indiana—"a perfect treat," said Orr, for "in every town that we stopped we were welcomed as *brothers*, inspiring us not only with encouraging words, but bestowing upon [us] without money or price all sorts of eatables[,] fruits &C." The reception by the womenfolk of Xenia, Ohio, was so hospitable—they "literally gave us more than we knew what to do with"—that many of the troops missed the regiment's train when it pulled out from the town and did not catch up with the 107th until a few days later at Chattanooga.

Under Union pressure, Braxton Bragg, who commanded the Confederate army that held Chattanooga, had withdrawn from the city in early September, just before Orr's regiment reached Tennessee. Federal troops, including the 107th, which was part of the XII Corps, immediately occupied the city. The 107th reached there too late to stop enemy cavalry from tearing up a section of the rail line. The New Yorkers chased the Confederates but without success.

The regiment finally went into what everyone hoped was winter quarters in mid-October. It was assigned to guard a makeshift railroad bridge across the Elk River that Union engineers built after Bragg's troops had destroyed the original. The entire XII Corps was scattered along what Orr called the "miserable old dilapidated ill begotten" rail line between Murfreesboro and Stevenson, Alabama. They were charged with protecting it from other Confederate raiders. Particularly vexing to the men was something new—bands of southern guerrilla fighters who appeared out of nowhere, inflicted damage, and then, their damage done, disappeared once again into the countryside.

Near the 107th's camp and close to the bed of a small creek were hot springs and what was left of a summer resort—"Gardens of Eden," in Orr's words—that once attracted "large numbers of the wealthy families of this Southern wilderness." Orr liked it in Tennessee: it was "better country" than Virginia. But his pleasure was short-lived. The regiment was ordered "up South," as the vernacular went, to Estill Springs. The men built "little houses" to serve as winter quarters there, but no sooner had they finished them, when orders came to "pack up for a march." It was "tough," said Orr, "yet nothing new to us."

During the next weeks, the men of the 107th marched to and fro, victimized by confusing and contradictory orders. First, for some reason that was not explained to them, they spent three days marching over a ridge of the Cumberland Mountains through "mud & storm" to a small town about a mile from the Alabama border. The next day, their orders were reversed, and they turned around and marched back to where they came from, but beyond where they had built their "little houses." Exasperated, the men were reluctant to build new quarters, fearing that they would not be permitted to stay where they were, and they were correct. A week later the regiment was on the move again.

The commander of the XII Corps, Major General Henry Warner Slocum, finally issued an order forbidding soldiers to destroy their quarters when they left them—"which," Orr said, "they (the soldiers) are quite apt to do in their fits of impatience & anger." As a result, the 107th found "pretty good huts" left by another regiment when it reached Wartrace Bridge, Tennessee, but that good fortune did not last long because the camp had to be moved to higher ground and "the boys" forced to build new shelters. "We have a Stove in our 'wall tent' which takes in 3 feet wood," Orr wryly commented, "so you see we are ready & prepared for the winter, but we may have to leave in three days, who knows? not I ha-ha."

The 107th's new encampment was near a rail line. Daily, trains rolled by, filled with southerners. They turned out to be Confederate soldiers captured in two major Union successes outside Chattanooga at Lookout Mountain and nearby Missionary Ridge in the last week in November. It was in the latter battle that David Armstrong was commended. Ulysses Grant, now in command of all federal western forces, directed both victories.

Every day, somewhere along the rail line, cars ran off the tracks.

Thanksgiving Day was no exception. Orr watched with horror as a train carrying Confederate officers, including the son and staff of General John Cable Breckinridge, jumped the rails. Four of the cars were totally smashed. All the casualties—four dead and six wounded—were members of the Union guard unit, the 2nd Tennessee Colored Infantry.

The incident gave Orr reason to pause. It was "unfortunate," he said, "that certain Brigades or Corps have to do all the fighting, while others do nothing that endangers their lives by exposure." The 107th "cannot see rougher times than we have," he said. Yet at the same time, he acknowledged that the "monotony of 'camp life' at times becomes almost insufferable." After all the fighting the regiment had gone through, Orr was sounding as eager as William Prentice was to get back into action. He wrote Tubbs that, although he preferred "this business to fighting because it is safe, yet I half wish I was back in Va."[3]

Prentice at the time was in southern Louisiana, not far inland from the Gulf of Mexico, and was not only feeling his usual lonesome self, but was paranoid as well. His life, he believed, was so different from that of his single friends from Osceola and Alfred University. Ever since he committed the "double crime of *Marrying* & enlisting," he said, he had lost friends. Except for his family, no one but Charles Tubbs ever wrote him, though "I am still flesh & blood, subject to joy & sorrow[,] Pains & Pleasure, as men who neither marry nor go *soldiering*." In addition, as he wrote Tubbs in the last week of October, the 161st New York had "followed the Rebs some over 100 miles but have not as yet succeeded in overtaking them, except for our occasional skirmish."

Prentice did not have to wait long to be in the thick of action again. His regiment became part of a diversionary force intent on drawing Confederate troops from Texas, where Nathaniel Banks was moving up the coast to Corpus Christi. The strategy worked. Southern troops under John B. Magruder rushed into Louisiana, hoping to block what they believed would be a federal invasion overland into Texas in support of Banks.

The 161st seemed to be on the move constantly. It fell back, drawing the Confederates, first from Vermillionville, then to Opelousas, and from there to Bayou Marie Croquand. The last leg, twenty-one miles long, made in rainy "dismal" weather, was what Prentice called "the hardest march I ever made." For one thing, the weather was "dismal." For another, Prentice was feverish again with malaria:

The last two hours it rained steadily and when about dusk we filed off into the timber on this side of the Bayou, I was too tired & sick to do anything but lie down under a tree. But here the proverbial generosity of the soldiers came to my help. Kind hands pitched my shelter tent & brought me a cup of Tea. with this, I lay down upon the ground, wet to my skin, & too sick with a burning Fever to eat or sleep. The night was tedious but passed away at last . . .

On our march our Brigade & Divis. took the advance, & so had all the skirmishing to do. On the retreat the 13th Corps was in the rear and had to take the brunt of the work. Most of the Corps was left at Carrion Crow and one Brigade . . . was attacked by an overwhelming force & for a time driven back, but being reinforced . . . finally defeated the Rebels with terrible slaughter.

We were on Picket at the time & at 12 Oc at night received notice to get under way in light marching order in an hour. We were ready at the time, but the Division did not get underway until 2 Oc A.M. Away we went at "Double Quick" most of the way, over the prairies toward Carrion Crow, the men as they have always been anxious for the prey: but we reached the battlefield only to learn that the . . . boys had been successful & driven the enemy clear back to Opelousas . . .

They were determined we should not get away safe & so followed us up in the hopes of cuting us to pieces, & it is exceedingly amusing to see their accounts of the different fights, everyone a defeat, they at Carrion Crow losing in killed & wounded at least 4 times our number, yet they magnify them all with "Splendid victories."

A month later, the 161st was encamped near New Iberia:

This is a queer country, being mostly rolling prairie and belts of timber skirting the numerous Bayous, which you see by the map f[o]rm a perfect network in Western La. Of these the Teche is one of the largest & is navigable for several hundred miles. At present, however, boats run only up to this point which is a pretty little town about the size of Addison, in Steuben Co NY, but now almost entirely deserted of its citizens. Here our army is at present gathered; the 13th Corps above town & the 19th below.

At present I am detached from the Regt & in command of two Co's doing guard duty over Quarter Master & Commissary's stores in town. Our quarters are in old negro huts, which however keep off the storm & keep us more comfortable than in Shelter tents. We have been here nearly a week & are quite likely to stay some time as there is no prospect that I can see of our moving on though it would be possible to ship the whole army to Texas in a very short time.

A boat arrives here every evening from Brashear⁴ & leaves at 9 Oc in the Morning. These Bayous are very deep & narrow & it looks queer enough to see a boat 100 feet long navigating a stream not as many feet wider.

"[T]he Blues," were getting to Prentice again, so much so that he feared that "they have become chronic." He did not mind the loneliness "while excitement was high," but "through these long evenings what would I *not* give for one sympathizing friend to help me pass among its hours."

For all his grousing, though, Prentice was living the high life. He had a servant—"my 'Boy' *Ben*" he called him—and he told Tubbs that if he came to visit him in Louisiana he could offer him "Beef Steak, Irish Potatoes, Onions, Wheat cakes smoking hot with tea or Coffee and Apple Sauce for a des[s]ert." For reading matter there was the "New Orleans Times," which says "Lincoln is a trump & Emancipation the only safeguard against disunion." Or there was "The Era, which says the same thing *only* tries to sugarcoat the pill in New Orleans by the idea that it would really be a good thing for the South [to adopt] our economical way since Slaves like all other things Southern have grown 'Mighty onsartin.' Or here is 'the Bee', which thinks the Union should be restored but cant tell how, since War has grown so unchristian that tis doubtful if it should be resorted to even in self defence. Then lastly we have the Picayune, which says 'Lincoln is a Despot, Banks a Tyrant & the Union humbug'."[5]

As the year drew to a close, David Armstrong was relishing a visit home, far from where his regiment was fighting in the South. He was among friends in Fremont, Ohio, on a sick furlough, recovering from the wound he received at Chickamauga. He was having "a good time at present," he wrote Tubbs. He chatted with neighbors, dallied with "some young ladies," and visited his "folks"—whose "health is not any the best"—at their home some forty-four miles from Fremont. Armstrong was sending almost all his army pay to his father to buy livestock and a secondhand wagon, but he was wondering whether it might not be better to start to save for himself.

During his absence, Armstrong said, the 49th Ohio fought another skirmish, losing heavily. He learned that those killed included six men from his unit, Company F. "[T]his is takeing of men at a great speed," he commented.

Undaunted by his wound or all the battles he had been through, Armstrong was considering reenlisting when his term was up in 1864. He was already under orders to report back to his regiment in January "to battle with the gray backs a gain and give them another chance at me and I at them."[6]

1864

CHAPTER 19

Decision Time

*I have not had a gun to go in battle only once and that
was on the skirmish line[.] I left the gray backs have
27 shots. I was out only one hour and a half when the
Lieutanant sent for me to come . . . he would tell me I
had no buisness out on the line and that I had one hole
through me and that was a nough.*

—*David Armstrong*[1]

The outcome of the Civil War may have seemed inevitable as the new year began, but few people were willing to speculate on how long it would drag on or how many more men on both sides would die. The war was now nearly three years old. For many Union soldiers, it was a time of decision. They had signed up for three years of service at the beginning of the war, or for two years' service in 1862. Should they reenlist, or should they return home? Four of Charles Tubbs' friends confided their dilemma to him. They wrote to him either at his home in Osceola or at Union College in Schenectady, New York, where Tubbs was a student now that he had graduated from Alfred University.

Since the summer of 1861, volunteers had received bounties, federal and sometimes state as well, for joining up. Three-year enlistees received $100 from the federal government, and that was raised to $300 in March 1863, prompting Mordecai Casson to rue that "large bounties" had "devoured" patriotism. "Money," he wrote Charles Tubbs, "is the primary object of private[s] as well as officers."[2] As an additional incentive, a veteran who reenlisted was granted a furlough home and often assigned for a time to recruiting duty in his neighborhood.

Despite Casson's cynicism, the lure of a bounty did not apparently tempt any of Tubbs' soldier friends, nor did it appear to be a consideration in his decision. Orville Kimball, for one, was moved by patriotism. He signed up again with the 103rd New York at the expiration of his two years of service in February 1864. "[W]ithout a country," he wrote Tubbs from South Carolina, "the noblest life is miserable and with a free country the poorest life is sweet." Still, said the twenty-one-year-old sergeant, "I have lost two years of the most favorable portion of my life and have degenerated rather than improved and now bid fair to lose three more just in the prime of life." Although he mourned the loss of his younger brother Harlan in the war and "often think of all those scenes of my earlier childhood," yet, he went on, "I wish to see the rebellion crushed any hour before I leave the service."[3]

David Armstrong, on the other hand, was in a quandary. He had nine months to decide, but he was already haunted by the choice ahead of him. He would be twenty-four years old in February, he wrote Tubbs, and regretted that he did not have "much schooling." Perhaps he should return home and get an education. On the other hand, he felt a loyalty to his fellow soldiers in the 49th Ohio.

Armstrong was in Louisville when he turned twenty-four in mid-February. He was just leaving a hospital there when his comrades in the 49th who had reenlisted passed through the city on their way home on veterans' furloughs. With the help of the regiment's captain, they induced Armstrong to return with them to Ohio and tried to persuade him to reenlist. He traveled with them to Tifflin, where the regiment was initially organized, and once there he was awarded a thirty-day furlough. Maybe, Armstrong thought, he would sign up again "if the doctor will take me."

Armstrong clearly did not want to spend more time as a cook. He wanted to fight and was concerned that his medical condition would keep him from battle:

[I] am willing to run a resk just for the sport of shooting some of those traitorish foes that has spilt so much of patriots blood on American Soil[.] yes and the very best of the Americans blood is being spilt[.] O how said [sic] it is to think upon [it.] It is a nough to make the blood of a Patriot boil in his vains[.][4]

But Armstrong was back in Louisville in March, lamenting that his health "will never be sound as it once was." He was with the 49th Ohio but "not able to perform as much duty as the rest of the boys" and was once again serving as cook for the officers.

Armstrong had not been in a fight since being wounded at Chickamauga. In July, two months before his tour of duty was up, his frustration got the better of him. The 49th Ohio, then part of the army of William Tecumseh Sherman, the new commander of federal western forces, was eleven miles outside of Atlanta when Armstrong grabbed a rifle and joined Company F on the skirmish line "just for the sport of

shooting some of those traitorship foes that has spilt so much of patriots blood on American Soil." Ordered back by his lieutenant, Armstrong felt impotent. It was the final straw. He finally decided to "go
home and enjoy the sweet comforts there" once his service was up in
September. If it had not been for his wound, he told Tubbs, "I should
have veteranised when the rest of the boys did." Armstrong said he
would leave the war to the young men who had stayed at home to
"take care of the farms and the Ladies." It was their turn to serve.[5]

John Orr was also reluctant to reenlist, but for quite a different
reason. By mid-February, Orr's "lively sort of wife," Melissa, was with
him in Wartrace, Tennessee. The couple were rooming in a private
home with another officer from the 107th New York and his wife. The
two couples were soon joined by a third, the 107th's captain and his
bride, a music teacher, who was able to find a piano and have it moved
to their shared quarters. "[I]t makes it very pleasant for us," said Orr.

By April, Orr was apologizing to Tubbs for not answering his letters sooner: "My wife is still with me; *that* I deem a sufficient explana-
tion." The regiment had its marching orders and expected to leave
Wartrace by the middle of the month. Officers were told to "send their
wives to the *rear*," but Orr doubted "ours will go a great while before
we leave, at least they say they 'wont[.]'" Orr said he witnessed many
regiments passing through Wartrace on trains, heading home north on
furloughs because they reenlisted, but he doubted that he would sign
up again: "if I live to see the end of a year from this date I do not think
that I shall feel that Patriotism or Duty will demand a renewal of my
services in the Army."[6] Besides, although he did not mention it to
Tubbs at the time, Melissa was pregnant. Their first child, a daughter
they named Phoebe, was due in October.[7]

George Scudder also had to decide whether to reenlist, but he
expressed no doubts or reservations. Like Armstrong, his tour was not
up until September. But he spent the first months of 1864 in New York
and Pennsylvania, recruiting—and bored to death. The truth was that
he was anxious to return to action. He had served several months on
the staff of Major General O. O. Howard and, more recently, at the
end of the year in 1863, as assistant provost marshal of the First Brigade, First Division, of the noted IX Corps. But even those assignments had left him champing at the bit. A first lieutenant and valued
member of the 45th Pennsylvania, he was used to being in action. He
had been through battles at Antietam and Fredericksburg, the siege of
Vicksburg, and fighting at Jackson, Mississippi.

Scudder wrote Tubbs from New York City in mid-March, where
he was hoping to induce young men to sign up with the 45th even
though it was a Pennsylvania regiment. From there he went on to Phil-

adelphia, where he came down with "a very bad case of 'dyptheria.'"
He was able to take a side trip to his family's old home in Equinunk.
But once he arrived, he became seriously ill and so helpless that his
mother came from Middlebury Center to care for him. For a week he
was virtually paralyzed, unable to move in bed without assistance.

As soon as he got better, Scudder went for walks through Equinunk, finding that it lacked the activity and excitement that he had
grown accustomed to. "There is a freshet in the River and the lumber is
passing by on its way to market by thousands," he told Tubbs. "All is
business and seemily dull."

He also missed his teenage friends, some of whom had gone off
to fight and die in the war:

> Sad though to relate it is not as plesant to me now as once[.] Those whom
> I associated with—most of them—are no more—. Four years has made a great
> change[.] When we lived here our little society numbered 5 in the town. Now
> four are in their graves while the others are scattered through the County. She
> with whom I used to join in the evening walk is among the dead and it sames
> oh'So lonely[.] Were she here I might write you of plesant times but now I can
> say no more than I enjoy myself the best I can under the circumstances[.]

The 45th, meanwhile, was regrouping at Annapolis, Maryland,
and, though Scudder did not like to boast, the regiment was "nearly
recruited up to the required maximum," in good part because of his
efforts, and "drilling very hard if reports are true." He wanted, he told
Tubbs, to go "off to the War again."[8]

That summer, one friend of Charles Tubbs' received a bounty for enlisting, but the money was not the inducement. He was a classmate
from Alfred University, Philip Taylor Vanzile. A native of Pennsylvania, Vanzile was living in Rochester, Ohio, and elected to serve in an
Ohio unit. He became the sixteenth of Tubbs' friends to enlist. He received $100 for signing up for a year's service.[9]

Vanzile had decided a year earlier to join up as soon as there was
a new call for volunteers. But when the call came in 1864, the quota for
his town was quickly filled, so he chose to enlist in Wooster, where he
had many acquaintances. "I am pretty near a full blooded buckeye now
but I shall never forget old Pennsyltuck," he told Tubbs. "I came to the
Army because I have long felt twas my duty[.]" He said that he felt he
was "doing Gods will[,] that I am defending everlasting truths[,] that I
am doing *duty* And knowing this is my happiness[.] I hope," he added,
"that I may do my duty as a soldier better than I did as a citizen[.]"

Vanzile was born in Knoxville, Pennsylvania, close to Osceola, in

Philip Taylor Vanzile.

July 1843. He entered Alfred in 1859, graduating in 1863 and speaking on the same commencement platform with Tubbs. His topic was "Martyrdom for Truth." Vanzile subsequently taught school in Osceola, but when he enlisted he was working as a railroad agent.

Vanzile was mustered into service in September 1864 in Battery E, 1st Light Artillery Ohio Volunteers, choosing to serve as a private in an artillery battalion rather than accepting an officer's commission in the infantry. He was his unit's bugler and soon also won the "good posish" of being its company clerk. Vanzile was twenty-one years old at the time. He was over six feet tall—almost six-two, according to one roster—weighed about 170 pounds, and was described as having gray or blue eyes, brown hair, and a fair complexion. He had cultivated a fringe of beard that circled under his chin.

Vanzile had planned to continue his education, but he wrote Tubbs that once he enlisted he did not expect to go further with his studies. He was, he said, "making few calculations for future execution."[10]

· CHAPTER 20 ·

A Matter of Viewpoint

[T]he officers are almost universally drunk *when going
into battle . . . It is enough to destroy all the patriotism that could exist in any mens brest to be used as
this army has been on this expedition. other armies are
having Victories but ours is defeated[.]*
                                    —*Mordecai Casson*[1]

*The affair at Mansfield or Sabine Cross Roads (It goes
by both names) has been magnified into a defeat, while
it was nothing of the sort.*
                                    —*William Prentice*[2]

Conflicting views of a battle are not unusual. A soldier's experience
is circumscribed by his immediate environment. Still, it is startling that
two soldiers on the same side in the same battle can view it in such
totally opposite terms. Two of Charles Tubbs' friends from Alfred University—William Prentice and Mordecai Casson—fought in the same
battle in Louisiana and came away with completely different impressions.
     One night in the second week of March 1864 near the small town
of Franklinton north of Lake Pontchartrain on a river called Bogue
Chitto, the two men crossed paths. Casson was surprised to be in Louisiana. The 2nd Veteran Cavalry, stationed just outside Washington,
was originally supposed to join the Army of the Potomac in Virginia.
But its colonel and the colonel of the 1st Veteran Cavalry, attached to
the Department of the Gulf, arranged a mutually-agreed-upon exchange
of assignments. The 2nd Veteran Cavalry left Giesborough Point in
midwinter for New Orleans, while the 1st Veteran Cavalry headed
north to Virginia. Casson found himself aboard a small vessel that was
so "badly crowded" that air "in the hold was very impure." He grum-
bled that sometimes during the unpleasant thirteen-day voyage he
could not remain below deck for more than five minutes at a time.

However, once in Louisiana, he wrote Tubbs. "If you see an account of the 5th Brig. Cav. Divis[ion] being in action or skedadling," Casson said, "you may calculate the 2nd Vets are in[.]"[3]

Casson and Prentice chatted, traded news about schoolmates from Alfred, then parted company. Both were aware that they were about to take part in a federal expedition in the northwestern section of Louisiana. The campaign was another Union attempt to seize control of that sugar- and cotton-rich portion of the state and establish a base for operations in Texas. Twice frustrated in attempts to achieve one or the other, Nathaniel Banks was planning, as the winter of 1863–64 drew to a close, yet another campaign up the Red River. His army of 17,000 men set off up Bayou Teche on March 12, headed for Alexandria, a major port on the river. There it was to link up with another federal army that was moving up the Red River, this one 10,000 men strong and commanded by William T. Sherman.

The 161st New York reached Alexandria in late March. After trudging through what the regiment's chaplain, William E. Jones, called "the very best sugar portions of Louisiana," the infantrymen arrived at the mansion of the state's rebel governor on March 25. From it, they could see "the smoke of our gunboats lying in the Red River, distant only eight miles" and soon after that the "cheering sight of the steeples of Alexandria greeted our eyes."[4]

The 161st's stay at Alexandria was brief. Advancing through pine woods, the regiment continued on to Natchitoches, reaching there on April 2 and encamping above it near the small town of Grand Ecore. The 2nd Veteran Cavalry was there, too, part of a division under the command of a former Kansas Supreme Court justice, Brigadier General Albert Lindley Lee. Casson's regiment was led by a first lieutenant named Dunn who Casson believed was the division's ablest officer.

Dunn rode in advance of the cavalry column as it proceeded down a road toward a wooden bridge that spanned a small stream. As he approached the bridge, he saw that the planks in the middle were torn up. Dunn raised his hand to warn the men behind him. Then a shot rang out and Dunn fell from his horse, dead, killed by a Confederate soldier concealed on the opposite bank.

The loss of Dunn was critical. Demoralized, the 2nd Veteran Cavalry continued slowly north on the narrow road, its speed hampered by the huge wagon train the division required to feed both the men and their horses. Trailing way behind them on the road, almost five miles back, was one of Banks' corps, the XIII, and even farther back on the road was the XIX, which the 161st New York was part of. It had broken camp on April 6, under orders to head for Mansfield, a town a little more than forty miles from the target of the expedition, the crucial river hub of Shreveport—"the place," Chaplain Jones said, "where the interest and destiny of the whole expedition culminated."

The federal cavalry and infantry continued through a scrubby pine barren of "wearisome montony," rough and rolling, traversed by only a "stumbling road,—so narrow as hardly to admit of vehicles passing each other." Although not a military man, the chaplain was shocked that the federal forces were so spread out: "[A]n able commander would, in such circumstance, see the necessity of giving his troops a greater compactness, and of keeping them well in hand, to be ready for any sudden surprise."

Prentice was shocked, too, because "an acquaintance" of his, a lieutenant in a New Hampshire cavalry regiment, reported to Albert Lindley Lee that "the enemy was in front in force." The general, Prentice said, refused to believe him and even went so far as to call the lieutenant "a *Coward*, & ordered him back to his Regt."

Neither Lee nor the general in command of the XIX Corps, William Buel Franklin, suspected anything. But down the road, waiting to intercept the Union troops, was a Confederate force led by General E. Kirby Smith, a former West Point professor and Indian fighter.

Suddenly, brisk artillery firing could be heard ahead, and infantrymen from the first of Banks' foot divisions rushed forward, one or two companies at a time, running past the federal cavalry toward a plain called Plumb Orchard. "[W]hen they were whiped" more soldiers were sent—"fighting by detail," Casson called it. Several soldiers who passed by told him that they were being sent ahead with only twenty cartridges "& when they were gone could get no more."

To prevent a retreat by the federal troops, Casson said, the entire cavalry division's wagon train was "shoved" up to the front to block the road. Then, he said, in a letter to Tubbs that was remarkably brief, considering the 2nd Veteran Cavalry's role in the ensuing battle:

Some of our artillery was drawn over a mile from the field & then had to be left. On the morning of the 9th our Brig. was ordered to form a line in front of the woods & hold the enemy back . . . our Skirmishers did not long remain in the woods & the Sharp Shooters opened on our line.

What Casson did not tell Tubbs was that, for some inexplicable reason, the cavalrymen spurred their horses and rushed forward against the Confederates and then, coming under fire, they turned and fled, panic-stricken.

Prentice was appalled by the behavior of the Union cavalry. The XIX Corps, he wrote Tubbs, had just gone into bivouac by a sawmill about eight miles in the rear. Almost immediately the order came for the men to fall in with two days' rations in their haversacks. The infantrymen sped down the road on the double-quick, but still it took them an hour before they reached Plumb Orchard. They arrived, Prentice said, just as the last line of the XIII Corps "was giving way & the victorious Rebels were pressing in on every side." He thought that "the Cavalry behaved badly."

I wish I could picture to your mind the scene that met our eyes when our Regt. forming the advance of the Corps came upon the little plain known as Plumb Orchard . . . There was the stampede not of whole Divis[ion], for there was not a Divis left, not of Wagon trains for they were all captured, not of batteries for not one was left. There were riderless horses, detached mules, single soldiers powder blackened, wounded & torn shouting like mad men, weeping at their defeat[;] there was a rush of broken, dismounted Cavalry, & there were grim soldiers still sending back from behind stump & tree their last few charges with their exultant & advancing foe, & we went upon the field torn with shot & shell & strewed with dead & dying with a wild cheer[,] our band playing the "Star Spangled Banner[.]" Old Col. [Nathan Augustus Munroe] Dudley (once our Brig commander) was shouting to the shattered remains of his once splendid Brig. "For God['|]s sake, Boys! Stop here! Here comes the 19th Corps that was never whipped."

The Cav was driven back in confusion upon the 13th Corps, which had hardly time to form but fell back fighting until at last our Corps came up & put a stop to the persuit. Lee had allowed his whole command to be drawn into a semi-circle of Rebel Inft. & Artilery, his trains, with a few mules on the rear wagons killed[,] entirely blocked up the way & all his artilery was captured.

Chaplain Jones said the mounted troops fled the battlefield "in the utmost disorder." The scene, he said "baffles description—

pressing their horses in hot haste, and dashing along the narrow road and through the skirting woods as if some pandemonium of evil spirits were after them, threatening to break through and scatter to the winds our advancing columns,—hatless, swordless riders shouting at their steeds, and riderless horses with saddles dangling at their heels.

Fixing bayonets to prevent being overwhelmed by their own retreating cavalry, Prentice's company and two others were detached and moved off to the right to lead as skirmishers as the rest of the regiment advanced to the edge of the opposite woods, "firi[n]g *into* the midst of the Rebels to try & hold them in check until the Division Could be formed."

Blocked in front, the Confederates tried to outflank the 161st, pouring such "a destructive crossfire" that it fell back as the rest of the corps came onto the field. The effect on the regiment was devastating.

"[I]t was not more than 20 minutes," Prentice related, "but in that time we lost 100 men, 5 Commissioned Officers & our Sergt Major, or one fourth of our whole Regt."

The fleeing federal cavalrymen lost at least twenty-two artillery pieces, large quantities of ammunition, nine hundred mules, and more than two hundred wagons. The Confederates captured nearly 2,500 infantrymen as well.

There were bound to be recriminations. Casson never went into detail about the cavalry's role in fleeing the battleground, nor did he mention a word about the behavior of Company C. He insisted that, except for their officers, who were drunk almost all the time, "I have never seen the 2nd Vets disgrace their state." It was his opinion "that if we had had a *General* our army would have been in Shreveport at this time." Yet, in the battle at Mansfield and even through the weeks of continued skirmishing that followed, his company suffered only minor casualties—two men slightly wounded, an amazingly low casualty toll.

Casson's brigade was ordered back to Grand Ecore with what little was left of the supply train. Both armies withdrew during the night, which was punctuated, Prentice said, by "a yell of defiance[,] a flash as of lightning circling the whole field & the deep roar of Musketry reverberating through those wild woods." As noiselessly as possible, the 161st gathered up its wounded and began its retreat.

Prentice's regiment did not stop until it reached Pleasant Hill, twenty miles away, at eight o'clock the next morning. Before pausing to make coffee and eat hardtack—they had not eaten in twenty-four hours—the men took up positions, ready to fight again. Dog-tired and sleepless, they had to wait until four o'clock in the afternoon before their next battle commenced. Prentice's brigade was on the right when

the ball opened with a heavy cannonade upon us without any damage however owing to our peculiar position.

But this was only a cover to their main attack which was made by a terrible charge upon our Left. Could th[e]y turn this th[e]y [would have] cut off all retreat & force [the] mome[n]t. I thought our case a foregone conclusion, but just as they thought the day won a masked battery opened a terrible fire of canister upon them, which cut them down by Regts. a heavy column of Inft. was then hurled upon the[m] & their rout was complete.

The Confederates were not through, though:

Their next attempt was upon our center. There they made a charge upon Battery L. 1st US Art.[,] killed all their horses & nearly eve[r]y man. They succeeded in capturing two pieces which were however recaptured . . . My Co dragged two Guns & one Cass[io]n from the field.

The next time Prentice wrote to Charles Tubbs it was April 26 and the 161st was back in Alexandria:

Another Retreat as you see, & several hard battles with more terrible marches. I am too tired to write, indeed cannot. If "a cat has 9 lives" there can not be more than the No[.] 1 part of a "Life" left in me.

For his part, Casson found "new difficulties awaiting" the 2nd Veteran Cavalry when it reached Grand Ecore:

[T]he River was to[o] low for our Gun Boats to opperate & Transports were running agroun & being hemed in by the enimies Sharp Shooters & land batteries. Our brigade relieved several. It soon became evident that our army could not long supply itself here. Our reg. burned hundreds of saddles, Carbines, Sabers & in fact eny thing that was not actually needed. Commenced our retreat at 5 P.M. of the 21st[.]

Casson's brigade led the left column of the retreat. It was briefly stopped twenty-five miles south of Grand Ecore when it ran into a Confederate unit and a skirmish followed. The brigade continued without many losses until it reached a river ford:

[H]ere they had a commanding position which they tried to hold. They had 6 of the pieces of artillry to work on us that they took at Mansfield. Our artillery . . . on their right flank Soon made it to[o] warm for them. from here they turned . . . & did not trouble us . . . until after we arrived at Alex[andria].
We had not been here long before they were on evry side of us[.] They kept harrassing on evry side but would not stand an engagement. Red rive was now from 17 to 20 ft. lower than usual at this period of the year[.] our gunboats were mostly above the falls. Nothing could be done except to dam the rive[.] this was done & by removing the iron clad & guns from the heaviest of the boats all except the largest & best boat was run over the 12th[.] this was burne[d.]

Casson did not realize it, but it was the 161st under Prentice's command that helped to dam the shallow river and save the federal fleet by an ingenious engineering feat—a series of wing dams such as lumbermen use. For more than a week, the regiment and other units from New York State as well as Maine worked day and night. Some men felled trees, others stripped mills of brick, iron, and lumber. The men made cribs filled with the brick and iron, then threw branches in front of the cribs and covered with them with bricks to stop up the crevices. The dams worked; the water rose. Both the 161st and Prentice were cited for their work in making it possible for the Union vessels to reach safety.[5]

Meanwhile, Casson's regiment rode through a desolate Alexandria. The port had been burned the day the federal infantry abandoned it:

Some worthless Soldier set fire to an old house which spread & before night the largest & best part of the town was in ashes. We remained in town all day to prevent more fires being set[.] I tell you Tubbs it was a hard sight to see the poor women lugging their all from house to house to keep it from the fire[.] Some were crying[,] others Swearing . . . Had this recd the Sanction of our officers it would have been a disgrace to our nation as the town was perfectly defenseless & contained none but Women [and] Childr[en.]

The 2nd Veteran Cavalry covered its brigade's rear as the army continued to retreat. One day, a Confederate force attempted to cut its train in two:

This is the only place where I know of the Colored troops being in action on this expedition . . . they moved in better order & were cooler under fire than any white soldiers . . . Our Co. was out as Skirmishers[,] were pressed pretty hard all day. the ball flew thick. Sometimes they wer[e] within 5 rods of us. We use Sharp Carbines & can Stand their Enfields as close as they can our carbines. they make a ball whistle but it takes a great deal of lead to Kill a man[.]

The two sides continued to harass each other until mid-May. Banks' supply wagons finally reached safety as the result of another engineering innovation: steamers were lashed together to bridge the 600-yard-wide Atchafalaya River.

Afterwards, Banks was relieved of his command. Franklin, who was wounded at Mansfield, left Louisiana, saying he was disgusted. The expedition drew an official censure from Congress. Casson insisted that it was not "the fault of the men" that the army returned defeated, "for they have never had an opportunity to fight."

Prentice, however, took a different tack. First of all, he told Tubbs, he believed from the start that the expedition was doomed:

[H]aving been successful in getting to Shrevesport, I could not see how the long line of the Red River was to be kept open unless several points upon its banks were occupied, for which we had not the requisite troops.

Prentice would not even consider using the word "defeat." "We met with a repulse (nothing more) at Mansfield. The 19th Corps was not, *never has been* defeated. It has been truly said that on that night our Corps 'snatched Victory from Defeat.'" And as far as Banks was concerned, Prentice said that although "accounts almost universally agree in condemning" him, "my faith in him has not been *shaken in the least.*"

It was the <u>Red River</u> that defeated us . . . Gen. Banks on the night of the 8th knew that the river had fallen so low that our transports could not proceed. The country there, you must recollect, is very <u>hilly</u>, covered with a dense forest of <u>pine</u>, & that for near one hundred miles in succession there is but one road leading over these hills & through this almost interminable forest. Banks has been blamed for not keeping his forces more concentrated, yet how could he do it on such a road & at the same time protect his train. His intention, however, was <u>not</u> to bring on a Genl. engagement at Mansfield, or not until he could bring up his forces.

In Prentice's view, the Battle of Sabine Cross Roads was definitely not a Union defeat "unless that is a defeat where the enemy leaves the field & sends a flag of truce, asking permission to bury his dead."

· CHAPTER 21 ·

The Price of Success

*[T]here is no deny that the coming campaign will wit-
ness battles that <u>for numbers engaged</u>[,] annihilation
of lives, & excrutiating torture of <u>soul</u> & body will
eclipse . . . Gettysburg. There is no disputing that the
"rebel army" is more formidable to day than it ever
was before, and ours is <u>surely much more so</u>[.]*
                                                    —*John Orr*[1]

In early spring of 1864, two major federal campaigns got underway: the Atlanta campaign in Georgia and the Wilderness in Virginia. Each proved fateful for one of Charles Tubbs' friends.

On May 1, John Orr and the unit he captained, Company F of the 107th Regiment New York Volunteer Infantry, was on the move in Tennessee, headed for Chattanooga and the border with Georgia. "Everything in this quarter indicates success," Orr wrote Tubbs. The 107th's colonel, a company captain, and ten enlisted men had been in upstate New York on a recruiting mission, and on the very night Orr penned his letter, fourteen new recruits arrived from Elmira. The regiment was already almost up to full strength—"about 800 strong & some 600 effective men"—chiefly because remnants of the battle-scarred 145th New York were consolidated with the 107th.[2]

As part of the Army of the Cumberland, the 107th was now attached to the Second Brigade, First Division, of Joseph Hooker's XX Corps. The XX was one of seven infantry corps of an army that rivaled in size the Army of the Potomac in Virginia. There were nearly 100,000 men in all, under the command of William Tecumseh Sherman. Sherman was under orders from Ulysses Grant—whom Lincoln had just made supreme commander of all fedeal armies—to move against and break up a more than 60,000-man Confederate army led by Joseph E. Johnston. He was told "to get into the interior of the enemy's country as far as you can, inflicting all the damage you can against their war resources."[3] Sherman's specific target was Atlanta.

"God grant that the 'Hero of Vicksburg' may infuse a concentration of strength and energy into our *Armies*," Orr wrote Tubbs that spring, his fingers crossed about Grant's ability to prod Union forces into aggressive action. "He who looks only for a moment into the future can infer the result of these two 'armies' coming in contact[.] To think of it is enough to make the bravest heart shudder." Orr said he realized that "there are many stronger & better hearts engaged in this war than mine."[4]

On May 7, Sherman began his advance into Georgia. A little more than two weeks later, on May 25, as his army approached New Hope Church, the backpedaling Confederates decided to make a stand. The two sides clashed at eleven in the morning. A federal cavalry unit and elements of Hooker's XX Corps led the attack on a strong enemy position, getting caught in the "Hell Hole," a massed crossfire of sixteen enemy cannons firing canister and five thousand Confederate infantrymen shooting at close range. Hooker quickly summoned the rest of his corps into action. The First Division, with Orr and the 107th New York, reached the battle scene in late afternoon and went immediately on the attack. But the massed fire of the enemy's artillery repulsed them.

In the midst of the raging fight, Orr fell, a musketball piercing the back and lower part of his right thigh. As the battle continued around him, the twenty-eight-year-old captain was carried off by stretcher to a temporary field hospital. There the bleeding from his wound was stanched, and his thigh was bandaged.

In the next two days, the federal forces regrouped, launched another attack, and were again repulsed. As the Union army maneuvered back to the railroad line it was following, licking its wounds, Orr was taken aboard a train to Chattanooga. There he was placed in an army hospital. Gangrene set in, and his condition worsened. Doctors were finally able to control the infection, and Orr, on crutches, was able to return home on sick leave to Tuscarora and his wife Melissa, who was four months pregnant, in June.

The 107th was with Sherman when, finally, he entered Atlanta in the first week of September, and it continued to march with him when he left the city that fall on his famous March to the Sea. But for Orr, the war was essentially over. Unfit for active service when he returned to the 107th, he evidently took on only administrative chores for the regiment.

Two days before Sherman's campaign against Atlanta began, hundreds of miles away the Army of the Potomac crossed the Rappahannock River into the Wilderness west of Fredericksburg, Virginia. Ostensibly,

A sutler's chit for "10 cetns."

the army was under the command of George Meade, but Grant was at his elbow and actually ran the operation.

The 45th Regiment Pennsylvania Volunteers was part of the army's First Brigade, Second Division, of Ambrose Burnside's IX Corps. The 45th crossed the Rappahannock at ten o'clock on the morning of May 5. By late afternoon it reached the Rapidan River at Germania Ford and continued its march through dense woods and almost impenetrable thickets. The men's spirits were high. They had a new flag. The regiment's old banner was so frayed by shots that it was difficult to read the names of the half dozen battles that the 45th had fought emblazoned on its stripes.[5]

In spite of the many setbacks suffered by the Army of the Potomac, George Scudder's zeal for battle continued unabated. And, although he did not brag about himself, he was never reluctant to praise his unit, Company F, or, indeed, the entire regiment. There was "little drunkenism or rowdyism" in either, the young first lieutenant said. In fact, the opposite—"asperity and good order"—was the rule. Scudder said that "nearly every cent" of the soldiers' pay was "sent home to those left behind" and the "sutlers tent or store is but very little patronised for petty things and he is not allowed to sell intoxicating drinks . . . & such stuff as spreads discord."[6]

In the latter part of May, the Army of the Potomac sparred almost daily with the Army of Northern Virginia in a series of minor skirmishes in which the 45th was involved only marginally. Then, on June 1, as the two opposing armies finally met head-on at Cold Harbor, the 45th was thrust into the thick of the fighting.

The fighting raged over three days. On June 3, the federal army, which outnumbered the Confederate army almost two-to-one, began a massive assault. The 45th was with the IX Corps on the federal right, near Bethesda Church. Its division was able to drive back the Confederate outposts there, but the enemy lines behind them held firm and, reinforced, the Confederates then counterattacked. The IX Corps was able to repulse the southerners but lost eight hundred men, thus adding to its reputation as "the wandering corps, whose dead lie buried in seven states."[7] Burnside planned to order his men to attack again at one o'clock in the afternoon, but he was overruled by Meade. Several federal attacks ensued along other parts of the battlefront, but each was repulsed.

By nightfall, when the battle was over, the Union counted up its dead and wounded in the past month of almost incessant campaigning since crossing the Rappahannock. Grant had lost more than forty percent of his army: 50,000 troops, killed, wounded, or missing. But they could be replaced by new recruits. Though Lee's losses were smaller— 32,000 men—they represented forty-six percent of his strength, and his losses were more critical. There was no way Lee could make up for them.[8]

In the deadly fighting at Bethesda Church on June 3 alone, the 45th Pennsylvania lost 163 men killed and wounded. Among its eighteen dead were two officers. One of them was Charles Tubbs' friend from Alfred University, George Scudder. He was twenty-three years old.[9]

· CHAPTER 22 ·

Politics and Pretense

Damnable intrigues. When you have Clement L. Va-
landigham praised & upheld as a "model" Unionist by
Rebels, who have fired their last round of cartridge at
your head you will understand my feelings exactly
. . . O for a besom of destruc[tion]—
                                        —William Prentice[1]

William Self stood beside the Chickahominy River in early June, surveying the battleground where the Bucktails had fought during the Peninsular Campaign. The Army of the Potomac was encamped on the very ground that it had struggled over two years before, only now the federal drive was directed at Petersburg.

The Bucktails no longer existed. On the expiration of their three years' enlistment, the men were mustered out of service, though a number—Self among them—chose to reenlist in the 190th Pennsylvania Volunteers. The regiment was part of the Ninth Division of Major General Gouverneur Kemble Warren's V Corps. The division was digging in, preparing for a siege, its lines so close to the enemy defenses, Self wrote Charles Tubbs, "that they can talk to one another and keep diging[.]" Both Union and Confederate soldiers had to be careful, because snipers of both armies "Shoot every head They see on each side." The Pennsylvanians had the advantage, though—new Spencer repeaters that they could fire eight times without reloading. They were even more accurate, Self said, than the breech-loading Sharps rifles the Bucktails had used since 1862.

A veteran of the twelve major battles with the Bucktails, Self was now thirty years old. He was still a private, perhaps because of his lack of education; he could barely write a simple declarative sentence. Self, however, believed it was because he refused to "Suck around an officer," which, he said, "I will never Doe[.]"[2] He boasted, instead, "There has been a good many Shot down [bes]ide of me While I whare only been knocked down by the explosion of Shell 3 times."[3]

Looking over the old battleground, Self caustically commented, "[W]e are not so close to Richmond as McClellan was." His remark was meant as a slap at Ulysses Grant. If George McClellan had had half of the men now assembled, Self declared, "he could have taken Richmond."[4] For all Grant's triumphs, he said, there still "Seemes to be enough of" the Confederates who remained to fight:

> *Still the Rebs Seeme to be as defyant as ever here[.] they say that they doe not Care for Grant[.] McClellan They Seeme to fear[.] I have talked with many of them[.] they say that their army has been Whiped worse by him than eny other General . . .*
>
> *I Cannot see the smart qualities about Grant[.] he has the power to Call out the Whol north and I think he has done it nerly and what has he done[?] . . . Why doe not the Millitary authorities say something about his Campain[?] no it would not doe this presant time[;] there is to[o] much at stake[.] elections is Close at hand.*[5]

Self maintained his strong support of the general he once fought under. "Three Cheers for McClellan," he wrote.[6] The general was currently being touted as a possible presidential nominee when the Democratic Party met in late August. Only a few days earlier, on June 8, Lincoln won the Republican nomination for a second term, and Self guessed that Tubbs would for vote for "Old Abe" in November. "I Suppose there are not many McClell men there but time will soon tell the Story[.]"[7]

Before he was wounded, John Orr expressed the opinion that he believed Lincoln would be reelected. "I think," he said, "he is the soldiers choice. If he could only crush this rebellion this Summer his election would be sure."[8]

Tubbs' friends debated with him in spirited terms through the mail about the virtues and flaws of McClellan as a general. But nothing raised the wrath of Tubbs' friends more than when the epistolary debate turned to politics—namely, the Peace Democrats and McClellan's association with them. The Copperheads opposed the Union's war policy and favored negotiating peace with the Confederacy.

Although the main strength of the Peace Democrats was in Ohio, Illinois, and Indiana, Orr groused about the Copperheads' success in the northeast and, in particular, "about the patriotism of NY[.] Truly may she be termed the Empire State of 'Coperheads' & 'dough faces[.]' " While not an out-and-out Copperhead, New York's governor, Horatio Seymour, was a foe of abolition, had denounced the Emancipation

Proclamation, and believed that army conscription was unconstitutional. He had close ties to Peace Democrats in New York City, who controlled a number of the city's leading newspapers. Its former mayor, Fernando Wood, who was now a congressman, was openly anti-administration. Voters in the city as a whole, in fact, voted against Lincoln in 1860 by a two-to-one margin (and would do so again in 1864). Politicians of the ilk of Wood and his brother Benjamin, who was also a New York congressman, were in Orr's opinion "valandigham Traitors." He told Tubbs that "Seymour & his 'Co-workers' deserve the maledictions of every loyal [citizen] & was justice meted out would be sent South . . . like Vallandigham."[9]

Lincoln had tried to suppress the Copperheads, using his executive powers to arrest its leaders, suspend the writ of habeas corpus, and censor the press. Clement Vallandigham was arrested in 1863 for treasonable utterances and banished to the Confederate states, but that did not stop him from running for governor of Ohio from exile that year. He lost, but, as the war dragged on into its fourth year, and Union death tolls mounted, his influence was still felt, and Copperheads were gaining strength.

Like Orr, David Armstrong was upset about the strength of the Peace Democrats in New York. Armstrong was tiring of the constant warfare, but he warned, "A person may think me a Copperhead but it would not be health[y] to tell me so at my face." Writing from a hospital in Louisville, where he was being treated for the wound he received during the Battle of Chickamauga, Armstrong theorized why the Peace Democrats were so strong:

> [T]he mo[s]t of the boys at home are copperheads or valandingham men[.] the reason of this is because the union boys have most all enlisted in the army[.][10]

William Prentice said he would "*gladly*" leave Louisiana to "go North to wage a war of *extermination*" against the Copperheads. They were, he said, "the most *contemptable* enemies of Freedom . . . the only hope of Southern Traiters." Prentice was particularly troubled to learn that Horace Greeley, the well-known editor and publisher of the anti-slavery New York *Tribune*, shook hands in Congress with "Fernando Wood & his fellow Traitors." Prentice believed the war would be over in "*one month*" if it weren't for them.[11]

It was the link of McClellan's name to the Copperhead faction that had alarmed George Scudder. Before he was killed at Bethesda Church, Scudder wrote Tubbs that he thought the low esteem in which McClellan was now held by "all good patriots and soldiers" was the result of "his connection" with the Peace Democrats. Scudder said the general, whom he once admired, "has lent himself to be used as a tool with this detested Peace Party."[12]

The soldiers' wrath regarding McClellan proved to be misguided. The Copperheads were able to push through a platform calling for peace at the Democratic convention, but McClellan repudiated it before he was nominated. Still, the opprobrium of being an appeaser clung to the general.

Writing from Little Folly Island, South Carolina, Orville Kimball told Tubbs, "I hope to see President Lincoln reelected to that proud office." Kimball believed that if Lincoln won reelection, "I do not expect to see rebellion in arms another two years."[13]

Kimball, however, had only negative news to report—while painting himself a bit of a hero in defeat. The 103rd New York and the 33rd U.S. Colored Troops had just returned from an unsuccessful attack on neighboring James Island in Charleston Harbor.

The two regiments set out on the night of June 30, crossing first over Tiger Island. The tide was low. Many of the men tried wading across but sank into the mud almost to their armpits. Company I was lucky. It got across on pontoon boats. At four in the morning the next day, as they sloshed through a swamp to reach James Island, a line of skirmishers from the 33rd leading the advance, several Confederate vedettes opened fire:

> [B]efore we had got across the swamp the rebel Pickets opened on us and we returned the fire of course[.] they ran out and we advanced across one line of rifle Pitts through some brush driving all before us and came into an open field 50 or 60 rods wide[.]
>
> I deployed ten men of company I as a second skirmish line[,] the first having strayed of[f] to the right and advanced across the swampy field two thirds the distance across when a masked battery opened on us with grape and canister double shotted[.] this caused some confusion in the rank[s] of the regt.[,] also among the negroes but they soon rallied and charged the battery and captured two guns 12 pds brass pieces[,] fine ones[,] and turned them on the enemy[.]

The 103rd lost ten men killed and seventeen wounded. Company I lost two dead—one of whom was Kimball's orderly clerk—and two wounded. Kimball himself "escaped intact except a lame foot[.] my boot though recieved a severe wound, the toe being tore with a grape shot[.] the only effect it had on my toe was making it sore and lame a day or two[.] however I mourn the *loss of my boot.*"

The 103rd was able to reach a third line of rifle pits, lying there until dark, when it withdrew to the lower end of James Island—"a wise though[t]," said Kimball, "for I believe if we had staid there we should have all been Killed or captured[,] which is about as bad[.]"[14]

The 103rd's commander, Major Joseph Morrison, saw the action, and Kimball's part in it, quite differently. In his official report on the attack, Morrison said:

> When I advanced on the island a few rods I halted the head of my column in order to enable the men on the left to close up, but before I could get the regiment in any shape I was ordered to advance. By this time the few skirmishers I had thrown forward had moved off to the right and were not to be found. I again halted. I sent my acting adjutant in search of the skirmishers . . .
>
> I had not more than halted when I was again ordered forward, and as my adjutant reported that he could not find the skirmishers, and deeming it unsafe to advance without them, I ordered Sergeant Kimball, of Company I, to take 10 men and advance as skirmishers. As the sergeant and his men knew nothing about skirmishing they were of no use, as they never advanced 50 yards in front of the column.[15]

Kimball did not mention the major's criticism to Tubbs.

William Self believed that Grant had to win battles to help Lincoln's election chances. "[Y]ou see," he wrote Tubbs, "he must keep doeing something in order to keep the people in good sprte and win their affections and thus Claim a Victory of it[.]" In fact, Self spent spent July and August fighting Confederates in one battle or skirmish after another as the Army of the Potomac struggled for a decisive victory that would help Lincoln win reelection.

The 190th Pennsylvania remained beside the Chickahominy River through most of the summer during the Petersburg campaign. In addition to a number of skirmishes, in late August the regiment fought along the Weldon Railroad when the V Corps tried to extend its lines in order to cut Confederate communications into Petersburg. The "Old Pa Reserve," Self reported, lost hardly any men killed or wounded, but a number were taken prisoner, and the entire Ninth Division suffered so many casualties that it was now down to some 300 men.

After the battle, the 190th returned to siege positions outside Petersburg. The federal line of battle was thirty miles long, but the men in the regiment hoped that if the Confederates attacked, they would concentrate their assault against the 190th's position:

[N]ow they drive the Pickets in this morning and we have been wishing they would Come out and try us on here but they will not[.] there is a very large field for them to come through and we are fortified up to the handle.

Every so often, as summer turned into autumn, the Pennsylvanians took the offensive, only to fall back. "[W]e go out them once in a while," said Self, "and get fleaced and thus fall back in our holes[,] a Strong line of Fortificaitons that we will defy the Devel himself to Come against[.]"[16]

The sparring between the two armies seemed endless. A decisive victory continued to elude the North.

CHAPTER 23

Life on the Mississippi

How the time slips. In August of 1862, I called on
you, a Recruit just of[f] for a three year cruise . . .
Now I stand, just as young in feeling a Veteran . . .
wondering if I am not mistaken after all and have only
gone to sleep in your old room over the book store to
wake up at the sound of the Chapel bell and the clatter
of recitation-bound students. Does it ever occur to
you[,] Tubbs, that we are grown to the years when
people have a habit of calling themselves men[?]
—William Prentice[1]

Most of the regiments that took part in the disastrous Second Red River Campaign in Louisiana were afterwards dispatched to western Virginia to fight under Philip Henry Sheridan in the Shenandoah Valley. Only a few units remained behind. One of them was the 161st New York. For the remainder of the summer of 1864, all of the autumn, and into the winter, the regiment was a river-based force. The men sailed aboard steamboats almost continuously up and down the Mississippi, disembarking every so often to chase guerrillas or to try to head off and catch the raiding forces of three of the Confederacy's most aggressive generals—Nathan Bedford Forrest, Sterling Price, and John Sappington Marmaduke.

Before the end of July, the 161st was at White River Landing, Arkansas, a forlorn community consisting of a single small store and a few huts on an island formed by the juncture of the Mississippi, Arkansas, and White Rivers. William Prentice led a detachment of fifty men and artillery charged with guarding the army supplies stored there. It was a dismal posting, and it took its toll on Prentice. He suffered from constant chills and fever, which he believed developed later into a serious case of pneumonia.[2]

As the 161st traveled north to White River Landing, it passed one of the long canals that had been built by Grant's engineers nearly two years earlier in an attempt to bypass the Confederate batteries at Vicksburg. Pen in hand, Prentice thought Charles Tubbs might be interested in "a kind of extract" from his diary:

Saturday July 23d pulled up stakes, got everything aboard the slow coach, Packet "Universe["] & bade farewell to Vicksburg without a sigh of regret. It is 9 miles around the "crooknecked squash shaped["] bend of the river here & just one mile across by the canal attempted first by Sherman & then by Grant. The "Ditch" can still be seen, but at the present low water mark it is some 20 feet above the level of the Miss. It was high water when Gen. Grant tried it, but the water commenced falling & fell faster than he could dig. Col. Bailey was employed by Gen. Sherman as Chief Engineer on that "Last Ditch" to turn the Miss from its chosen course. The Mountain would not move from Mohamet, so Mohamet went to the Mountain & Grant found another way to V.burg, & 'The Father of Waters' still goes "on his winding way to the sea."

Night came on at last, clear & bright & after the last straggler had been gathered to the arms of ["]Morphius" I spread my blanket[,] wrapped my cloak about me and lay down upon the bow of the boat to sleep. A stiff but not unpleasant breeze swept the deck and I lay till long after Midnight listening to the wild songs of the Negro boatman[.] There was a stanza, a solo[,] then a shrill but musical whoop & then the wild chorous "Ho! Hi! A!; Hi! Ha! Ho!; Ah! Ho!; Ho Hi! O! Hi! Ho! Ah! Ho!" First loud and wild it swept over the waters and then in low plaintive notes that scarsely waked the echoes upon the broad green shores.

Toward morning however I fell asleep & only woke after sunrise to find my boat saturated with the damp fog which almost shut the river from view, and through which the Sun could be but direcly seen.

The scenery here is the tamest possible[,] nothing to be seen but the broad, quiet river, and the low, wooded shores. Last night we passed a place where we sail 12 miles to gain 80 yards. A man can throw a stone across the neck or one boatman from his lofty pilot house can hail another, yet he must sail near two hours to get around.

Sunday July 24th—Still slowly steaming up the river. At 9 Oc our wood & coal had both given out, and we tied up to the shore to get a supply of rails. *If you were to ask the Captain how he paid for them, he would reply "By a note, payable in Southern Shin Plasters six months after the recognition of the Southern Confederacy.["] The men improved the opportunity to make Coffee & soon 200 men were bringing rails from a fence a quarter of a mile away[,] the long line going & coming so industriously[,] reminding me of the industrious little insects who invade my mess chest & soon transfer 16 oz of sugar to their underground magazines. Ah Solomon! You must have been a soldier of a more philosophic turn of mind than myself, or you could never have said "go to the*

Ant. Thou sluggard, consider her ways & be wise," for it requires all the Moral forces I can bring to bear to keep from saying "Go to the D——l you stinking Pis Mires, keep out of my sugar & sav your lives["] . . .

The Coffee was just steaming in the kettles when Whiz-zz-z cam a bullet & looking out a hundred Rebel Cavalry were discovered in line of battle just across a little lake. Five Co.s were immediately sent ashore when the Trans-Grand-Lake party consulted discresion & retired. Every available spot being piled with the needful rails we got underwy again. Every precaution was taken. The Regt was yet under arms & stood to their guns until we [passed] Columbia & Grenville, noted Guerrilla haunts[,] but we were not disturbed . . .

"Monday July 25th["] During the forenoon we reached White River land-ing and tied up to the Shore . . . We now form a part of Gen. [Frederick] Steele[']s Army, but have no idea of what our destination is. At present Maj. [Willis E.] Craig is in command of the post, which consists of some 20 negro huts, a log store, two or three Steam boats and a few acres of cotton. Beyond us for miles is nothing but the dense cane brakes & forest of Ark. abounding with wild animals of almost every Species known to North America & infested with Mosquitoes, Rattlesnakes & Guerrillas. I have been tramping all the forenoon, trying to establish a Picket line through it . . . We hop not to stay here long, as the situation is not pleasant . . .

I send you a Cotton Blossom picked close by my tent.[3]

There was one diversion—"a joyful time," as, tongue in cheek, the 161st's chaplain, William Jones, put it. In mid-August, the regiment and the 23rd Wisconsin boarded vessels to sail to Mobile Bay, off the Gulf of Mexico. There a federal fleet under Admiral David Glasgow Farragut was attacking Fort Morgan, a strong fortification mounting 140 heavy guns that guarded the entrance to the bay and the city of Mobile. The two regiments were to aid in the assault. But by the time the two regiments arrived on the morning of August 23, the fort had just capitulated. The vessel with the soldiers of the 161st New York aboard sailed in close and weighed anchor. The men could see the fort's Confederate defenders, now prisoners, drawn up in a line while the Union flag was raised on a temporary flagstaff "and unfurled to the breeze to the music of the guns of the forts and fleet."[4]

The 161st had nothing to do, but orders to return to the Missis-sippi did not come through for several days, so—to the soldiers' dis-gust—the regiment went into camp across the bay at Cedar Point. The area was infested with mosquitoes. The men started fires every few yards in a fruitless attempt to ward them off. The water there was brackish, as well, making tea and coffee "almost unbearable." Then the regiment's provisions gave out. Ever afterwards, the men spoke of Cedar Point as "Point Misery."[5]

By mid-October, on a day "too dark and foggy to run," Prentice wrote Tubbs again. He was now aboard the steamboat *Baltic*, on the Mississippi again, fifty miles above Vicksburg. Pickets were ashore, to guard against a surprise attack by guerrillas. The 161st and two other regiments—"baggage, horses, mules and wagons"—were aboard transports so crowded that "every available inch is occupied and every place where a man lie, sit, stand or *hang* is filled." After Mobile Bay, the men had spent two months conducting "raids in different directions none of which accomplished anything but some of which were very severe on our muscle." On one march, the regiment started out from camp at sundown and tramped fifty miles in twenty-four hours. The physical strain of such marches, the extremes of warm days and cold nights, and frequent and severe thunderstorms took their toll on Prentice. The twenty-eight-year-old captain confided to Tubbs, but did not tell his wife, Myra, that his health "seems to be somewhat impaired (though *this* must be betwen *you* & *me*)[.] I am *now* just recovering from a severe attack of Typhoid Fever, and have but litt[le] strength."[6]

Before the year was out, Prentice and the 161st New York were back at White River Landing. His health was restored, but Prentice was now bored again with the interminable routine of duty:

Our life . . . has only been a repetition of that before. Up and down the river we have been, traveling more than 4000 miles on steamboat since the termination of the Red River Campaign.

The frustration was especially galling because Sterling Price's forces had been expelled from Missouri, and John Marmaduke had been captured. The 161st had nothing to do with either success. And then, when Nathan Bedford Forrest threatened Memphis, the regiment quickly sailed there and spent weeks futilely trailing after him as Forest headed first to Paducah and then moved on to Columbus, Kentucky. The 161st never caught up with the elusive Confederate.

The regiment took up winter quarters at Columbus, but it remained there only a month before it was sent on to Memphis, where the men were promised they would stay all winter. They put up $2,000 of their own money to purchase lumber to build log cabins, only to be told to pack up and be ready to board a packet bound for New Orleans.

In the two and a half years since the 161st New York was organized, the war had taken its toll:

We left Elmira with over 900 men. since then we have received more than 300 recruits. Our aggregate Enlisted is now 709. So you see how the soldiers go . . . Of our original Orderly Sergts., only one remains: the others dead[,] discharged[,] promoted & reduced to the ranks.

"H" Co. started with 80 enlisted men. Of these 13 have died of disease[,] 2 been killed in battle, 6 have deserted[,] 5 transfered[,] 12 discharged, and 1 promoted. Ths winter I hav recd Recruits enough to bring our number up to 80 again. We have been the most fortunate co. in the Regt. in deaths, though several of the discharged are permanently disabled by wounds.[7]

Prentice did not know it at the time, but the 161st New York was headed back to Mobile Bay.

· CHAPTER 24 ·

Adventures of a New Recruit

*My Dear Old Chum[,] I hardly know how to write as
a soldier. The style of my letters must be so different
from those I used to scribble off on the old round table
in No. 18, M.S. South College Union[.] Then as you
are well aware I used to spend considerable time scrib-
bling to ——— while at the opposite side of the table
you were as busily engaged in framing tender mes-
sages to ——— (fill the blanks at your leisure).*
                                                    —John Andrews[1]

In mid-September 1864, John Tuttle Andrews—a classmate of Charles
Tubbs' at Alfred University and his roommate at Union College—enlisted in Elmira as a second lieutenant in Company D, 179th Regiment
New York Volunteer Infantry. He was the seventeenth—and last—
friend of Tubbs' to join up.

A native of Reading Township on the western side of Seneca Lake
in rural, hilly Steuben County, Andrews was born March 9, 1842, into
a distinguished upstate New York family. His father, a descendant of
Aaron Burr, was a member of the 25th Congress. Afer attending several upstate private schools, Andrews entered Alfred in 1861. Speaking
at commencement exercises in July 1863, in ceremonies during which
Charles Tubbs and Philip T. Vanzile also spoke, Andrews delivered a
talk entitled "American Patriotism." He and Tubbs subsequently matriculated as seniors at Union, where both majored in classical studies,
graduating in the spring of 1864 with a bachelor of arts degree. But
while Tubbs chose to go on to law school in Michigan, Andrews elected
to join the army.

Andrews sported a moustache and sideburns and was of average height—five-foot-seven—but considered himself a short man: he
referred to himself as "The Little Lieutenant."[2] For some inexplicable
reason—unless his enrollment officer made a mistake—he gave his

169

John Tuttle Andrews.

age as twenty-three when he enlisted although he was actually twenty-two.

Before joining the regiment in Virginia, Andrews spent his first weeks working as an enrollment officer, trying to sign up other recruits. Soon afterward, in company with the 179th's chaplain, a minister named Taft, he left Elmira, headed for "the front" in Virginia.[3]

The two men traveled on the first leg of their trip south by rail to New York City and there switched to a train for Baltimore. They had little time to tour Baltimore, and what little they did see, said Andrews, "was the very worst portion. It had been raining, and the streets were nastier than were those of New York when we visited it. Here we began to see *niggers* and we've seen plenty of them ever since."

Leaving the city aboard the U.S. mail steamer *Adelaide*, Andrews and Taft reached Fortress Monroe, on the tip of the Peninsula on Chesapeake Bay, early the next morning. They remained there "only long enough," Andrews said, "to eat the vilest mess ever sat on a table for man to eat, and for which I was charged the modest little sum of one dollar." They then boarded another U.S. mail boat, the *Webster*, and started up the James River on a slow, almost ghostly voyage through an area ravaged by the war. In Hampton Roads, they passed close by the wreck of the 24-gun sloop *Cumberland*, rammed and sunk by the Confederate ironclad *Merrimac* more than two years earlier. Its hulk rose a little above the water.

Proceeding farther upriver, the *Webster* continued past "places which have become points of interest during this war" but were "of no importance aside from their historical value[.]"

Harrison's Landing so famed during McClellan's Peninsular Campaign is merely a landing—it can claim but one building and that one a modest two story brick dwelling house. A few soldiers were also stationed here. All around were the woods in which [George] Stonemans Cavalry operated, and far back in the distance we could see Malvern Hills.

City Point which we reached about two o'clock in the afternoon was once perhaps a quiet little village of five or six hundred inhabitants, but war has made sad havoc with it. It was so recently taken from the rebs that some of its buildings still show the effects of our shells. It is now a great military depot. A military railroad runs from it up to "the front["]—at least up as far as the Weldon R.R.

The 179th had been organized in upstate New York four months earlier. Most of the men in Andrews' unit, Company D, were from the area around Dunkirk on Lake Erie, and the company was originally called the "Dunkirk Company."[4] When Andrews reported to the regiment in Virginia, it had already participated, as part then of the XXII Corps, Army of the Potomac, in battles at Cold Harbor and Globe Tavern and in an assault on Petersburg.

The regiment was now camped near Poplar Springs Church, where it had just fought as part of the First Brigade, First Division, of the IX Corps. The IX Corps was the same "wandering corps, whose dead lie buried in seven states."[5]

Andrews suddenly found himself thrust from student to warrior with no preparation, no special training, not even rudimentary orientation. As an officer, he was not even told what was expected of him, and there was no time to acclimate. The 179th was already playing an active role in the Petersburg campaign. For Andrews, it was a baptism by fire. Fortunately, he wrote Tubbs, he was "among friends at the very outset." One, a lieutenant named Force, who had been a school-mate when both of them were teenagers, ordered supper for him and shared his blankets. It was a totally new experience for Andrews:

> *I sleep on the ground with nothing but a rubber blanket under me—shiver all night and roast during the day. I eat dirt, drink dirt, and am covered with dirt; and yet I feel as well as when I left home. The whole army is lousy but I haven't found any on my person* yet—*I suppose I shall have them though—don't you envy me my situation?*

Early in the morning, only two days after Andrews reached the regiment, it was formed in line of battle, everyone expecting to make an advance. The 179th remained under arms till three o'clock in the afternoon but made no move other than to extend its picket line a mile and a half. Some shots were exchanged in a desultory fashion, but the shooting did not seem to faze Andrews. "The 'Johnnies' fell back without showing much fight," he told Tubbs. "We lost a few men killed and wounded. I only saw two of the wounded men come in—both wounded in the head. One had a beautiful flesh wound in the cheek. It will leave a scar that he will be proud of."

The next day, Andrews went out on the picket line and, to his amazement, discovered that it was very close to the Confederate picket line, so close that the opposing pickets conversed with one another and exchanged newspapers and other articles. "I saw a group of rebel officers within a stone's throw," he remarked. "They were a dirty look-ing lot of scoundrels."

While out on the picket line, Andrews stumbled on his first close-up view of the horror of war: the body of one of the regiment's men, killed in the battle for Poplar Springs Church. "The rebs had covered his face, and called that a burial," said Andrews. "There he lay, partly in a stream . . . a dead patriot, food for worms, millions of which were feasting upon his remains."

Andrews was struck by the pomp and ceremony of another re-pugnant aspect of war: the execution of a deserter from a Maryland regiment. Desertion was a major problem for both armies. Somewhere in the neighborhood of 200,000 men fled the Union army alone, many of them bounty jumpers. In fact, two days before the execution that Andrews witnessed, five men from the 179th, nearly all new recruits who had received large bounties, secretly stole off in the night from the regiment's encampment. Andrews said that "reb pickets" had "informed our pickets that all deserters would be furnished free transportation to Europe."

Desertions by men thought to be comrades-in-battle prompted angry comments from a number of Tubbs' friends. George Scudder was alarmed that desertions were frequent in regiments raised in New York State and New Jersey. "[W]ould to God," he wrote back in 1863, "that the deserters were brought back and suffer ther doom[.]" Scudder said he despised "a coward—a sneak and deserter[.] And as true as there is a God in Heaven do beleive I could pull trigger on them with a good conscious."[6]

Both deserters and slackers drew the ire of William Self. He complained about two of the latter, fellow Bucktails who were "sick whenever there is a little fighting to do . . . neither one have ever seen eny fighting[,] always sick or lame[.]"[7]

Early in the war, Self witnessed the drumming out of a man who had deserted twice. "[H]e was brought out of jail and upon the praid ground and a company of nearly five thousand around him and eighteen drums behind." The man was so distraught by the disgrace that afterwards he tried three times to drown himself.[8]

As the war progressed, penalties for desertion became harsher. The man whose execution Andrews witnessed was one of 147 federal soldiers executed during the war for desertion:[9]

The victim was a member of the 2nd Maryland Reg.[,] had twice deserted to the enemy. After his second desertion he was taken prisoner in battle fighting against us. He was tried by Court Martial and sentenced to be shot. The whole division were ordered to be present at his execution.

It was a beautiful sight to see those thousands of men, with glittering bayonets, colors flying and bands playing march to the scene of execution and form in a hollow square around the newly dug grave. Then came the prisoner attended by two chaplains, followed by the guard who were to shoot him and preceded by four men bearing his coffin and by a band playing a mournful death march. They entered the square and marched all around it. They then marched to the grave—he sat down on his coffin, his sentence was read to him, his eyes bandaged[,] the guard leveled their peices, fired and he fell back upon his coffin[.] The blood streamed from his head down over the side of his coffin—and he died without a struggle. Then the Division marched away, the bands playing lively airs.

The man died "game". He marched around the square with a firm step, and seated himself upon his coffin with an unconcerned air. I was surprised at myself, that I could look upon such a scene and remain unmoved but such was the case[.] Everything was done with such military precision that there was nothing at all to shock one.

By the time Andrews described the deserter's execution to Tubbs, he himself was in deep trouble.

One day, while in command of a portion of the picket line, Andrews was asked by a superior officer to obtain a Richmond newspaper. The day before, Confederate pickets had violated an unspoken agreement. They had taken prisoner a man from the 179th who had gone out to exchange some foodstuffs and newspapers with them. So when Andrews saw a Confederate picket waving a newspaper from across the no-man's-land between the two armies, he informed his men that in retaliation he was going to go out and bring the Confederate in. Hiding a revolver in his shirt, Andrews approached the enemy soldier. There was a second Confederate behind the first. Hoping to entice him to come forward, too, Andrews offered to purchase a Richmond paper for a dollar. Hearing this, the second Confederate stepped forward. Andrews then drew the revolver and ordered the two Confederates to return with him to the Union line as prisoners.

The commander of the 179th, Colonel William M. Craig, wanted to promote Andrews to first lieutenant on the spot. But when the incident reached the attention of the provost marshal, Craig was ordered instead to arrest Andrews for violating orders against communicating with the enemy. Andrews was placed under what amounted to house arrest and brought before a military board. He refused counsel and, pleading his own case, was acquitted.[10]

Andrews was still facing the court-martial when the 179th took part in late October in a "reconnoissance in force"—an engagement known variously as the Battle of Burgess' Mill, the Battle of Boydton Plank Road, or the Battle of Hatcher's Run. Suspended from his regular duties because of the proceedings against him, Andrews could not take part in the action, but curiosity got the better of him"[11]:

> I will give you a short account of what I _saw_ of it, inasmuch as I am to be hence forth your "special correspondent, with the Army of the Potomac".
>
> For several days before the movement began, the camp was full of rumors as to where it would _strike_. Six days' rations were given out and a hundred rounds of cartridges per man, all baggage not absolutely needed turned over to the Quarter Masters, and they with their trains sent back to City Point. We thought a big battle was about to be fought and felt confident that the victory would be with us. Col. Gregg advised me—being a _non combattant_—to go to City Point and remain there until the movement was over with, but I "couldn't see it" and remained.
>
> At half past three in the morning (Oct 27) the army was in motion. I[t] went out in two columns—the 9th Corps comprising one, and the 2d & 5th the other. I stopped at Fort Cummings (which is at the extreme left of our line) and

saw them move by. The "Dirty 9th" passed by at the right of the fort and formed in lines of battle in the wood beyond; the 2d & 5th Corps passed by at the left and forming other lines of battle passed out of sight, taking a direction farther to the left than the 9th Corps.

Firing commenced as soon as our troops entered the woods but it kept sounding farther and farther off. I remained at the fort an hour or two and then not being able to restrain my curiosity longer I "mosied" off through the woods to find my reg. I came up with it about a mile beyond in an open field holding some breastworks just vacated by the rebs. A short time after they were moved farther on into a piece of woods and set to throwing up breastworks and cutting down the woods in front of them.

The negro division of our Corps was in the advance, and we could hear a constant popping from where they were. I listened awhile and my curiosity became excited to know what it all amounted to, and I followed along the line about a mile through the woods till I came to a little ten acre lot and there I found the fight. My curiosity was very soon satisfied and I came back.

All the afternoon the men stood at the breastworks expecting an attack every moment from the rebels, but they came not. We could hear the firing of the other column, and we knew from it that they were meeting with considerable resistance, much more than ours did . . .

It had rained at intervals all through the day but at night it poured down. I wandered around till about nine o'clock when I found a laying down place in a tent alongside of a half dozen other officers, and although I had no blankets, I slept soundly till morning. The next morning after eating our breakfast Lieut Force (my tentmate) and myself found that our "six days' rations" were gone, so I took a large haversack and started back to get a new supply at some sutler's.

Before I got back to Fort Cummings I began to fall in with stragglers from the 2d Corps. I questioned different ones and they all told the same story. They said the rebs kept falling back all the afternoon the day before, they followed and just at night came into a small field and found theirselves surrounded by rebs in the woods on all sides. Here they said they were badly cut up and that every one of them would have been taken prisoner had not the 5th Corps cut a way open for them. They were then ordered to fall back as best they could to the "Yellow Tavern"—two miles back within our old lines.

I found a sutler about a mile and a half below the fort, got my haversack filled and started back . . .

Reaching the road near the fort I met the stream of stragglers coming back. The road was full of them; many officers were along; they were completely disorganized. They were all from the 2d and 5th Corps.

Farther on I met Gen. Meade accompanied by two Major and three Brig. Generals.—The Army was falling back. By noon the 5th Corps had fallen back past us into our line of fortifications, then the 9th Corps commenced falling

*back, first forming many lines of battle and then the front line falling back to
the rear of all the others.*

*It so happened that our brigade was the rear guard for our Corps as it
marched through the woods in front of Fort Cummings, back within our old
lines. The reb skirmishers followed close. Our brigade was in an open field
through which ran a line of breastworks. Our skirmishers had fallen back to the
shelter of these breastworks and from behind them kept up a constant fire at the
reb skirmishers who were dodging from tree to tree about twenty or thirty rods
beyond. Several shots passed over the brigade. Gen. Griffen [Charles Griffin]
and his aids kept riding from point to point hurriedly giving orders and the
brigade commenced falling back, every man feeling <u>mad</u> to think they should
thus retreat and have perhaps only a few hundred "gray backs" following close
at their heels firing at them[.]*

*I went up to the breastworks to see <u>what I could</u> see. While gaping
around I heard the peculiar <u>zip</u> of a bullet and the dust rose up from the ground
less than a rod in front of me. A rebel sharpshooter was trying his skill upon
me[.] I beat a retreat well satisfied with what I had seen.*

*At four p.m. we were back again on our old camping ground. Our loss
was <u>one man wounded</u>.*

*This movement is called in the papers a <u>reconnoissance</u> but the <u>army
knows better</u>. The 2d Corps acknowledges that it was badly whipped, and the
men swear they will not fight any more this fall. The Richmond paper is right
when it says our army has got "winter quarters on the brain".*

Andrews—like William Self, who, with the 190th Pennsylvania,
was also taking part in the Peninsular campaign—believed that the
truth about the engagement would not be made public:

*Tubbs[,] you know that at the time of this movement it would not have
done to have acknowledged a defeat for mere political reasons, but we were
never the less <u>defeated</u>, and there is a great deal of despondency in the army on
account of it. I really believe that the 9th Corps, at least, would not go into
battle now with one quarter the enthusiasm or confidence that they would two
weeks ago.*[12]

Despite the fact that the soldiers groused about the defeat, Andrews predicted before the presidential election on November 8 that
men of the Army of the Potomac would vote for Lincoln rather than
their former commander, McClellan. "The army is all Lincoln," he
wrote Tubbs.[13]

Andrews' assessment was correct. Lincoln was reelected, receiving well over 75 percent of the total military vote—nearly 117,000 votes
to fewer than 34,000 for McClellan.[14]

George Pratt Scudder used this envelope, reflecting Lincoln's popularity with the army, to mail a letter to "Lieut" Charles Tubbs.

By then, Andrews had learned at least one thing—not to publicize any doubts or questions he had about the way the army was run. He told Tubbs that he was writing "just as *I please* to *you.*" He would not dare to do so "to every one."[15]

CHAPTER 25

The Last Major Battles in the West

*In Art[iller]y one is generaly shure of a good shelter
and can carry enough blankets to keep him warm As
all such are loaded on the Cassins and pieces. And
what men have not got horses can ride on the Gun
carriages so that it is not just like carr[y]ing your bed
clothes and horse on your back and going a foot at that
through the mud and wet.*

—Philip Vanzile[1]

Neither John T. Andrews nor Philip T. Vanzile—classmates at Alfred University until Andrews left for Union College—thought the other was doing well. Andrews said that Vanzile's job as company clerk in the Ohio 1st Light Artillery "don't amount to anything scarcely." He explained to Charles Tubbs that the position "excuses one from some camp duties but it does not from drill nor from going into battle whenever the co. goes."[2]

For his part, Vanzile scoffed at Andrews' being a foot soldier, even though an officer. "I was sorry to hear that John T. had gone into the infantry," he wrote Tubbs.[3] "If you could see infantry men even Captains down here and then see us, you would not say foolish as I expect you will say now. Artillery is the nicest part of the U.S. service."[4]

Both friends were worried about each other, though. Andrews had not heard a word from "P.T.," and Vanzile did not know where to address "John T." They both asked Tubbs to get word to the other.

Vanzile was totally unaware that autumn that Andrews was facing court-martial charges for fraternizing with the enemy. At the time, he was with the 1st Light Artillery outside Nashville. The Ohio battery, organized at the beginning of the war, had seen extensive duty, chiefly in Tennessee, and had even been briefly captured by Confederate cavalry led by Nathan Bedford Forrest. Its most recent posting was as the garrison artillery at Bridgeport, Alabama.[5] Now, the 1st Light Artillery was part of the defenses of Nashville and had been completely re-armed and refurbished with new guns and fresh horses.

While stationed outside Nashville, Vanzile was able to take time off to ride into the city and had the unusual "pleasure" of hearing Lincoln's running mate, Vice President–elect Andrew Johnson, a Tennessee resident, speak twice:

> The last time was a grand old time[,] twas a torch light procession of the Collored People. I tell you there is a string of them here[.] They call Andy Johnson their Moses and he did talk to them like a Moses[.]
>
> I went down on horseback to the City and rode up on a little eminance in front of the Capital and had a good chance to hear him And see him[.] he speakes with quite a good deal of force But one can perceive that he is not a well educated man[.] Pronounces some words wrong[.]

The torchlight parade and speeches were not without incident, though. There was a Peace Democrat in the crowd:

> I see one Copperhead get his change that night[.] After Johnson spoke Col Mussey the organizer of the Collored troops in this Department get up and was making a splendid speech when this chick with a brazen head made some re-mark[.] When the Col said that there was a fellow in his sight that did not agree with what he was saying And says he "May be he be born to Mc[C]Lel-lans bosom[.]" The fellow shortly after Commenced bel[l]owing[,] Said Andy Johnson was a darned old Traitor and threw a stone at the Col. About this time the little lead things commenced going for him and he went down[.] I will not say how many shots were fired[;] 17 balls were found to have taken effect in his body.
>
> This is merely a soldriss Compliments to a Copperheads and may they all enjoy the God given <u>blessing</u>.[6]

In mid-November, Vanzile's unit, Battery E of the 1st Light Artillery, was assigned to the Army of the Cumberland, commanded by Major General George H. Thomas. The men moved their cannon and caissons into Fort Huston, one of the numerous fortifications circling Nashville:

> We now man 9 Guns in all. We retain over eight Field Guns and horses so that we can if necessary move out and take the field at any time[.] We have enough Men now to man the guns of the fort and Also our Batry. Our Company now numbers 150 Men and good solid fellows at that. Tis a nice place here about the defences of this City[.] Fort Huston is one a line of forts that extend nearly around the City[.] This fort is not done yet[.] There are 100

laborers working on her now. I suppose when tis finished we will have more heavy guns[.] The heaviest we have now is a 24 pds. siege gun 4 12 pds. brass pieces and 4 6 pds. Field riffles for our battery.

Vanzile, who as company clerk made out all the requisitions, expected to see action soon. "[W]e are drawing some Shot & Shell &c.," he informed Tubbs.[7]

But Vanzile was wrong. It was months before the Ohio battery was ordered into action.

In September, a Confederate army led by John Bell Hood abandoned Atlanta to Sherman. In the weeks that followed, Hood, in a series of engagements, tried to lure federal forces north, away from Georgia. By November 30, he reached Franklin, south of Nashville. The move forced Vanzile's outfit into battle.

Vanzile was not looking forward to any fighting because of his commander, a first lieutenant, "a man that thinks more of a bum than his Company." Vanzile said that he, Vanzile, would "rather try to get along with almost any kind of man but one of this stamp." He confided to Tubbs, "[H]e sprees it nearly every day . . . And a Man that is drunk has no business commanding a Battery of Artillery."[8]

Now Charles[,] I had no Idea of a battle untill I see one fought. And from reading discriptions of writers one cannot get a very good one. In a fight 'tis generally every chick for himself. The excitement of Gen Hood's march began upon the Citizens (And to please same) about the 20th of November and some of them were badly scared[.] It did not effect the Millitary untill the 30 of November When they began to fix things for his reception by moving Troopes into position And reinforcing picketts.

About ten oclock in the morning just as the Most of our boys were having their first dreams an Orderly from Gen. [John Franklin] Miller rode up to our Head Quarters and brought orders for us to report on the Hillsborough Pike (Which is south west of the City and on the right of the line) at one oclock the next Morning. About 11 o.c. we had reveille and then Boots-an-Saddles (which is to hitch up) And soon were on the way expecting a little row in the morning but nary [a] reb. After lieing on the ground all night in the morning we came back to camp but only to return with the night.

The Confederates suffered a disastrous defeat at Franklin. Afterwards, Hood's depleted force retreated north and took up a position close to the federal defenses of Nashville. Hood hoped to be reinforced there. But, in the meantime, the federals seized the initiative. The 1st Light Artillery was supposed to be held in reserve, Vanzile reported, but instead it was the first battery ordered to engage the enemy. The men "had to fight like the D——l and came near getting gobled at that," he said.[9]

> On the 1st of December in the Morning we were ordered to the left And sent away out in Advance of the line of battle about one Mile And not a bit of support[.] This we and everybody considered a mistake (And so it turned out to be) but we went to work and here I had a chance to display my fine qualities of Snatching thing[s]. And twas in the Shape of Shovels from Citizens Around about . . . I could steal rather more picks and shovels than the boys could use so we went to pressing Nigs And by dark we had nice little works thrown up in front of each gun. And lots of tools for more so we Lay down by the Guns and slept.
>
> The next day the Johnnies made their appearance on a high hill in our front and grubed away some but few came out and seemed mostly to be Laying out a plan for works. But that P.M. they began to move up and get rather thick[.] We just fed one of our guns a shell and let him spit his compliments At them[.] Well they stuck their ears up some but we put down more shell and drove them Out, but soon found a good force of them in a piece of woods on our left. Well now if we did'nt give them goodly I wish you could have seen them climb.
>
> We were here for [f]lour days every moment expecting support but none comeing. And had the Rebs know this they could just sent out a Regt of Infantry just at dusk and gobbled us up. The last night we were here Liet Will Welsher and me slept in a house close by. But we were might watchfull And arose quite early in the Morning.
>
> That P.M. we were moved back on the main line where we were safe as far as support was concerned. But oh how we suffered here with Cold. It was awfull cold and we have nary a tent And there was snow on at that[.]
>
> On the 10th we got permission to go into our old Camp. We staid there untill the night of the 14th when we moved out on the Nollensville Pike on the left of the line[,] took position on the 15th at day break And found a fine lot of Rebs in our front.

With twice the number of troops at his command than Hood, Thomas launched a federal attack on December 15. Vanzile was "sixlie" that morning, suffering a "billious fever." He thought at the time that it was "nothing more than one of those old headaches" he was accustomed to getting, so he decided to stay at his post. "I did not leave the Battery which was then on the line of Battle booming away at the Rebs old Hood[.] Twas pretty rough but I could not see sacrificing so much fun." The 1st Light Artillery

gave the Rebs Haile Columbia that day but the Nigs did the gay old fighting[.]
One Regt. or Brigade went for a battery of the Rebs just in front of us. They
went up as steady And the Rebs had their pieces all loaded and lay behind their
works untill they came up just the right distance and then they let loos[e.] The
volley killed dead 19 men in one Regt. but six they never wounded but went
with a shout and took the works but they could not hold them[.] I tell you they
fight[.][10]

The battle ended the next day in a decisive victory for the Army
of the Cumberland. It had eliminated the major western Confederate
army as an aggressive force. Losses on both sides were relatively small,
but by then Hood's army was so decimated that its effectiveness as an
offensive force was over.

After the Battle of Nashville, Vanzile conceded that his commander—
the first lieutenant about whom he had complained—performed well.
He was "a good man in a fight," said Vanzile, "or any place where
whiskey was scarce."[11]

The Ohio 1st Light Artillery was subsequently turned into an even
more effective fighting force—a "Horse (or flying) Artillery," Vanzile
reported. "Every Man is mounted as Cavelry and have our big guns
besides. So we are able when necessary to do Cavelry duty[.]" Vanzile
said Battery E was "intended to accompany Cavelry on raids where it is
dashing into the heart of a C[o]untry and out[,] doing All the damge
That a yank is capable of doing[—]Just what I shall like[.]" Then he
added:

"How I would like to be sent in to help capture old Lee."[12]

1865

CHAPTER 26

"The Bright Sunlight of Peace"

*At present there is a good prospect before us[.] our
armies are victorious on almost every quarter[,] gradually tightening the grip on the monster Secessia . . . it
is a happy time for all especially for the soldier who
has borne the hardships and fatigue of the march and
the dangers of the campaign when there is a prospect
of our success over all our misfortunes.*

—*Orville Kimball*[1]

The new year began on an optimistic note in the North. The Union
now had massive armies in all three critical areas of the war. Grant was
at Petersburg, battling the dwindling Army of Northern Virginia. Thomas
controlled Tennessee. Just before the year 1864 ended, Sherman occupied Savannah, Georgia, and less than two months later, both Charleston, South Carolina, and Wilmington, North Carolina, were in federal
hands.

A decisive Union victory finally seemed near. But the Confederacy still clung to the hope of an honorable settlement, its expectations
resting primarily on Robert E. Lee. Before the month of January was
out, he was named General-in-Chief of all Confederate armies.

On January 1, eight of Charles Tubbs' friends were still in the
service. But just two weeks later, Dr. William Humphrey, chronically
ill with diarrhea, was discharged for medical reasons. Between periods
of active service, first with the Bucktails and then with the 149th Pennsylvania and the Third Division of the I Corps, Humphrey was hospitalized twice, spent time on different occasions recovering at the home
of a private physician in Washington, and returned home to Oceola
three times on sick leave.[2]

Spurred once more by patriotism, Leonard Kimball volunteered
again, his third enlistment. Two weeks before the end of 1864, Lincoln
had issued a last call for volunteers—300,000 men to replace Union

casualties. Kimball and eight other Osceola men immediately signed up. They were told to report to Williamsport, some fifty miles away, in March, but floods prevented their travel, and by the time their muster-in was rescheduled, they were no longer needed.[3]

Meanwhile, the rest of Tubbs' friends were scattered about the country, and, interestingly, as the war drew to a conclusion, their letters to him and his letters to them became sporadic.

In February, Leonard Kimball's half-brother, Orville, transferred to Company B Battalion outside Petersburg, where he took on administrative duties for the 103rd New York. Both the durable private, William Self, and the "Little Lieutenant," John Andrews, were in Virginia, too, fighting with the Army of the Potomac. Andrews' commander had recommended that he be brevetted a captain, saying that "no officer" of the 179th New York was "better entitled" or the promotion "more worthily earned."[4]

Philip Vanzile with Battery E of Ohio's 1st Light Artillery had been shifted from Nashville to Chattanooga. Though confined to administrative duties, John Orr was still with the 107th New York when the regiment took part in Sherman's March to the Sea and the siege of Savannah in the late fall of 1864; it was now stationed in the Carolinas. Farther south, Mordecai Casson, who was promoted to sergeant on New Year's Day,[5] was seeing action as a scout with New York's 2nd Veteran Cavalry on expeditions and raids in Georgia and Alabama.

William Prentice was also in Alabama. The 161st New York was participating in the siege of Mobile after barely recovering from a shocking accident. On January 8, the 161st left the mouth of the White River in Arkansas, embarking on the steamer *John H. Dickey*. The regiment was under orders to report to New Orleans. The trip down the Mississippi began uneventfully. Then, in midafternoon, the vessel was fired on by guerrillas from the shoreline; no one, though, was injured. The *John H. Dickey* reached Vicksburg the next day, took on coal, and resumed her voyage about five in the afternoon. Chaplain William Jones remembered how everyone in the ship's cabin was in the best of spirits:

> [H]ere, a group were singing patriotic songs; there, some were reading; others were engaged in pleasant intercourse, when suddenly, about 7 o'clock, in the midst of all this pleasure, there came a stunning blow, as if the steamer had bolted against some massive substance; then, crash, crash! as if every timber in the boat was being crushed to atoms, followed by clouds of steam rushing in the cabin.

Another steamer, the *John Raine*, had collided with the *Dickey*. The collision, on the larboard side near the bow, tore away the *Dickey*'s lower boiler and hurricane decks. Her wheelhouse was crushed and the wheel left hanging "by shreds" to the vessel's side. For some moments, utmost confusion prevailed:

In their fright, many of the men leaped into the water to swim ashore, but three were drowned in the attempt, and twenty-three others were injured by the collision, two of whom died a few days afterward.

The *Raine* rescued the rest of the regiment and conveyed the men to an encampment twelve miles above New Orleans. There, it joined other units as the XIII Corps rendezvoused in preparation for a general advance against Mobile.[6]

In the third week of March, the 161st tramped overland into Alabama. At one point, the troops had to cut down trees and lay corduroy roads made up of the logs in order to get their supply wagons and artillery across swamps and quicksand. It took four days of work day and night to travel fifteen miles. Wet for days on end, Prentice suffered an attack of rheumatism.[7]

Nevertheless, Prentice stayed at his post as captain of Company H, when on March 28 the XIII Corps, in cooperation with a naval fleet, succeeded in completely surrounding the strong fortifications on the east side of Mobile Bay. The federals were now in command of the main channel to the city:

The Bay was so full of Torpedoes that after losing three gunboats, the navy gave out and left the work to the land forces. From the 28th to the 8th of April we were conducting the operations of a regular seige, but as the navy could not cut off their [the Confederates'] communications with the city, an assault was ordered and the work carried, though a part of the crew escaped on launches to the swamps across the narrow channel and thus got away. That same night reinforcements were sent to [Maj. Gen. Frederick] Steele, who was investing Blakely, & on the night of the 9th that was also assaulted and carried. Our loss was only about 2000 in these two assaults, which is small considering the nature of the ground. Our captures amount to only about 5000 men on account of the chanc[e] which they had to get away into the swamps of the upper bay.

The next night our Division went down to Starks Landing 15 miles[,] crossed the bay on Transports, landed at Dog River Bar, and occupied the city which had been evacuated of necesity after the capture of the forts on the East side. Since then, we have been in camp at this place, doing Picket, Guard and Provost Duty.[8]

The siege of Mobile began on March 25. Four days later, in Virginia, Grant began his Appomattox campaign, and four days after that, the Confederate government was forced to abandon Richmond.

On a Sunday, in the second week of April, elements of the Army of the Potomac and the remnants of the Army of Northern Virginia stood opposite each other at Appomattox Court House. William Self—who boasted that "there is not a man in the whole Regt that has been [in] the number of engagements that I have"⁹—was out on the skirmish line of the 190th Pennsylvania. The men of the regiment were called, like their predecessors in the original 13th Pennsylvania, Bucktails. One of them described the dramatic events of that day:

About noon on the ninth of April we got the order, "Bucktails to the front—double quick, march," and away we went, past our own division, past the first division, past the advance, out into an open field. "Battalion into line—deploy as skirmishers—forward—double quick—march" rang along the line. The order seems to ring in my ears now.

Away we went. Sheridan's cavalry was just coming out as we went in. Soon we got sight of the rebels and they of us. We advanced double quick and they fell back. They opened on us with a battery from the brow of a hill, first with shells and as we got closer with canister, and just as we were about charging on the battery, up over the brow of the hill in front came a horseman, then another, and another.

*The first bore a white flag. "Cease firing," "Cease firing," was the order, and the rider bearing it passed down through the lines. "They have surrendered, they have surrendered" was repeated from to man until the whole army knew the glad tidings, and cheer after cheer rent the air. The glad hour for which we had been battling for four long years had come.*¹⁰

Later, Self was one of the men who stood guard outside the home of Wilmer McLean as, inside, Robert E. Lee and Ulysses Grant discussed the terms of the surrender.

Self had marched more than twelve hundred miles and been in twenty-nine battles and skirmishes in the four years since he first enlisted.¹¹

Philip Vanzile was at Chattanooga with Battery E of Ohio's 1st Light Artillery on the night of April 9, writing Tubbs about the "noise in this Army" when news of the capture of Richmond was announced. "The air was full of cheers and at Sun down they opened their big guns and made some racket." Suddenly, in the midst of writing, word came that Lee had surrendered at Appomattox:

All you can hear is cheering all around going from one Command to another until it dies away in the distance[.] Well I am affraid now more than ever that we will not get a good pop at the Rebs[.] Again I would like one good raid.[12]

Vanzile never got the opportunity for that "one good raid." One by one, in the weeks that followed, Confederate armies in the south and west surrendered. Little more than a month after Appomattox, Battery E was disbanded; its armaments were turned over to another unit. Two friends of Vanzile's, one of them his tentmate, had both been promoted and reassigned to another battery.

Vanzile was eager to return home. His mother had been injured, apparently in a fall, and he confessed to Tubbs that he was "somewhat anxious" about her health. Otherwise, his mind was on women, and in a rare salacious spirit he wrote:

Well I heard how that new Lib Barker there[—]you know her dont you down there, Why yes of Course you do, What did I ask that for[—]Why she has now gone and and and why "done it[.]" Yes got married[.] Yes thats why I mean by done it—you know now[,] dont think I want "that[.]"—what you are thinking about. Bully for Elizabeth Barker[.] I wonder if her man got wounded the first night from any of her preminent points. Well I have one consolation[,] Evaline is left pine "virtuous" and undefiled and no thieves have broken through and Stolen[,] No I repeat it[,] Not a one . . .

Now with me if Miss Tirte to Tirte Tirte or any other of her happy interesting shemale sisters was here to ask me to eat with them Why I should except and show them that I could eat a soldiers rations[.]

Vanzile said that "the last gay old news" his regiment received was the capture of the fleeing Confederate president, Jefferson Davis, on May 10. "I suppose things up north begin to assume their old accustomed posish and that peacfull times begin to take the place of the warlike[.]"[13]

When he wrote his last letter to Tubbs in July, Vanzile was at Camp Dennison, outside Cincinnati. Battery E had been officially mustered out only a few days earlier and the men were awaiting their pay before returning home:

Well my soldiering is about played out now for this war And I have one thing to regret and that is that I did not ge[t] in seconds[.]

But tis war And once more the bright sunlight of peace comes beaming in upon us through the dark clouds of carnage that for the last four years has enveloped us[.] We are all glad and as one common people n[o]urished in the fighting can in coming time rejoice together and talk over the brave deeds and hard trials of the bully boys in blue in the "Great Rebellion of 1861[.]" But Oh the many vacant places[,] The Many Patriot Mothers and Fathers that will listen long with vain hoping for the return of some brave who went forth when his Country called And thus will the[y] look & hope and thus hoping and wishing will pass over the river And away yonder in the other side will meet once more that hero boy.[14]

Writing from Mobile, William Prentice was ecstatic. He wished, he said, to ignore the war "as a horrid Night Mare from which we have gradually been escaping until today we are fully wakened."

Peace! You can hardly know how joyful a word it is to the soldier, three years (almost) an exile from Home, congenial persuits, and all he loves. Today, we say, the sun which dawned on the 10th of April has fully risen. . . . Four years of bitter bloodshed have dragged their slow length along and the Bright Morn of Peace is upon us! Oh how the heart leaps up at the glad thought, and utterance is almost choked, for joy that the glad day has come at last! Companions of many a bloody & trying hour grasp one anothers hands whenever they meet like long absent friends, and looks not words speak the great joy which has dawned upon us: while more sedate but equally demonstrative men say "let's take a glass of Lager."[15]

On Good Friday, April 14, five days after Lee's surrender and two days after the surrender of Mobile—on the very day that the Union flag was raised once more on Fort Sumter—Lincoln was mortally wounded by John Wilkes Booth. Surprisingly, only two of Tubbs' correspondents mentioned the tragedy in their letters. One, William Prentice, implied that he was too shocked to comment: "Of the assassination of the President I can say nothing."[16]

Orville Kimball was more voluble:

The joys consequent on the closing scenes of the rebellion were only dampened by a cold.-blooded most foul and cowardly assassination of Our honored Chief Executive Abraham Lincoln[.] But although this threw the whole nation in mourning it will not relax one single effort to the total extinction of the rebellion and its causes and in this fact we have a proud thought after four years war unparalelled in history[:] our endeavors are crowned with a glorious sucess[.][17]

CHAPTER 27

Homeward Bound

[L]et us not trample on the right of the southern peo-
ple though they are in our power[.]
—*Orville Kimball*[1]

The victorious federal armies paraded down Pennsylvania Avenue in late May. There were so many soldiers marching in splendid order from the Capitol to the White House, their scarred battle colors flying, that the spectacular celebration took two days.

As thousands of citizens lined the broad street and cheered the troops on, William Self and John Andrews marched in a Grand Review of the Army of the Potomac on May 23. The next day, John Orr and the 107th New York, which had witnessed the surrender of Joseph E. Johnston's Confederate army to William Tecumseh Sherman outside Durham, North Carolina, strode down the avenue in a second Grand Review.[2]

Orville Kimball remained in Virginia, working in the army's commissary department at Surry Court House well into the autumn. He doled out provisions to soldiers and destitute southerners and gave "an immense number of rations" to newly freed blacks.[3] He was not certain what he thought about Reconstruction. "Tis surely a knotty question," he said, "and I would not[,] could I[,] interfere with its settlement." He did not believe blacks were capable of governing either themselves or others. As for those white southerners who had waged the war, he said:

[L]et us show them that we are magnanimous as we have been brave in
the fierce struggle[.] The Black man are not the only true Unionist of the
south[.] there are others[.] The people are submissi[ve] and willing to submit to
the powers that be and let us not give them cause to complain by taking from
them the right of suffrage and giving it to the negro. Let there be the people of

the proud American Union and that is enough[.] they have been rebels but one now repentent though[.][4]

William Prentice, meanwhile, was responsible for guarding three of the conspirators who had taken part in the president's assassination. On August 1, the 161st New York began duty at Fort Jefferson, an immense fortification on Garden Key in the Dry Tortugas, southwest of Florida in the Gulf of Mexico. The fort, surrounded by a seventy-foot moat, had long been used as a prison for military offenders.

When the 161st took over command of the fort from another New York regiment whose term of enlistment was about to expire, there were more than four hundred prisoners within its walls.[5] Among them were three men convicted in the plot to kill Lincoln, Michael O'Laughlin, Samuel B. Arnold, and Dr. Samuel A. Mudd. Arnold, a Maryland farm worker who had known Booth in his youth, insisted that he was innocent. Dr. Mudd also maintained his innocence. He had set the broken shinbone of John Wilkes Booth's left leg, injured when the assassin jumped onto the stage of the Ford Theatre after shooting the president.

For a time, Prentice was in command of the fort and during it he developed a relationship with both Mudd and Arnold. On the day before the regiment itself was mustered out in late September and Prentice left the island, he gave the doctor a copy of Victor Hugo's novel, *Les Miserables*. In return for "the token" of Prentice's "friendship and kindness," Mudd, a Catholic, gave him a small medal depicting the Virgin Mary.[6]

After the 161st left, replaced by the 82nd United States Colored Troops, Mudd tried to escape, and Arnold was implicated in the attempt. He had been entrusted to work as a clerk in the fort's provost marshal's office, but that privilege was taken away and he was put in the fort's guardhouse. Twice, in October and November, Arnold wrote Prentice. He protested any complicity in Mudd's escape attempt and asked Prentice to intercede on his behalf. "I know nothing," he insisted. Arnold said that he was "only permitted to look upon the bare wall and chilly floor" of his cell, listening to "the slow and measured tread of the sentry as he walks his beat both day and night before our quarters, now [no] intercourse with outside—all is monotony."[7]

Whether Prentice did anything in Arnold's behalf is not known. President Andrew Johnson pardoned both him and Mudd in February 1869. The doctor was commended for being instrumental in fighting an outbreak of yellow fever in 1867, during which O'Laughlin had died.

In contrast with the grand reviews in Washington, the return that fall of the 161st New York to Elmira, the site of the regiment's organization three years earlier, was a quiet affair. Chaplain Jones described the remnants of the returning regiment as "a little band, with war-worn countenances and thinned ranks." The 161st had lost 18 men killed in action; an additional 11 men, part of the 96 wounded in battle, died afterwards of their injuries.[8]

The citizens of Elmira treated the surviving members of the regiment to a public reception, a "sumptuous dinner provided by the ladies of the city," on October 12. Five days later, the noncommissioned men received their pay and were discharged. William Prentice and the other officers were paid and discharged the next day and sat down that evening to a final "elegant supper" hosted by the 161st's major, Willis E. Craig.

The regiment, Jones noted with pride, had traveled "eleven thousand miles by water, and twelve hundred by land, carrying its tattered flag, torn by the enemy's bullets, over the burning plains of the South, into the thickest of the fight, and into seven different States, and come home with not an act to regret, with not a stain on its banners, and with a history for endurance and heroism untarnished and glorious."[9]

Epilogue: When the Colors Fade

Amid all our rejoicing we should remember . . .
Mothers & Fathers. And when I celebrate the victories
of this war I would go farther to find such an one if I
could comfort them[.] For tis the last request of most
all true Soldiers And this request I would grant.
                                        —Philip Vanzile[1]

The news of Lee's surrender on April 9 reached Osceola the next day, prompting an instant celebration. The elated townspeople ran to churches to ring bells; others fired off guns. The Cowanesque Valley echoed with shouts of rejoicing. According to one resident, "Men gave themselves up to the most extravagant expressions of the delight they felt at the good news."[2]

The citizens of Osceola were proud of the town's contribution to the War of the Rebellion. Sixty-eight of its young men served in the war, either in the infantry or the cavalry, and every one of them was a volunteer. "From first to last," Charles Tubbs wrote afterwards, "no drafted man served in the ranks from Osceola."[3] Of those sixty-eight, eighteen were dead: ten were killed in battle; two men died in Confederate prison camps, one of them at the infamous one in Andersonville, Georgia; and six men died of disease or infection. The dead ranged in age from fourteen to forty.[4]

Overall, the residents of Tioga County were proud, too. At the outbreak of the war, the county's population stood at roughly 31,000 persons, 6,000 of whom were adult males. An unusually large number of the men, almost half of them, served in federal armies—a ratio of almost one in ten citizens. Of the total, 445 of the men—one in almost every seven who served—lost their lives in battle, from infections and disease, or died in prison camps in the South.[5]

Four of Charles Tubbs' letter-writing friends were dead—Orrin Stebbins and George Scudder killed in battle, Samuel Stevens and Harlan Kimball of diseases they picked up in the army. During the war, four others had been discharged for medical reasons—William Humphrey, Leonard Kimball, Henry Maxson, and Allen Van Orsdale. Two others—David Armstrong and Asa Spencer—served until the expiration of their terms of enlistment but left with impaired health, Armstrong still suffering from a wound, Spencer plagued with chronic diarrhea.

Almost without exception, even those who served to the end of the war suffered from illnesses they contracted during their years in the army, or so they stated in applying for a government pension. Yet, amazingly, considering the health problems they enumerated on their applications and the state of medicine in the nineteenth century, most of them lived long lives. Eight of the thirteen soldier friends of Tubbs' who survived the war lived into their seventies, three into their eighties.

By some strange quirk of fate, William Self—the indestructible private who had fought in more battles than any of the others—died at an early age, about forty-two. One of the first of Tubbs' Osceola friends to enlist at the start of the war in April 1861—and the lone member of the 13th Pennsylvania still on active service at its conclusion[6]—Self was mustered out at Arlington Heights, Virginia, on June 28.

Almost immediately after returning home to Osceola, Self was troubled by respiratory difficulties. He came under the care of William Humphrey, suffering from bronchitis and "disease of the lungs"—consumption—which the doctor had treated him for while he was still in the service. Despite the doctor's ministrations, he continued to suffer from severe bleeding of the lungs and was unable to work much.

Self married Julia Campbell of nearby Nelson in January 1869 and subsequently moved to Michigan, where the couple had a son, born in 1871. He came under Humphrey's care again when he returned to Osceola in 1873 following the death of his wife while giving birth to a daughter in October of that year. Self was so poor that he had to borrow decent clothes to attend Julia's funeral. He himself died of consumption on January 31, 1875, leaving the two children to the guardianship of Charles Tubbs' uncle, George Tubbs, an Osceola attorney.[7]

Little is known about Asa Spencer, who also died at a relatively early age. The one-time Osceola schoolmaster and "Comander in chief of the Rat Department" at Columbian Hospital in Washington, returned to his wife, Betsey, in Jasper, New York, after being mustered out of the 136th Pennsylvania.[8] He evidently did not return to teaching but instead farmed on 123 acres of land he owned in the town. At the time of his death from heart failure on January 9, 1892, Spencer was in his mid-50s.[9]

Dr. William T. Humphrey, before his death in 1897
at the age of seventy-two.
Courtesy of Tioga County Historical Society, Wellsboro, Pennsylvania.

Dr. Humphrey, who left the army due to ill health in mid-January 1865, not only continued to practice as a physician but also pursued a political career. As soon as he returned home to Osceola, he ran as a Republican and was elected to the Pennsylvania State Legislature. He was reelected the following year and also served in the legislature from 1874 to 1876.

Humphrey and his wife, Mary, had three children. Charles Tubbs had helped the couple to purchase their home in Osceola in 1863, when Humphrey was in the field.[10] Mary died in March 1883 at the age of fifty-eight. A year later, when Humphrey remarried—his second wife, May Baker, was twenty-one years his junior—Tubbs served as a witness at the ceremony.

A month before his second marriage, Humphrey, then fifty-eight years old, applied for a government pension. He claimed that, as a result of the chronic diarrhea he had contracted in the army, he had been unable in the past six to eight years "to do more than ½ of my former labor as a physician." His constant attacks of pain and "distention of the bowels continue to grow more frequent & it is with great difficulty that I can procure a passage when my bowels become constipated. The rectum lessens in calibre & I am obliged frequently to use warm water injections."[11]

Humphrey never fully recovered. He suffered continually until his death, at the age of seventy-two, on July 31, 1897.[12] Charles Tubbs attended his burial in Fairview Cemetery in Osceola.[13]

For William Prentice, the war left a bitter aftertaste and, like Humphrey, a legacy of constant pain and illness. Shortly after being mustered out with the 161st New York, he returned to Jasper, his plans for the future, he wrote Tubbs, simple: "When I get *home* I must see you & have a long talk over the events through which we have both passed since . . . we both drank the last glass of Cider & parted for three years."[14]

Prentice's experiences in the army had embittered him. He rued that the feeling of "joyful anticipation" upon returning home when a student at Alfred University "has nearly died out now and the future has a dread." He had "grown misanthropic," he said, "and distrust men too much."[15]

Prentice still suffered from rheumatism, which he had contracted when the regiment advanced on Mobile in the spring of 1865. But bouts of it failed to keep him from becoming a teacher and working for some years at his alma mater.[16]

Over the years, Prentice and his wife, Myra, lived in a number of towns in upstate New York. In the early 1890s, he sought a government pension on the grounds of both rheumatism and lung trouble, but his application was rejected. Prentice's health deteriorated after that. He suffered ankylosis—an abnormal bone fusion—of both shoulders that left him unable to dress himself without help, and then his eyes began to fail. Sometime during this period, Myra apparently died. By 1900, as the result of a detached retina, Prentice was virtually blind, unable, he said, to continue work as a teacher or even "to recognize my most intimate friends." By 1906, he could no longer care for himself and had to hire help to tend to his everyday needs. He was then awarded a $12-a-month pension. Prentice died on July 15, 1909. He was seventy-three years old.[17]

In a way, Henry Maxson was fortunate. He was discharged after the 85th New York fought a series of battles in the "swamps of Virginia" in the late spring and summer of 1862. He was suffering from typhoid, bronchitis, and diarrhea at the time, but at least he was alive. A total of 326 men in his regiment died of disease during the war, almost ten times the number of those killed in combat.[18]

Even before he left the army, Maxson wondered whether farming was his "true place."[19] Now he was so disabled that, though he returned to farm in upstate New York, he soon found that he was unable to make a living by manual labor. In addition to chronic diarrhea, he developed ulcers. So he decided to follow the only career he could think of that he could manage: he became a doctor. He started studying medicine in the early 1870s, becoming a doctor in 1877. His first patient was himself.

Before then, Maxson lived with his family in Minnesota and New Jersey. He married Olive Palmer in March 1866 in Ashland, Minnesota. The couple had three sons. The family later settled in Kansas, first at Nortonville and then in Cunningham.

Maxson testified as a doctor on his own behalf in applying for a disability pension in 1891. He died on May 30, 1910, at the age of seventy-one.[20]

A year after Maxson died, another friend of Tubbs' from Alfred University, Allen Van Orsdale, died. Van Orsdale had returned to his home in Jasper after his medical discharge from the Bucktails in May 1862 to serve as the town's army enrollment officer. He subsequently was a commissioner on the draft board of the 27th Congressional District in Elmira until the end of the war.[21] Soon after, in mid-December 1865, he married Sarah Deck. The couple had one son.

Over the next forty-five years, Van Orsdale taught school in Jasper and several other Steuben County towns. He applied for an invalid's pension in 1890, when he was fifty-three years old. He claimed he could no longer do any manual labor because of "Prolapsus ani or Piles and General Debility." Van Orsdale was receiving $15 a month at the time of his death in Hornell on April 9, 1911, of arteriosclerosis and mitral insufficiency. He was two months shy of his seventy-fourth birthday.[22]

Although he volunteered twice more after his medical discharge from the 34th New York in June 1863, Leonard Kimball continued to be troubled by deafness. As early as 1869, Kimball, a farmer, applied for a government pension. Among the doctors who testified to his inability to hear well due to catarrh—an inflammation of the mucous membranes of the nose and throat—was William Humphrey. The doctor swore in an affidavit that Kimball's health problem prevented him from "performing manual labor to any extent." Another doctor said Kimball also suffered frequent attacks of inflammatory rheumatism. A third said he did not have "so strong a constitution as some." Kimball was awarded a pension of $27 a month. He tried to have that increased in 1883 as a result of what he called total deafness but evidently was unsuccessful.

Kimball had married Julia Kimball in February 1866. A native of

County Limerick, Ireland, she was the adopted daughter of an uncle of Kimball's.[23] The couple had six children.

Kimball died of heart disease and old age on July 17, 1914.[24] He was seventy-six years old.[25]

Two of Tubbs' friends died in 1916—his childhood friend David Armstrong and his roommate at Union College, John Andrews. Little is known about what happened to Armstrong, the self-confessed "poor scholar" who was the color bearer of Company F, 49th Ohio Infantry. Though wounded at Chickamauga in late summer 1863, Armstrong had remained with the regiment until his three-year term of enlistment expired in September 1864.[26]

Armstrong had written Tubbs from Atlanta in 1864 that he would like to get married—to a "nice young Lady . . . neat[,] han[d]some and virtuous[,] also acquainted with work and willing to do the womans part as it should be."[27] Between Christmas and New Year's Eve of 1865, Armstrong married Josephine Hollinger, and sometime afterward the couple moved, first to Constantine, in southern Michigan, and then across the state line to South Bend, Indiana. The couple had two children. Armstrong, who worked as both a carpenter and a locksmith, began applying for a disability pension in 1867, but the application became lost during the family's moves. In reapplying in 1879, he claimed that he had contracted a disease "known as *Salt Rheum*," which had spread over his hands, arms, and other parts of his body. His death, on June 18, 1916—when he was seventy-six years old—was attributed to a form of syphilis called locomotor ataxia. At the time, Armstrong was receiving a pension of $36 a month.[28]

On the other hand, a great deal is known about John Andrews. He was mustered out with Company D, 179th New York, on June 8 near Alexandria, Virginia,[29] and returned home to upstate New York to lead a varied and prosperous life. At first, in 1866, he joined his brother-in-law in the furniture business in Dundee, on Seneca Lake. He left two years later to study law in the office of two attorneys in nearby Penn Yan and was admitted to the bar in December 1869. But rather than pursuing a law career, Andrews turned his attention to business. He owned a linseed-oil mill and, later, a mill that made butcher's wrapping paper, and a flour mill. An ardent Republican, he served as a member of the New York Assembly in 1882 and was postmaster of Penn Yan from 1890 to 1893.

Andrews married Arville Raplee of Dundee in July 1866. His wife died thirty-six years later, in 1902. The couple had four sons, the second of whom was named for Andrews' college roommate—Charles Tubbs Andrews.

Andrews, who had recently returned from a trip around the world, was motoring to Buffalo from Penn Yan with another of his sons on September 4, 1916, when he suffered a stroke. He died early the next morning in a Buffalo hospital. He was seventy-four years old.[30]

While still in the service, Philip Vanzile debated whether he should become a lower-school teacher or continue his academic studies. "I am lost to know what to go into when I get home," he wrote Charles Tubbs.[31] He eventually decided to continue his studies and earned a Ph.D.[32]

Vanzile's unit, Battery E of Ohio's 1st Light Artillery, had suffered incredibly few casualties in the single year in which the company served. At the time of its mustering out at Camp Dennison outside Cincinnati on July 10, it had lost only three enlisted men killed or mortally wounded in battle. Twenty-nine others, however, died from disease, and Vanzile claimed that he contracted muscular rheumatism while fighting in Tennessee.[33]

Vanzile returned to Rochester, Ohio, and in December 1865, between Christmas and New Year's, he married Lizzie A. Jones. The couple moved first to Charlotte, Michigan, where Vanzile's sister resided and where they spent the first thirteen years of their marriage. In subsequent years, they lived in Salt Lake City, Detroit, in Charlotte again, and finally in Detroit once more after 1890. The couple had four children, only two of whom survived.[34]

Vanzile's occupations changed almost as often as his place of residence. For a while, he was a judge.[35] At another time, he worked as a sawyer.[36]

In 1892 Vanzile applied for a government pension. He said that the muscular rheumatism he suffered often forced him to take to his bed. He also claimed that he suffered a "disease of the rectum." Evidently, Vanzile's application was denied, because he submitted another application in 1915, when he was seventy-one years old. This one was approved. Vanzile received $19 a month until his death from pernicious anemia on October 26, 1917, at the age of seventy-four.[37]

John Orr's war wound continued to bother him, so much so that in 1879, when he was only forty years old, he applied for a government pension. He claimed that he was partially disabled.

Orr, who was mustered out with Company F of the 107th New York on June 5, 1865, at a camp outside Washington,[38] had returned to his wife, Melissa, in Addison, New York. There, he settled into the life of being, at various times, a farmer, a merchant, and a teacher in both Addison and Tuscarora. The couple, who already had one daughter—Phoebe, born during the war in 1864—had three more children.

Orr was receiving a pension of $30 a month when he died of exhaustion following a case of bronchitis on September 15, 1918, in

Orville Samuel Kimball about 1900,
when he was in his late fifties.
Courtesy of New York Public Library.

Phoebe's home in Minneapolis. He was buried in Lakewood Cemetery there. Orr was a month shy of eighty-two years old at the time of his death.[39]

Orville Kimball, who was the last of Tubbs' friends still on active service to be mustered out after the end of the war, changed his career several times. The 103rd New York was not disbanded until December 7, 1865.[40] Kimball returned home to Osceola, laboring on his father's farm for three years before settling in town and working as a wagon-maker. In the meantime, he married Mary Cameron in October 1866. The couple had three children; one, a son, Ernest, bore the middle name Harlan in memory of Orville's younger brother who died of chronic diarrhea and malaria during the war.[41]

While living in Osceola, Kimball joined the town's Cornet Band and, early in 1876, the local post of the Grand Army of the Republic, the same veterans' post that his half-brother Leonard Kimball and William Humphrey were members of.[42] Orville served as its commander for three years.[43]

Kimball returned to the farm in 1880 to take care of his father when the old man took ill. He was elected to a five-term term as justice of the peace in Osceola that year and reelected in 1885. He also served as one of the town's school directors.

Kimball, who began sporting a walrus moustache, remained on the farm until his father died in 1893. He then moved to nearby West-field, where he became involved in the weekly *Free Press* and worked as a photographer. He was elected justice of the peace there, too, in 1902 and was reelected in 1907.[44]

The reason for Kimball's change in career can be traced to 1890, when he was forty-seven years old. Orville claimed then that he could no longer do any manual labor because of "a creek in the back" that made him lame, at times even prostrating him so that he was "entirely helpless and unable to feed himself." He could not, he stated in applying for an invalid's pension, follow his "usual occupation (that of a farmer)." He was awarded a pension of $6 a month and sought an increase in that amount after the turn of the century, saying he had become further disabled by varicose veins in his left leg and deafness in his left ear. A physician recommended that he warranted a pension of $10 a month. By the 1920s, Kimball's condition had deteriorated so much that another doctor certified that Kimball had trouble in maintaining his equilibrium, often fell and had to be helped to his feet, and needed assistance to dress. He attempted to walk with a cane but, seized with vertigo, would fall nonetheless. At the same time, his weight—which he gave as 201 pounds in 1904—fell to 174 pounds by 1923.

Despite his hobbling condition, Kimball lived until he was eighty-two years old, dying on February 25, 1925. He was buried in Fairview Cemetery, Osceola.[45]

The last of Charles Tubbs' letter-writing friends to die, Mordecai Casson, suffered constantly from rheumatism and fell ill with an incredible number of ailments and injuries, yet he lived until 1926.

Casson was mustered out with New York's 2nd Veteran Cavalry at Talledega, Alabama, in the fall of 1865. He returned to upstate New York to work as a farmer. Until he retired in 1908, Casson lived in Tuscarora; after that, in Addison. He and his wife, Helen, whom he married in 1883, had two sons. Sometime after the birth of the second child, Helen died.

In the mid-1870s, a decade after the Civil War ended, Casson began to complain not only of rheumatism but of asthma as well. Later, he severely injured his left knee while removing a stump fence, and by March 1923 he was suffering from high blood pressure and kidney

Charles Tubbs, in later life.
Courtesy of Tioga County Historical Society, Wellsboro, Pennsylvania.

trouble. He required a practical nurse to help him get around but eventually, with the aid of a cane, managed to walk short distances. Casson was then awarded a government pension of $23 a month. The following year, he broke his hip in a railroad accident. The injury left him entirely helpless. He applied for a pension increase, claiming also the debilitating effects of hardening of the arteries and disability due to old age. Casson received $72 a month until his death a few days before Christmas 1926 at the age of eighty-seven.[46]

Charles Tubbs' friends who had encouraged him to finish his studies during the war rather than serve in the army would have considered themselves justified by his life and career in the half century after the conflict ended. He maintained an active, even passionate interest and involvement in politics and government, serving his community and state in many appointed and elected offices.[47]

Tubbs earned a law degree from Michigan University in 1867, but he did not seek admittance to the bar in the county seat of Wellsboro until 1882. He waited eleven more years before seeking to practice in federal courts and until 1903 before he sought admittance to the Supe-

rior Court of Pennsylvania at Harrisburg. Instead, he took an active
role in Republican politics in the county and the state.

Almost immediately after graduating from Michigan, Tubbs was
appointed transcribing clerk of the Pennsylvania House of Representatives, serving in the years 1869 and 1870. He was himself a member of
the House, representing Tioga County, from 1881 to 1885, and served
on committees dealing with the judiciary and judicial appointments,
local elections, and federal relations. He voted consistently in favor of
the rights of labor and the interests of education, and just as consistently against schemes devised by oil, telegraph, and railroad monopo-
lies.[48]

In addition, Tubbs presided at Republican county conventions in
1876 and 1878 and represented Tioga County at state conventions in
1879, 1883, and 1891. He was a candidate for the U.S. Senate before a
joint session of the state legislature in 1899; he received 52 votes, but
the lawmakers failed to chose a senator. Tubbs subsequently cam-
paigned for the post in 1901 but lost. Five years later, Tubbs was nominated for Congress but for some reason he withdrew his name before
the election. In the following year, 1907, he was appointed by Pennsylvania's governor to the Commission on Public Records. Moreover,
Tubbs was a director of the Wellsboro National Bank, president of the
Cowanesque Valley Agricultural Society, and Osceola's solicitor until
his death.

It was Orrin Stebbins who, shortly before his death in battle, attributed to Charles Tubbs the sobriquet "historian."[49] All his long and
varied life, Tubbs remained interested in—and active in preserving—
the history of Osceola and Tioga County. He was a founding member
and first president of the Tioga County Historical Society as well as a
member of other historical societies in the state.

Tubbs' library included some seven thousand books, and he himself wrote extensively on local history and took part in many community celebrations. He and William Humphrey both spoke at a dinner
commemorating the completion of the Keystone Telegraph linking Osceola to the outside world in 1878.

In 1884, the local post of the Grand Army of the Republic asked
Tubbs to deliver an address to veterans of the Civil War at its annual
Memorial Day celebration. Pleased by the presentation, the post afterwards sought Tubbs' permission to publish his speech. Tubbs agreed,
but believing it necessary now to make it a complete history of Osceola's contribution to the war effort, he traveled extensively to inter-
view surviving veterans, exchanged correspondence with others, and
added to his manuscript excerpts from some of the letters he had re-

Charles Tubbs, standing in front of the Tubbs home in Osceola,
Pennsylvania, on a fall day many years after the Civil War.
Courtesy of Tioga County Historical Society, Wellsboro, Pennsylvania.

ceived during the war—after editing them for spelling and grammar.
The result was the 52-page *Osceola in the War of the Rebellion*, which was
published in 1885.[50]

Tubbs married Sylvina Bacon in the fall of 1879. The couple had
one son, Warren, born in 1882. Charles Tubbs inherited the Tubbs
homestead and farm upon the death of his father in 1900. He continued to supervise the farm—it covered some five hundred acres—until
his own death.

When in his early sixties, Tubbs toured the British Isles and Europe with his family, and in 1905 he took an extended trip to the Rocky
Mountains and Pacific Coast country.

Tubbs' younger brother Henry—who was also a friend of a number of Charles' correspondents in the Civil War—died in March 1912 at
the age of sixty-seven and was buried in Fairview Cemetery, Osceola.

Charles died in Buffalo on January 25 of the following year. He
was sixty-nine years old. He was also laid to rest in Fairview Cemetery.[51]

Charles Tubbs, sometime before his death
at the age of sixty-nine in 1913.
Courtesy of Tioga County Historical Society, Wellsboro, Pennsylvania.

In an "Appreciation" published in the *Tioga County Agitator*, a friend wrote in part:

In public life no one thought of questioning his fidelity to any trust. He had no groveling ambition in politics, but measured all questions by high ideals, and put the public interest above all other interests . . .

He was a scholar, happy in the acquisition of knowledge . . .

In all his civic and social relations he bore the high mark of excellence and attracted and maintained close friendships.[52]

Appendixes
Notes
Bibliography
Index

The Letters

Please excuse this ill Composed letter an Poor writing
for I have no place to Write on.
—William Self[1]

The letters quoted in this book are part of a privately held collection, an album entitled "One Hundred & Sixty-Seven Letters From the Boys 1861–5." Actually, the collection contains 177 letters and a poem (see Appendix B). With the exception of one letter, all the letters were written by the seventeen friends of Charles Tubbs identified in the book. The exception is an almost illiterate scrawl by an anonymous author who facetiously signed it Winfield Scott, the septuagenarian who was General-in-Chief when the Civil War started; the handwriting does not match the penmanship of any of the other letter writers.

The stationery the seventeen soldiers used varied, depending on what they could purchase from a sutler or what they could scrounge. "I will trust you will excuse this writing material," wrote one soldier from Harpers Ferry, whose penciling was smudged. "The paper is a blank leaf out of a Secesh account book and I have no ink here."[2] Writing after the Battle of Cold Harbor, another soldier apologized for writing "on Such a dirty Sheet and with a lead pencil." He explained that "I would not have had This had I not got it from a Reb the other day. They charged on our Division and got drove[.]"[3]

Besides the accountant's ledger and soiled paper, the stationery the soldiers employed ranged from ruled five-by-eight-inch paper to eight-by-twelve-inch foolscap. Sometimes the paper was blue. A few sheets bear patriotic motifs—generals' portraits, flags, shields, and military scenes—that were often printed in red and blue against a white background. Such themes appear more frequently on the envelopes in which the soldiers enclosed their letters, many of which Tubbs also saved. More often than not, the letter writer used every bit of space a sheet of paper provided, finishing sentences up the margin of the page, writing above a dateline, and, in more than one case, writing perpendicularly directly over what he had already penned.

Photographs and ambrotypes accompany the letters of ten of the correspondents: some depict the men in uniform; in others they are in civilian garb.

One Hundred & Sixty-seven
Letters
From the Boys.
1861-5.

The title page of the album containing the collection of letters.

Tubbs sent photographs of himself to many of them and evidently requested those of the soldiers that appear in the album.

Except for a few, all the letters were expressly written to Tubbs. Those not addressed to him, six in all, were addressed to his younger brother, Henry, but retained by Charles. Six others were addressed to members of the Orophilian Lyceum at Alfred University. It is obvious that the latter, also six in number, were meant to be read by Charles to his fellow society members at Alfred.

It is similarly clear from the letters that were written to him that Charles Tubbs' taste in friends was eclectic and democratic. Semiliterate farm boys as well as college students or fellow budding teachers wrote him. At the start of the war, the youngest was seventeen years old, the oldest thirty-six; five of them were married. The letters writers addressed Tubbs in a variety of ways, most often as "Dear Chum," "Dear Friend," or "Friend Tubbs." An exception was a young farmer who initially began his correspondence "Dear sir." However they addressed him, Tubbs remained a vital link to the world they had left.

All the letters were once glued inside an old, decaying picture album. Its current owner, Peter C. Andrews, had them rebound on special acid-free paper inside a single, carefully bound album. Mr. Andrews, grandson of one of the letter writers, John Tuttle Andrews, is, however, unaware of how his family came into possession of the album. Charles Tubbs evidently still had them in his possession in 1884, when he quoted, after extensively editing, several of the letters in a Memorial Day address he delivered about Osceola's contribution in the Civil War.

The collection indicates a prolific correspondence between Tubbs and the soldiers; other letters are referred to and some missives between them were lost in the mail or perhaps even discarded. Not one letter of the many that Tubbs wrote back to the soldiers survives, though one can surmise a little of what they contained because a soldier friend would write, "You wanted to know about . . . " or "I agree with you that . . ."

The actual number of letters written by the individual correspondents is as follows. In parenthesis, when incorrect, is the number that Tubbs indicated in the album that each wrote:

John T. Andrews, 3; David Armstrong, 19 (17); Mordecai Casson, 4; William T. Humphrey, 2 (1); Harlan Kimball, 4 (1); Leonard L. Kimball, 4 and a poem (4); Orville S. Kimball 20 (15); Henry R. Maxson, 5; John Orr, 13; William R. Prentice, 19 (18); George Scudder 19 (21); William Self, 28; Asa Spencer, 9; Orrin M. Stebbins, 14 (including remarks he wrote in joint letter with Allen A. Van Orsdale); Samuel Stevens, 2; Allen A. Van Orsdale, 3; Philip T. Vanzile, 8; anonymous, 1.

A Poem

*To you Charles[,] one of the few men among all my
early companions in whom I have learned to place implicit trust[,] whose friendship I have proved and
whom I highly esteem for mental worth, this is most
humbly inscribed*

—Leonard L. Kimball[1]

Lines

Swiftly, Charles, the days are passing.
Days of boyhood, yon peace and glee[,]
Hopes and dreams, too[,] are they massing
No swifter than the days they flee
Like ripples down the restless river
In sunlight glisten, gone forever.

Oft in sadness now I ponder
Our school day scenes so blithe and gay
Follow where we used to wander
In boisterous, artless, childish play
Beneath the beach [sic] and basswood shadow
Up in that pasture, and the meadow.

Rank the thistle, and the elder;
Are growing where the school house stood,
Where with rules that sore bewilder
We pondered over the tense, and mood
While all that now remains a token
Is that old Dear stone, rudely broken[.]

Yes, the stone that used to patter,
With bare feet when our sports forsook,
Loud we heard the teacher clatter
Upon the window with a book,

Oh how the arms and limbs went flapping[.]
We ran and cried "the school marm's rapping."

Scattered like our dreams, some sleeping
Those early playmates, (laughing train)
Memory, though in her keeping
Can never give them back again,
Can not restore to me that Brother,
Nor fill the void, can any other.

Little knew we then the anguish
So soon to shroud our smiling Land
Little thought those friends must languish
Beneath grim war's red dripping hand
Their blood be poured, Oh such libation,
A willing ransom for the nation.

Days though gone, and youth's dream scattered
Yet Charles one jewel from the wreck
Comes through time, undim[m]ed, unscattered
No years com[r]ades, no change can speak
Tis Friendship tried and proved: Outlasting
The Heart of flesh, which death is wasting[.]

Like the one in furnice [sic] lighted,
Tis tried by passion[']s melting flame
Burnt the dross, the gold as united
And hardened in a brighter gleam
A ray amidst life's wildering mazes,
The desert[']s fountain, life's oasis.

Notes

*I cherish your friendship deeply because I know you
are <u>noble</u> & true. It would do me good to clasp your
hand again[.] I think I should recognize you by your
gripe [sic] even in the dark.*

—*John Orr*[1]

The following abbreviations are used on second reference in the footnotes:

AU	Herrick Memorial Library, Special Collections, Alfred University, Alfred, N.Y.
Album	Album of letters and photographs, the basis for this book, in the possession of Peter C. Andrews, Washington, D.C.
Bates	Samuel P. Bates. *History of Pennsylvania Volunteers, 1861–5.* Wilmington, N.C.: Broadfoot Publishing, 1993–94.
Brown	*History of Tioga County, Pennsylvania.* Vols. 1–2. N.p.: R. C. Brown, 1897.
C.T.	Charles Tubbs
Munsell	*History of Tioga County[,] Pennsylvania.* New York: W. W. Munsell, 1883.
NA, RG94	National Archives, Record Group 94: Records of Volunteer Union Soldiers Who Served during the Civil War.
NYAG	New York State Adjutant General's Office. *Registers of New York Regiments in the War of the Rebellion.* Albany: Wynkoop, Hallenbeck, Crawford; J.B. Lyon; Oliver A. Qualyle, 1896–1904.
NYSA	War Service Records, New York State Archives.
OR	*War of the Rebellion: A Compilation of the Official Records of the Union and Confederate Armies.* Washington, D.C.: U.S. Government Printing Office, 1880–1901.
Sypher	J. R. Sypher. *History of the Pennsylvania Reserve Corps.* Lancaster, Pa.: Elias Barr, 1865.
TCHS	Tioga County Historical Society, Wellsboro, Pa.
Tubbs	Charles Tubbs. *Osceola in the War of the Rebellion.* Wellsboro, Pa.: Agitator Book and Job Print, 1885.
UC	Schaffer Library, Union College, Schenectady, N.Y.

Epigraph

1. Excerpt from "Lines," a poem written by Leonard Leverne Kimball that appears in the album of letters and photographs in the possession of Peter C. Andrews, Washington, D.C. For the full text of the poem, see Appendix B.

Introduction

1. The background for Charles Tubbs and the Tubbs family is an amalgam of several sources, including: John W. Jordan, ed., *Genealogical and Personal History of Northern Pennsylvania* (New York: Lewis Historical Publishing Company, 1913), 2: 670–73, and 3: 1162–64; *History of Tioga County[,] Pennsylvania* (New York: W. W. Munsell, 1883), 340–64; Decennial Register, Officers and Alumni, 1836–1886, Herrick Memorial Library, Special Collections, Alfred University, Alfred, N.Y.; Bill Book, 1864, Alumni File, Schaffer Library, Union College, Schenectady, N.Y.; photocopy of Charles Tubbs obituaries, personal files, Tioga County Historical Society, Wellsboro, Pa. Originally, the Tubbs family was from New England. Charles could trace his family to Litchfield County, Connecticut, where his paternal ancestor, Samuel Tubbs, first settled in 1663. In 1762, his great-grandfather, also named Samuel, moved to Wyoming Valley in what is now northeastern Pennsylvania but which, at the time, was part of Connecticut. This Samuel Tubbs served during the entire Revolutionary War, taking part in the Battle of Brandywine, surviving the winter of 1777–78 at Valley Forge, and leading a command that was, unfortunately, days short of reaching the Wyoming settlement before Loyalists and Indians attacked its inhabitants, massacring many of them, including his father-in-law. His own aged father, Lebbeus Tubbs, one of the old men who defended the Wyoming settlement, escaped unharmed, but after the war the family was dispossessed, losing its property, along with other Connecticut settlers, in a bitter boundary dispute that pitted Connecticut against Pennsylvania. Samuel moved farther west, to Elkland in the Cowanesque Valley in Pennsylvania abutting the New York State border. One of his sons purchased a farm in a section of Elkland that would one day form the village of Osceola, and he was followed by a brother and his son. Soon, sons, grandsons, uncles, and cousins were playing a prominent role in the development of the community. A descendant of Samuel's was among four men from Osceola who volunteered to serve after the British burned Buffalo during the War of 1812, but he never saw action because the British withdrew. Later, in 1848, a James Tubbs commanded a company of Pennsylvania militia that included four other Tubbs family members. It was a Robert Tubbs who established a brickyard in Osceola in 1827, then lime and tar kilns and, in 1839, a potash works. He and his sons were the principal lumbermen for many years. Another family member, Benson Tubbs, opened the first general store in 1836, and still another, Hoyt Tubbs, was co-founder of a tannery. Robert Tubbs was county treasurer in 1820 and sheriff in 1827. Two of the early directors of the school built in 1845 were Tubbs men, and the year before the Civil War began a John Tubbs was one of the town supervisors.

2. *Tioga County Agitator*, Apr. 24, 1861.

3. John Nelson Norwood, *Fiat Lux: The Story of Alfred University* (Alfred, N.Y.: Alfred University, 1957), 2.

4. 1836–1876 catalogue, 79, General Catalogues, 1836–1900, AU.

5. John T. Andrews to Charles Tubbs, Oct. 15, 1864, Album.

6. Leonard Kimball to C.T., June 30, 1861, Album.

7. Orrin M. Stebbins to C.T., Apr. 17, 1861, Album.

8. Stebbins to C.T., May 17, 1861, Album.

9. Stebbins to C.T., Sept. 15, 1861, Album.

10. David Armstrong to C.T., May 18, 1862, Album. Armstrong said that he had not "tasted of any birch bark Since and I have not seen any Since[.]"

11. Armstrong to C.T., Mar. 3, 1862, Album.

12. William R. Prentice to C.T., undated, Album. This letter appears in the album between letters written Dec. 12, 1863 and a brief, also undated letter that is probably a continuation of it. The next dated letter in the album is dated Jan. 27, 1864.

13. Prentice to C.T., Jan. 6, 1865, Album.
14. Prentice to C.T., Oct. 15, 1864, Album.
15. John Orr to C.T., Aug. 23, 1863, Album.
16. Orr to C.T., Feb. 16, 1864, Album.
17. Orville S. Kimball to C.T., Nov. 25, 1864, Album.
18. Prentice to C.T., Jan. 27, 1864, Album.
19. Orville Kimball to C.T., Apr. 18, 1863, Album.
20. Asa Spencer to C.T., Nov. 14, 1862, Album.
21. Prentice to C.T., Jan. 27, 1864, Album.
22. Spencer to C.T., Nov. 14, 1862, Album.

Prologue

1. Prentice to C.T., Dec. 12, 1863, Album.
2. Allen A. Van Orsdale to C.T., Sept. 15, 1861, Album.
3. Andrews to C.T., Nov. 9, 1864, Album.
4. Orr to C.T., May 22, 1863, Album.
5. Orr to C.T., May 13, 1863, Album.
6. Henry Maxson to C.T., Mar. 6, 1862, Album.
7. Stebbins to C.T., June 5, 1861, Album.

1. The Call to Arms

1. William T. Humphrey to C.T., July 12, 1862, Album.
2. Philip T. Vanzile to C.T., May 16, 1865, Album.
3. Charles Tubbs, *Osceola in the War of the Rebellion* (Wellsboro, Pa.: Agitator Book and Job Print, 1885), 8–9.
4. Munsell, 358. The postman was Edward Wescott, who served the town from 1848 to 1874.
5. Ibid., 352.
6. Tubbs, 9–10.
7. Humphrey's background is an amalgam of Munsell, 362; Tubbs, 10–12, 23, 50; *History of Tioga County, Pennsylvania* (N.p.: R. C. Brown, 1897), 1: 391; Personal File and Cemetery Records, Fairview Cemetery, Cowanesque Valley, TCHS; Pension File, National Archives, Record Group 94: Records of Volunteer Union Soldiers Who Served during the Civil War; War Service Records, New York State Archives.
8. Samuel Stevens addressed C.T. as "Cosin Charles" in a letter to him on Nov. 3, 1861, Album.
9. Stevens' background and description is an amalgam of Tubbs, 10–12; Samuel P. Bates, *History of Pennsylvania Volunteers, 1861–5* (Wilmington, N.C.: Broadfoot Publishing, 1993–94), 2: 925; J. R. Sypher, *History of the Pennsylvania Reserve Corps* (Lancaster, Pa.: Elias Barr, 1865), 711; Muster Rolls, NA, RG94. According to a pension form, NYSA, Stevens' wife's name was Mary; interestingly, he never mentions her in his letters to Tubbs.
10. Certificate of Disability for Discharge, Jan. 19, 1863, NA, RG94.
11. William Self to C.T., Jan. 18, 1862, Album.
12. Tubbs, 10, 12, 15. Self's wife's maiden name was Julia Campbell, pension application, Jan. 20, 1881, NA, RG94. He comments about saving his pay in a letter to C.T., Feb. 11, 1862, and speaks of himself as "Tough as a bear," Apr. 25, 1862. Both, Album.
13. Stebbins to Tubbs, June 5, 1861, Album.

14. Ibid., Van Orsdale. Van Orsdale and Stebbins penned separate sections of this letter to Tubbs.

15. Richard E. Matthews, *The 149th Pennsylvania Volunteer Infantry Unit in the Civil War* (Jefferson, N.C.: McFarland, 1994), 17–20.

16. Brown, 219. The officer was Gen. Robert C. Cox.

17. Self to C.T., undated, Album. The letter, the first one of his letters in the album, was obviously written sometime in late May, about six weeks after he reached Camp Curtin. Self's next letter is dated Aug. 16, 1861.

18. Tubbs, 9–11.

19. Leonard Kimball's background is an amalgam of Brown, 2: 811–12; Tubbs, 26, 46–47; NYSA; and L. N. Chapin, *A Brief History of the Thirty-Fourth Regiment N.Y.S.V.* (n.p., n.d.), 134. Chapin's book, apparently published in 1902, says Leonard has "since died," but Cemetery Records, Fairview Cemetery, Cowanesque Valley, TCHS, give the year of his death as 1914. Some references to Kimball give his first name as Leverne, but his gravestone reads Leonard L. Kimball.

20. Clark Kimball identifies Leonard as a law student, pension application affidavit, Apr. 7, 1869, NA, RG94. A pension certificate from the War Department in the same file gives his age on enlistment as twenty-one, which is incorrect.

21. Leonard Kimball to C.T., June 6, 1861, Album.

22. Ibid.

23. Leonard Kimball to C.T., June 30, 1861, Album.

24. Stebbins' background and description is an amalgam of William H. Tuttle, *Names and Sketches of the Pioneer Settlers of Madison County[,] N.Y.* (Interlaken, N.Y.: Heart of the Lakes Publishing, 1984), ix; Decennial Register, AU; Tioga County, Pennsylvania Records, vol. 9 (1828–1878), 57; Brown, 418; and the *Tioga County Agitator*, Sept. 10, 1862, which carried his obituary on its front page. The business card is mounted along with Stebbins' letters, Album. Stebbins and Tubbs taught at Union Academy in 1859 and 1860.

25. Stebbins to C.T., Apr. 17, 1861, Album.

26. Stebbins to C.T., May 17, 1861, Album.

27. Ibid.

28. Stebbins to C.T., Sept. 15, 1861, Album.

29. Stebbins to C.T., Mar. 28, 1862, Album.

30. Ibid.

31. Company Muster Roll, NA, RG94.

32. Pension application, NA, RG94.

33. Van Orsdale's background and description is an amalgam of Bates, 2: 924 (where his name is given as A. V. Vanarsale); Sypher, 711; Decennial Register, AU; and *War of the Rebellion: A Compilation of the Official Records of the Union and Confederate Armies* (Washington: U.S. Government Printing Office, 1890), series 3, vol. 5, 896. Van Orsdale's remark about the "purs[u]its of science and peace" is from a letter to C.T., Sept. 15, 1861, Album.

34. Van Orsdale to C.T., Aug. 15, 1861, Album.

35. Ambrose Bierce, *An Occurrence at Owl Creek Bridge and Other Stories* (London: Penguin, n.d.), "One of the Missing," 59.

36. Van Orsdale to C.T., Aug. 15, 1861, Album.

37. Stebbins to C.T., April 17, 1861, Album.

38. Stebbins to C.T., Aug. 14, 1861, Album.

39. *Tioga County Agitator*, Feb. 5, 1862.

40. *Tioga County Agitator*, Apr. 2, 1862.

41. *Tioga County Agitator*, Apr. 30, 1862.

42. Ibid.

43. Van Orsdale to C.T., Aug. 15, 1861, Album.
44. *Tioga County Agitator*, July 10, 1861. This first column of Stebbins' appeared under the initials O.M.S. Subsequent columns were signed with variations of "Colonel Crocket" such as "Col. Crocket," and simply "Crocket" or "Crockett."

2. First Blood

1. Self to C.T., Oct. 9, 1863, Album.
2. Stebbins to C.T., July 1, 1861, Album.
3. Ibid.
4. *Tioga County Agitator*, July 24, 1861.
5. *Tioga County Agitator*, July 31, 1861.
6. George Scudder to C.T., Dec. 24, 1861, Album. Scudder found the people of Maryland "very enthusiastic but more so in the Country than City."
7. Robert D. Hoffsommer, "The Pennsylvania Bucktails," *Civil War Times Illustrated* 4 (Jan. 1966): 18.
8. Stebbins to C.T., Aug. 14, 1861, Album.
9. Van Orsdale to C.T., Aug. 15, 1861, Album.
10. Stebbins' description of Manassas is an amalgam of two articles he wrote for the *Tioga County Agitator*, Apr. 23 and 30, 1862.
11. *Tioga County Agitator*, Aug. 7, 1861.
12. Self to C.T., Aug. 16, 1861, Album.
13. *Tioga County Agitator*, Aug. 21, 1861.
14. *Tioga County Agitator*, Oct. 6, 1861.
15. *Tioga County Agitator*, Sept. 11, 1861.
16. Van Orsdale to C.T., Sept. 15, 1861, Album.
17. *Tioga County Agitator*, Sept. 18, 1861.
18. *Tioga County Agitator*, Sept. 25, 1861.
19. John P. Bard, "42d Regiment Infantry (Thirteenth Reserves, First Rifles)," *Pennsylvania at Gettysburg: Ceremonies at the Dedication of the Monuments* (Harrisburg: Harrisburg, Publishing, 1906), 307.
20. *Tioga County Agitator*, Dec. 4, 1861.
21. Self to C.T., Dec. 22, 1861, Album.
22. Self to C.T., undated, Album. This letter follows that of Dec. 22, 1861, in the album. Self's next dated letter is that of May 25, 1862.
23. *Tioga County Agitator*, Jan. 8, 1862.
24. Stevens to C.T., Nov. 3, 1861, Album.
25. *Tioga County Agitator*, Jan. 8, 1862.

3. Rumors and Recruits

1. *Tioga County Agitator*, Jan. 8, 1862.
2. *Tioga County Agitator*, Nov. 13, 1861.
3. Stebbins to C.T., Nov. 6, 1861, Album.
4. Orville Kimball to C.T., Apr. 7, 1862, Album.
5. Scudder to C.T., Dec. 24, 1861, Album.
6. Carl Sandburg, *Abraham Lincoln* (New York: Harcourt, Brace, 1939), 1: 61, and 2: 199.
7. Stebbins to C.T., Mar. 6, 1862, Album.
8. Scudder's background and description is an amalgam of Brown, 2: 1136; Com-

pany Muster Rolls and furlough applications, NA, RG94; and OR, series 1, vol. 36, part 1, 183.

9. Scudder to C.T., May 7, 1861, Album.

10. Scudder to Lt. Col. Nicholas Bowen, Apr. 1863, Camp Dick Robinson, Kentucky, NA, RG94. No specific day in April is given.

11. Scudder to C.T., Oct. 15, 1861, Album.

12. Scudder to C.T., Feb. 17, 1862, Album.

13. Scudder to C.T., Dec. 24, 1861, Album.

14. Scudder to C.T., Jan. 22, 1863, Album.

15. Armstrong's background and description is an amalgam of pension file, NA, RG94, and *Official Roster of the Soldiers of the State of Ohio in the War of the Rebellion, 1861–1866* (Cincinnati: Ohio Valley Company, 1889), 519. He described his decision to enlist in a letter to C.T., Mar. 7, 1862; his weight, May 17, 1863; and referred to himself as a "poor scholar," Apr. 11, 1863. All, Album.

16. Maxson's background is an amalgam of Norwood, *Fiat Lux*, 18, 22–23, 26–27, 30, 45–47, 57, 92; New York State Adjutant General's Office, *Registers of New York Regiments in the War of the Rebellion* (Albany: Wynkoop, Hallenbeck, Crawford; J. B. Lyon; Oliver A. Qualyle, 1896–1904), 30: 1059; NYAS, and Decennial Register and Organizations File, AU. He referred to Tubbs as his "Livy . . . classmate" in a letter to C.T., Feb. 20, 1862; and worried about his health and vocation, Apr. 15, 1862. Both, Album. One Maxson with the 85th New York was captured during the war and died in the notorious Confederate prison camp at Andersonville, Georgia.

17. *Tioga County Agitator*, Jan. 8, 1862.

18. *Tioga County Agitator*, Dec. 29, 1861. The New York regiments were the 33rd and the 49th.

19. *Tioga County Agitator*, Dec. 18, 1861.

20. Mark Mayo Boatner III, *The Civil War Dictionary* (New York: David McKay, 1962), 624.

21. Self to C.T., undated, Album. Written in pencil on top of the first page of the letter, apparently by Tubbs, is "Nov 1861."

4. Casualties

1. Stevens to C.T., Nov. 3, 1861, Album.

2. Orville Kimball to C.T., Aug. 9, 1861, Album. Orville learned of Leonard's enlistment in a letter from a friend long after Leonard was discharged, so it is clear that the two men, and Harlan Page Kimball as well, were not close.

3. Orville Samuel Kimball, *History and Personal Sketches of Company I, 103 N.Y.S.V., 1862–1865* (Elmira, N.Y.: Facts Printing, 1900), 6. Kimball gives the baron's name as Fred W. Van Egloffstein.

4. NYSA gives Orville Kimball's age as twenty-one. However, there are often discrepancies in age in the records of other soldiers, as well.

5. Orville Kimball's background is an amalgam of his own book, *History and Personal Sketches*, 82–84; Tubbs, 26–27, and Brown, 2: 811–12.

6. Three of Harlan Kimball's letters are addressed to Henry Tubbs.

7. Harlan Kimball's background is an amalgam of O. Kimball, *History and Personal Sketches*, 139–40; Tubbs, 26–27, 38; and NYSA.

8. Self to C.T., undated, Album. See chap. 3, n. 21.

9. *Medical and Surgical History of the Civil War* (Wilmington, N.C.: Broadfoot Publishing, 1990, originally published as *Medical and Surgical History of the War of the Rebellion (1861–1865* [Washington: Government Printing Office, 1870–1888]) 1: iii–xii, xliii, and 3:

2. The records of Dr. Humphrey's operations are in 10: 555, 629, 712, 724; 11: 219, 256, 263; and 12: 450, 500 (Page citations are to the 1990 edition).

10. Munsell, 362.

11. Tubbs, 47. Tubbs gives Leonard Kimball's discharge date as March 1862. According to Chapin, 134, and NYAG, 22: 1010, the date was Feb. 11, 1862. But note that Kimball's last letter to C.T., from Harpers Ferry, is dated Feb. 28, 1862, and he does not mention in it that he has left or is leaving the army.

12. Leonard Kimball to C.T., Feb. 28, 1862, Album.

13. Pension affidavit by Capt. Henry Baldwin, Mar. 15, 1869, and Certificate of Disability for Discharge, Apr. 21, 1862, NA, RG94.

14. Stebbins to C.T., Nov. 6, 1861, Album.

15. Stebbins to C.T., Mar. 6, 1862, Album.

16. Stebbins to C.T., Sept. 15, 1861, Album.

17. Stebbins to C.T., Nov. 6, 1861, Album.

18. Stebbins to C.T., Mar. 27, 1862, Album.

19. *Tioga County Agitator,* May 14, 1862.

20. Certificate of Disability for Discharge, NA, RG94, gives Stevens' discharge date as Jan. 19, 1863. In the album, preceding the letters Stevens wrote, Tubbs noted that he had "died of disease contracted in the Army July 1862."

21. Orr's background is an amalgam of NYAG, 34: 119; Decennial Register, AU; and NYAS. Orr spoke of the botched vaccination in letters to C.T., May 22 and June 3, 1863, Album. Pension application, Mar. 23, 1914, gives the date of his marriage and name of his wife, Melissa. Her last name is given as both Kinne and Kinney. His remarks about her are from a letter to C.T., Feb. 16, 1864; his comment about being "fleshiest," Aug. 23, 1863; and that of being "the happiest of men," Dec. 4, 1863. All, Album.

22. Prentice's background is an amalgam of Chapin, 22; Decennial Register and University Commencements, AU; NYSAG, 40: 856; NYAS; Personal Files, TCHS; and pension application, June 5, 1906, NA, RG94.

23. Spencer's background is an amalgam of Tubbs, 21 (and footnote); Decennial Register, AU; and pension affidavit, Apr. 20, 1892, NA, RG94. The affidavit says Spencer and Betsey Wright were married Sept. 10, 1859. His reluctance to tell his wife about his illness is in a letter to C.T., Oct. 18, 1862; his friendship with Prentice, Jan. 1, 1863. Both, Album.

24. Spencer to C.T., Jan. 1, 1863. The letter is actually dated "First 1863." He had just received a letter from Tubbs, he stated, "written in 1862 and recd in 1863[.]"

5. Friends and Enemies

1. Prentice to C.T., Mar. 10, 1864, Album.
2. *Medical and Surgical History,* 1: iv.
3. Scudder to C.T., Jan. 23, 1863, Album.
4. Orville Kimball to C.T., Aug. 13, 1862, Album.
5. Orville Kimball to C.T., Jan. 30, 1864, Album.
6. Orville Kimball to C.T., Feb. 29, 1864, Album.
7. Stebbins to C.T., Mar. 6, 1862, Album.
8. Stebbins to C.T., Nov. 6, 1861, Album.
9. Stebbins to C.T., Sept. 15, 1861, Album.
10. Armstrong to C.T., Mar. 11, 1863, Album.
11. Armstrong to C.T., Mar. 27, 1864, Album.
12. Armstrong to C.T., July 14, 1864, Album.
13. Scudder to C.T., Mar. 1, 1862, Album.

14. Self to C.T., Feb. 11, 1862, Album.
15. Armstrong to C.T., July 14, 1864, Album.
16. *Tioga County Agitator*, Feb. 12, 1862.
17. Prentice to C.T., Oct. 16, 1862, Album.
18. Scudder to C.T., Jan. 22, 1863, Album.
19. Self to C.T., Dec. 25, 1862, Album. The battle was that of Fredericksburg.
20. Self to C.T., July 9, 1864, Album.
21. Scudder to C.T., Jan. 22, 1863, Album.

6. Generals

1. Van Orsdale to C.T., Mar. 30, 1862, Album.
2. Scudder to C.T., Sept. 20, 1862, Album.
3. Orr to C.T., Sept. 29, 1862, Album. The letter was written from Harpers Ferry after the battle.
4. Self to C.T., Dec. 1, 1862, Album.
5. Stebbins to C.T., Mar. 6, 1862, Album.
6. Stebbins to C.T., Mar. 28, 1862, Album.
7. Orville Kimball to C.T., Aug. 9, 1862, Album.
8. Armstrong to C.T., Jan. 14, 1863, Album.
9. Self to C.T., Nov. 19, 1863, Album.
10. Scudder to C.T., Mar. 3, 1863, Album.
11. Self to C.T., Mar. 9, 1863, Album.
12. Self to C.T., Jan. 23, 1863, Album.
13. Self to C.T., Oct. 26, 1862, Album.
14. Scudder to C.T., Sept. 20, 1862, Album.
15. Armstrong to C.T., Nov. 30, 1862, Album.
16. Self to C.T., Dec. 1, 1862, Album.
17. Self to C.T., Jan. 20, 1863, Album.
18. Self to C.T., Apr. 18, 1863, Album.
19. Scudder to C.T., Dec. 24, 1861, Album.
20. Armstrong to C.T., Nov. 30, 1862, Album.
21. Armstrong to C.T., May 17, 1863, Album.
22. Self to C.T., Mar. 31, 1862, Album.

7. On the Offensive at Last

1. Armstrong to C.T., May 18, 1862, Album.
2. Self to C.T., Feb. 11, 1862, Album.
3. Armstrong to C.T., Mar. 7, 1862, Album.
4. Armstrong to C.T., Apr. 17, 1862, Album.
5. Armstrong to C.T., May 18, 1862, Album.
6. Maxson to C.T., May 12, 1862, Album.
7. Maxson to "Brother Oro's and sister Athenaeums," undated, Album. This letter was obviously written during the Peninsular Campaign in the latter part of May and before the Seven Days' Battles that started on June 25. It follows a letter of May 12, 1863, and is the fifth and last of Maxson's letters in the album.

8. "The South"

1. Orr to C.T., Nov. 9, 1863, Album.
2. *Tioga County Agitator*, Apr. 30, 1862.

3. *Tioga County Agitator*, June 11, 1862.
4. *Tioga County Agitator*, June 4, 1862.
5. Spencer to C.T., Oct. 5, 1862, Album.
6. Orr to C.T., June 3, 1863, Album.
7. Orr's description of Tennesseeans is an amalgam of two letters to C.T., Oct. 22 and Nov. 9, 1863, Album.
8. Orr to C.T., Feb. 16, 1864, Album.
9. The description of New Berne is an amalgam of two letters from Orville Kimball to C.T., Apr. 7 and May 9, 1862. Both, Album.
10. Except for Harlan Kimball's remarks about the sentry pacing on duty, his description of Cape Hatteras that follows is an amalgam of two letters, that of June 4, 1862 to Henry Tubbs and that of June 9, 1862 to C.T. Both, Album.
11. Orville Kimball's description of Cape Hatteras is an amalgam of two letters to C.T., June 1 and 10, 1862. Both, Album.
12. Harlan Kimball to Henry Tubbs, Apr. 6, 1862, Album.
13. Orville Kimball to C.T., Aug. 9, 1862, Album.
14. Harlan Kimball to C.T., Aug. 14, 1862, Album.

9. Death in the Afternoon

1. Stebbins to C.T., Jan. 17, 1862, Album.
2. *Tioga County Agitator*, July 16, 1862. This was, the newspaper noted, "Crockett's Last Letter."
3. The account of the battle that follows is an amalgam of two letters, Self to C.T., July 12 and Sept. 26, 1862, Album.
4. Spencer to C.T., Oct. 18, 1862, Album.
5. The description of the battle in which Stebbins died and those of Stebbins' morbid thoughts in the paragraphs that follow are an amalgam of two letters, Self to C.T., July 12 and Sept. 26, 1862, Album.
6. The letters referred to are Stebbins to C.T., July 1, 1861, and Mar. 6 and 27, 1862. All, Album.
7. *Tioga County Agitator*, June 11, 1862.
8. *Tioga County Agitator*, May 28, 1862.
9. *Tioga County Agitator*, June 25, 1862.
10. Humphrey to C.T., July 12, 1862, Album.
11. Self to C.T., Sept. 26, 1862, Album.
12. Maxson to C.T., Apr. 15, 1862, Album.
13. Pension application, June 4, 1877, NA, RG94.

10. Chance Encounters

1. Scudder to C.T., Jan. 22, 1863, Album.
2. Self to C.T., Sept. 26, 1862, Album.
3. Scudder to C.T., Nov. 1, 1862, Album.
4. Self to C.T., Apr. 18, 1863, Album.
5. Orr to C.T., Sept. 29, 1862, Album.
6. Spencer to C.T., Nov. 14, 1862, Album. The man with Orville Kimball was William Eugene Cilley. Cilley had just turned twenty-one when he was wounded on May 6, 1864, during the campaign in the Wilderness. A fragment of a shell struck him in the head. Cilley was sent to a field hospital that was subsequently captured by the Confederates and died there on May 9, according to Tubbs, 36 (and footnote).

7. Self to C.T., Oct. 25, 1862, Album.
8. Spencer to C.T., Oct. 18, 1862, Album.

11. Ringing Out the Old

1. Armstrong to C.T., Jan. 14, 1863, Album.
2. Self to C.T., Dec. 1, 1862, Album.
3. Self to C.T., Dec. 25, 1862, Album.
4. Ibid.
5. Armstrong to C.T., Nov. 30, 1862, Album.
6. Armstrong to C.T., Jan. 14, 1863, Album.
7. Self to Tubbs, Dec. 25, 1862, Album.

12. Emancipation

1. Armstrong to C.T., Mar. 11, 1863, Album.
2. Munsell, 341.
3. *Tioga County Agitator*, Sept. 4, 1862.
4. Harlan Kimball to C.T., Apr. 6, 1862, Album.
5. Orville Kimball to C.T., Sept. 28, 1865, Album.
6. Scudder to C.T., Feb. 17, 1862, Album.
7. Scudder to C.T., Mar. 1, 1862, Album.
8. Scudder to C.T., Mar. 6, 1862, Album.
9. Orr to C.T., July 18, 1863, Album.
10. Orr to C.T., Aug. 23, 1863, Album.
11. Prentice to C.T., Jan. 16, 1863, Album.
12. Armstrong's feelings about blacks is an amalgam of four letters to C.T., Feb. 3 and 7, Mar. 11, and Apr. 11, 1863. All, Album.
13. Prentice to C.T., Jan. 27, 1864, Album.
14. Prentice to C.T., May 5, 1865, Album.
15. Orville Kimball to C.T., July 15, 1865, Album.
16. Boatner, *Dictionary*, 584.
17. Orr to C.T., Nov. 9, 1863, Album.
18. Orville Kimball to C.T., July 15, 1864, Album.
19. Orville Kimball to C.T., Jan. 1, 1863, Album.
20. Scudder to C.T., May 12, 1862, Album.

13. Tourists and Politicians

1. Spencer to C.T., Feb. 19, 1863, Album.
2. Spencer's remarks about his health problems and his description of Columbian Hospital are an amalgam of two letters to C.T., Nov. 14, 1862, and Jan. 1, 1863. Both, Album.
3. Spencer's description of his visits to Washington and his remarks about the rats are an amalgam of four letters to C.T., Jan. 1, Feb. 19, Mar. 9, and Apr. 2, 1863. All, Album.
4. Orville Kimball to C.T., Sept. 2, 1864, Album.
5. Van Orsdale to C.T., Aug. 15, 1861, Album.
6. Leonard Kimball to C.T., Feb. 28, 1862, Album.

14. Frustrations

1. Prentice to C.T., Jan. 16, 1863, Album.
2. Prentice mentions the pneumonia relapse in a pension application, Mar. 27, 1906, NA, RG94.
3. Prentice to C.T., Jan. 16, 1863, Album.
4. Ibid.
5. Scudder to C.T., Jan. 22, 1863, Album.
6. Scudder's remarks about Burnside, McClellan, Peace Democrats, and Hooker are an amalgam of two letters to C.T., one dated Mar. 3, 1863, the other undated but written after the Battle of Fredericksburg in mid-December 1862. Both, Album. The undated letter, four pages long, is affixed in the album on the same page and behind his fourteenth letter to C.T., also of four pages, which is dated Jan. 22, 1863. However, the January letter ends on the top of page four, leaving adequate room for Scudder to continue if he wished to add to that letter at a later date, as sometimes the letter writers did. That Scudder would start another four pages at the time, or a little later, and include all eight in the same envelope is doubtful.

15. Defeat and Disappointment

1. Armstrong to C.T., Apr. 11, 1863, Album.
2. Orr's remarks after Chancellorsville are an amalgam of three letters to C.T., May 13 and 22, and June 3, 1863. All, Album.
3. Orville Kimball to C.T., Apr. 18, 1863, Album.
4. Armstrong to C.T., Apr. 11, 1863, Album.
5. Armstrong to C.T., May 17, 1863, Album.
6. Whitelaw Reid, *Ohio in the War: Her Statesmen[,] Generals and Soldiers* (Columbus: Eclectic Publishing, 1893), 2: 302–303.

16. Gettysburg: Two Views

1. Self to C.T., Aug. 10, 1863, Album.
2. Tubbs, 24. The regiment was the 35th.
3. John D. Imhof, "Two Roads to Gettysburg: Thomas Leiper Kane and the 13th Pennsylvania Reserves," *Gettysburg*, no. 9 (July 1993): 56.
4. Self to C.T., Aug. 10, 1863, Album.
5. Pension application, Feb. 3, 1883, NA, RG94.
6. Bates, 7: 618.
7. "Bucktail Images: Keystone Riflemen in the Collection of Ronn Palm," *Military Images* 8, no. 6 (May-June 1987): 27.
8. Bates, 2: 612–613.
9. Tubbs, 50–51.
10. Self to C.T., Aug. 10, 1863, Album.
11. Orr to C.T., July 18, 1863, Album.
12. Tubbs, 51.
13. Orr to C.T., July 18, 1863, Album.
14. Boatner, *Dictionary*, 339.
15. Orr to C.T., July 18, 1863, Album.
16. Tubbs, 24.
17. Prentice to C.T., June 18, 1864, Album.
18. Prentice to C.T., July 25, 1864, Album.

17. Raising the Flag in the South

1. Prentice to C.T., Sept. 20, 1863, Album.
2. Prentice to C.T., July 25, 1863, Album.
3. Boatner, *Dictionary*, 833.
4. Prentice to C.T., Sept. 20, 1863, Album.
5. Orville Kimball to C.T., Aug. 24, 1863, Album.
6. Orville Kimball to C.T., Apr. 18, 1863, Album.
7. Orville Kimball to C.T., Aug. 24, 1863, Album.
8. Reid, *Ohio in the War*, 303.
9. O.R., series 1, vol. 31, part 2, 278. The report was written by Maj. Samuel F. Gray.
10. Muster Rolls and Company Descriptive Book, NA, RG94.
11. Casson's background is an amalgam of Decennial Register, AU; NYAG, 7: 285; pension records, NA, RG94; and Hamilton Child, *Gazetteer and Business Directory of Chemung and Schuyler Counties, N.Y., for 1868–9* (Syracuse: *Journal*, 1868), 77.
12. Casson to C.T., Nov. 6, 1863, Album.
13. Casson to C.T., Jan. 11, 1864, Album.

18. On All Fronts

1. Orville Kimball to C.T., Aug. 24, 1863, Album.
2. Self to C.T., Nov. 19, 1863, Album.
3. Orr's comments and the 107th's movements are an amalgam of three letters to C.T., Oct. 22, Nov. 9, and Dec. 4, 1863. All, Album.
4. Brashear is now called Morgan City.
5. Prentice's reactions and the 161st's movements in Louisiana are an amalgam of three letters to C.T., Oct. 25, Nov. 22, and Dec. 12, 1863. All, Album.
6. Armstrong's doings and remarks are an amalgam of two letters to C.T., Dec. 23, 1863, and Jan. 14, 1864. Both, Album.

19. Decision Time

1. Armstrong to C.T., July 14, 1864, Album.
2. Casson to C.T., Jan. 11, 1864, Album.
3. Orville Kimball's remarks about reenlisting are an amalgam of two letters to C.T., Jan. 30 and Apr. 2, 1864. Both, Album.
4. Armstrong to C.T., July 14, 1864, Album.
5. Armstrong's quandary about reenlisting is an amalgam of five letters to C.T., Jan. 14, Feb. 17, Mar. 27, June 8, and July 14, 1864. All, Album.
6. Orr's comments about his wife and reenlisting are an amalgam of two letters to C.T., Feb. 16 and Apr. 5, 1864. Both, Album.
7. Bureau of Pensions form, Mar. 22, 1915, NA, RG94.
8. Scudder's remarks about reenlisting are an amalgam of two letters to C.T., Mar. 13 and Apr. 14, 1864. Both, Album. His service with O. O. Howard's staff and as assistant provost marshal are from Company Muster Rolls, NA, RG94.
9. Muster and Descriptive Roll, NA, RG94.
10. Vanzile's name is often misspelled Van Zile, including in the album itself. His background is an amalgam of Decennial Register and Commencements, AU; Munsell, 348; *Official Roster . . . Ohio*, 10: 392; and Muster Rolls, NA, RG94. He spoke of rejecting a commission in the infantry in a letter to C.T., Sept. 16, 1864; his remarks about being a

"buckeye" and "doing Gods will," Nov. 27, 1864; his remark about "future calculations," Jan. 30, 1865; the fact of his being Battery E's company clerk, Oct. 27, 1864. All, Album.

20. A Matter of Viewpoint

1. Casson to C.T., May 28, 1864, Album.
2. Prentice to C.T., June 5, 1864, Album.
3. Casson to C.T., Mar. 12, 1864, Album.
4. The incidents described in the Second Red River Campaign are an amalgam of William E. Jones, *The Military History of the One Hundred & Sixty-first New-York Volunteers, Infantry, from August 15th, 1862, to October 17th, 1865* (Bath, N.Y.: Hull & Barnes, 1865), 22–32; Casson to C.T., May 28, 1864, and three letters, Prentice to C.T., Mar. 10, Apr. 21, and June 18, 1864–all, Album.
5. OR, series 1, vol. 34, part 1, 221. Rear Admiral David D. Porter's official report cited Prentice and the 161st.

21. The Price of Success

1. Orr to C.T., Apr. 5, 1864, Album.
2. Orr to C.T., Feb. 16, 1864, Album.
3. Boatner, *Dictionary*, 30.
4. Orr to C.T., Apr. 5, 1864, Album.
5. Richard A. Sauers, *45th Infantry*, Advance the Colors: Pennsylvania Civil War Battle Flags (Harrisburg: Capitol Preservation Commission, 1987), 121.
6. Scudder's remarks are from an amalgam of two letters to C.T., Dec. 24, 1861, and May 12, 1862. Both, Album.
7. Boatner, *Dictionary*, 192.
8. Ibid., 165.
9. Bates, 2: 1068.

22. Politics and Pretense

1. Prentice to C.T., Oct. 25, 1863, Album.
2. Self to C.T., Sept. 16, 1864, Album.
3. Self to C.T., Jan. 20, 1863, Album.
4. Self to C.T., June 10, 1864, Album.
5. Self to C.T., Oct. 12, 1864, Album.
6. Ibid.
7. Self to C.T., Sept. 16, 1864, Album.
8. Orr to C.T., Apr. 5, 1864, Album.
9. Orr's remarks about Copperheads and New York politicians are an amalgam of two letters to C.T., Aug. 23 and Dec. 4, 1863. Both, Album.
10. Armstrong's remarks about Copperheads are an amalgam of two letters to C.T., April 11, 1863, and Jan. 14, 1864. Both, Album.
11. Prentice's remarks about Copperheads and Greeley are an amalgam of two letters to C.T., Oct. 25, 1863, and June 18, 1864. Both, Album.
12. Scudder to C.T., Mar. 3, 1863, Album.
13. Orville Kimball to C.T., Apr. 2, 1864, Album.
14. Orville Kimball to C.T., July 15, 1864, Album. Kimball's letter is also quoted in Tubbs, 26–27, where it is heavily edited for mistakes in spelling and grammar.
15. O.R., series 1, vol. 35, part 1, 78–79.

16. Self's remarks about the fighting on the Weldon Railroad and about Grant are an amalgam of two letters to C.T., Sept. 16 and Oct. 12, 1864. Both, Album.

23. Life on the Mississippi

1. Prentice to C.T., Jan. 6, 1865, Album.
2. Pension affidavit, Mar. 27, 1906, NA, RG94.
3. Except as otherwise noted, the story of Prentice's trip to White River Landing is from a letter from Prentice to C.T., July 27, 1864, Album.
4. Jones, *Military History*, 37.
5. Ibid., 37–38.
6. Prentice to C.T., Oct. 15, 1864, Album.
7. Prentice to C.T., Jan. 6, 1865, Album.

24. Adventures of a New Recruit

1. Andrews to C.T., Oct. 15, 1864, Album.
2. Andrews' background is an amalgam of newspaper obituaries, Personal File, Alumni Files, UC; Child, *Gazetteer*, 65–67; Decennial Register and University Commencements, AU; and NYSA. He referred to himself as "The Little Lieutenant" in a letter to C.T., Nov. 9, 1864, Album.
3. Andrews to C.T., Oct. 15, 1864, Album. Unless otherwise noted, descriptions of Andrews' trip to join the 179th New York, his experiences with it, and his witnessing of an execution of a deserter are all from this letter.
4. *History of the 179th Regiment NYSV* (Ithaca: E. D. Norton, 1900), 18.
5. Boatner, *Dictionary*, 192.
6. Scudder to C.T., Jan. 22, 1863, Album.
7. Self's comments on slackers are from two letters to C.T., one undated, which follows the letter of Mar. 25, 1862, the other Sept. 26, 1862. Both, Album.
8. Self to C.T., undated, Album. This letter is in the album before a letter dated Aug. 16, 1861.
9. E. B. Long, *The Civil War Day by Day: An Almanac 1861–1865* (New York: Doubleday, 1971), 714.
10. The story of Andrews' court-martial is from an account written by Thomas H. Fearey, class of 1863, Union College, Personal File, Alumni Files, UC.
11. Andrews to C.T., Nov. 9, 1864, Album. The lengthy description of the Battle of Burgess' Mill that follows is from this letter.
12. Ibid.
13. Ibid.
14. Long, *Civil War*, 594.
15. Andrews to C.T., Nov. 9, 1864, Album.

25. The Last Major Battles in the West

1. Vanzile to C.T., Nov. 18, 1864, Album.
2. Andrews to C.T., Nov. 9, 1864, Album.
3. Vanzile to C.T., Nov. 18, 1864, Album.
4. Vanzile to C.T., Oct. 27, 1864, Album.
5. Frederick H. Dyer, *A Compendium of the War of the Rebellion* (Dayton, Ohio: Morningside, 1979), 1482.
6. Vanzile to C.T., Nov. 18, 1864, Album.
7. Vanzile to C.T., Sept. 16, 1864, Album.

8. Vanzile's remarks about his commander are an amalgam of two letters to C.T., Oct. 27, 1864, and May 16, 1865. Both, Album.

9. Vanzile to C.T., Apr. 9, 1865, Album.

10. Except as noted, Vanzile's description of the actions at Franklin and Nashville are an amalgam of two letters to C.T., Nov. 18, 1864, and Jan. 3, 1865. Both, Album. The latter letter was actually dated 1864 by Vanzile, an obvious mistake, which Tubbs corrected by writing in pencil below his dateline the correct year, 1865.

11. Vanzile to C.T., May 16, 1865, Album.

12. Vanzile to C.T., Apr. 9, 1865, Album.

26. "The Bright Sunlight of Peace"

1. Orville Kimball to C.T., Nov. 25, 1864, Album.

2. Pension affidavit by Humphrey, Feb. 3, 1883, NA, RG94.

3. Tubbs, 29.

4. Transcript copy of service record of J. B. Sloan Post, No. 93, Grand Army of the Republic, Milo Town Clerk. The copy is in the possession of an Andrews descendant, Robert Winters of Highstown, N. J. Andrews joined the post Apr. 7, 1870. The commander was Brevet-Brigadier Gen. William W. Gregg.

5. NA, RG94. In the album, Tubbs gives Casson's rank as corporal.

6. Jones, *Military History,* 40–41.

7. Pension affidavit by Prentice, Mar. 27, 1906, NA, RG94.

8. Prentice to C.T., May 5, 1865, Album.

9. Self to C.T., June 10, 1864, Album.

10. Tubbs, 14–15. I have separated the long account into paragraphs. This letter does not exist, either edited or unedited, in the album. Tubbs does not identify who wrote it, but it is likely that it was written in the 1880s, when Tubbs sought out survivors of the Civil War in order to flesh out his account of Osceola in the war.

11. Tubbs, 15. Tubbs says erroneously—repeating a myth—that "Lee laid down his sword to Grant under the famous apple tree."

12. Vanzile to C.T., Apr. 9, 1865, Album.

13. Vanzile to C.T., May 16, 1865, Album.

14. Vanzile to C.T., July 16, 1865, Album.

15. Prentice to C.T., May 5, 1865, Album.

16. Ibid.

17. Orville Kimball to C.T., May 13, 1865, Album.

27. Homeward Bound

1. Orville Kimball to C.T., July 15, 1865, Album.

2. Dyer, *Compendium,* 1447.

3. Orville Kimball to C.T., Sept. 28, 1865, Album.

4. Orville Kimball to C.T., July 15, 1865, Album.

5. Jones, *Military History,* 49–50.

6. Saml. A. Mudd, M.D., to Capt. W. R. Prentice, Sept. 19, 1865, Personal File, AU. Mudd added, "With many regrets at your early withdrawal from the Chief Command of the Post and contemplated departure homeward—a pleasant trip—a happy future."

7. Arnold's appeal is based on the typescript of two letters, Sam B. Arnold to Capt. W. R. Prentice, Oct. 20 and Nov. 10, 1865, Personal File, AU. The October letter was accompanied by an Oct. 15, 1865, letter to Arnold from "Cap. and Provost Marshal"

Henry A. Harris noting Harris' "regret" at being "compelled to loose [*sic*]" Arnold's services as clerk. Harris wrote that "a higher authority has ordered me to discharge you from office." He also said that he had found Arnold "a good man and moral man, attentive to your calling and in every way honest deportment[,] gentleman[l]y and in every way have given full satisfaction."

8. Jones, *Military History*, 52–54.

9. Ibid., 51.

Epilogue: When the Colors Fade

1. Vanzile to C.T., July 16, 1865, Album.

2. Munsell, 352.

3. Tubbs, 34–39. In an entry, "Osceola Township," written by Charles Tubbs for Munsell's history of Tioga County, 353–55, Tubbs gave the figures as sixty-three having served in the war, and fourteen dead—six in action, one at Andersonville, and seven from disease. Presumably, after further research, he revised those figures for his own book, which was written a few years after the Munsell piece.

4. Ibid. Thirty-four of the Oceola men who served in the war were in the cavalry; thirty served in the infantry, and four in both infantry and cavalry. None was in the naval service or the artillery branch of the army. Four Osceola citizens furnished substitutes, none of whom came from the town. The substitutes were not included by Tubbs in his statistics.

5. Brown, 1: 248–49.

6. The original Bucktails, the 13th Pennsylvania, suffered total losses of 252 men—eleven officers and 151 enlisted men killed or mortally wounded, and two officers and 88 enlistees dead from disease, according to Dyer (*Compendium*, 1583).

7. On behalf of Self's children, William and Jennie, there are six undated Origin of Disability and pension affidavit applications—one of which is stamped received on May 5, 1884—submitted by, among others, William Humphrey. There are also personal affidavits from, among others, George Tubbs. His is dated June 25, 1880, NA, RG94.

8. Bates, 7: 318–34. Though the 136th Pennsylvania served only a year, it lost 26 men killed or mortally wounded, and 23 more from disease. Almost all those killed in combat as well as 28 men who were wounded were struck down during the Battle of Fredericksburg in December 1862. Brown (232–33) has Vanzile incorrectly listed as being in the 126th Pennsylvania.

9. Spencer's pension file, NA, RG94, includes a widow's application dated Jan. 9, 1892, submitted by Betsey, as well as a general affidavit and declaration submitted by her in the summer of 1900. The couple's daughter was named Gertrude. Betsey inherited the farm and rented it out. In initially applying for a widow's pension, she noted that she received a meager $130 a year from her tenants. The government awarded her $8 a month and later increased that to $12 a month, which she was receiving upon her death in January 1910 when she was in her late sixties.

10. Humphrey to C.T., Mar. 31, 1863. Humphrey said he would give Tubbs $550 to buy "the Vanzile House & lot" provided Tubbs immediately gave possession of it to his wife. She was to pay Tubbs $200 down, and Humphrey to pay $200 in June 1863 and the balance in August. Humphrey said he had expected to buy the "Beagle House" but had not heard from its owner.

11. Pension application, Feb. 3, 1883, and General Affidavit submitted by Humphrey, stamped Jan. 3, 1884, NA, RG94.

12. Cemetery Records, Fairview Cemetery, Cowanesque Valley, TCHS.

13. Widows' Application for Accrued Pension, Aug. 5, 1897, NA, RG94. May

Humphrey was receiving a pension of $17 at the time of her death in November 1912, aged sixty-seven. Humphrey's three children were Gertrude, Jennie, and Wilmot. The last also became a doctor.

14. Prentice to C.T., May 5, 1865, Album.
15. Prentice to C.T., Oct. 15, 1864, Album.
16. An heir donated to Alfred University two swords and three bayonets that Prentice brought back from the war (*Alfred Reporter*, 4, no. 3, [June 1980], AU). It is also likely that it was Prentice who returned home with the unusual newspaper, *The Natchitoches Union*, that was evidently given to Charles Tubbs and subsequently handed over, together with the album of letters, to the Andrews family. As Chaplain Jones explained in his history of the 161st New York, "some enterprising Yankee soldier, with a corps of assistants, took possession" of a vacated newspaper printing office and issued the newspaper. It was printed on the glued side of scraps of wallpaper. The newspaper is dated April 4, 1864, and identifies its editor as Lt. Thos. Hughes, a supporter of the Lincoln-Johnson ticket. Articles include stories about escaped Union prisoners, the murder of a soldier from Iowa by "a citizen," an account of "Rebel Brutality" against Union prisoners in Texas, the latest news from the various battle fronts, and items of interest about Natchitoches. Jones said the demand for the newspaper "was far greater than the supply" (Jones, *Military History*, 24).

17. Declaration for Original Invalid Pension, Mar. 27, 1906, and pension applications, Mar. 27 and June 5, 1906, NA, RG94.
18. Dyer, *Compendium*, 1439.
19. Maxson to C.T., Apr. 15, 1862, Album.
20. Pension application, June 4, 1877; Inability Affidavit, Apr. 17, 1891, and Pension Claim, undated, NA, RG94. It is unclear whether Maxson received a pension when he applied in 1877 and 1891. His wife, Olive, received a widow's pension—how much is not recorded—before she died in December 1928 at the age of eighty-three. The couple's three sons were Ira, born 1870, who also became a doctor; William, 1883; and Albert, 1887.
21. Declaration for Invalid Pension, July 28, 1890; Standard Certificate of Death, Apr. 10, 1911; Declaration for Widow's Pension, May 11, 1911, NA, RG94. OR series 3, vol. 5, 896, says Van Orsdale served on a draft board as a commissioner from Oct. 7, 1864 to May 8, 1865.
22. Pensioner Dropped form, Aug. 5, 1915, NA, RG94. Van Orsdale's wife, Sarah, who received a widow's pension of $12 a month, died in June 1915 when she was sixty-nine. Their son, Edward, was born in 1871.
23. Jordan, *Genealogical and Personal History*, 2: 812.
24. Affidavits by Dr. William Humphrey, Jan. 22, 1869; Capt. Henry Baldwin, Mar. 15, 1869; Clark Kimball, Apr. 7, 1869; Dr. H. C. Bosworth, Apr. 8, 1869; and pension application, Leverne L. Kimball [*sic*], Dec. 26, 1890, NA, RG94.
25. Cemetery Records, Fairview Cemetery, Cowanesque Valley, TCHS. Leonard Kimball's wife, Julia, died in 1926, when she was seventy-eight. The couple's children were Hannah, born 1867; Irving, 1868; Clark, 1872; Clara, 1875; Eva, 1877; and Mary Faith, 1884.
26. Robert S. Harper, *Ohio Handbook of the Civil War* (Columbus: Ohio Historical Society, 1961), 62. Armstrong's regiment, the 49th Ohio, served another year after his discharge. It lost 202 men in battle, 161 to disease.
27. Armstrong to C.T., July 14, 1864, Album.
28. Pension records, NA, RG94. The couple's children were Mary, born 1869, and Charles, born 1876. Armstrong's widow, Josephine, died in the spring of 1933, when she was eighty-eight years old. She was receiving a widow's pension of $40 a month.

29. Dyer, *Compendium*, 1470. During the less than fourteen months that the 179th New York was in the field with the Army of the Potomac, it lost 186 men—seven officers and 61 enlisted men in battle, 118 to disease. However, *History of the 179th Regiment* says the regiment lost 191 men, but its figures of those killed add up to 186. It also says that twenty-five of those who died of disease were prisoners "in the hands of the enemy" (5).

30. Obituary clippings, Personal File, Alumni Files, UC. Andrews' surviving sons were Edwin, Charles, and Clarence. Edwin was with Andrews when he suffered the stroke. The National Archives has no pension file for him, probably because he never applied for one. Andrews was well-to-do and evidently felt no need for a pension.

31. Vanzile's ambivalence and indecisiveness about his future is an amalgam of two letters to C.T., May 16 and July 16, 1865. Both, Album.

32. Annual Report, 1902–3, 31, AU.

33. Dyer, *Compendium*, 1485.

34. Pension applications, Jan. 11, 1892, and Jan. 18, 1915, NA, RG94. Vanzile's children who survived were Hortense, born in 1868, and Donald, 1885.

35. Annual Report, 1902–3, 31, AU.

36. U.S. Census, 1870, Charlotte, Eaton County, Mich.

37. Bureau of Pensions, Dec. 23, 1921, NA, RG94. Vanzile's wife, Lizzie, lived to be seventy-eight years old, dying three days after the fourth anniversary of his death in 1921.

38. Dyer, *Compendium*, 1447. In all, the 107th New York lost 222 men—four officers and 87 enlisted soldiers in battle, 131 others to disease. Orr's promotions were directly linked to the fortunes of another officer in the regiment, John F. Knox (vol. 34, 119, NYAG). Each time Knox was promoted, Orr rose a notch behind him. He became a captain when Knox, then a captain and the company's commander, died at Dallas, Georgia, in the same battle in which Orr was wounded.

39. Declaration for Original Invalid Pension, Aug. 12, 1879; pension affidavit signed by George G. Ruggles, Sept. 29, 1880; and pension application, stamped received Feb. 18, 1907, NA, RG94. Orr's children were Horace, born 1868; Hortense, 1871, and John, 1873. His wife, Melissa, died in April 1919.

40. Dyer, *Compendium*, 196. The 103rd New York lost 168 men—five officers and 61 enlisted killed or mortally wounded, two officers and 100 to disease.

41. Brown, 2: 922. Orville Kimball's other children were Ida Grace and Bessie May.

42. Tubbs, 42. Orville Kimball joined the group—Alfred J. Sofield Post, No. 49, Department of Pennsylvania, Grand Army of the Republic, on Feb. 8, 1876. Humphrey joined Feb. 18, 1875, "Leverne L." Kimball on Mar. 15, 1882.

43. Jordan, *Genealogical and Personal History*, 2: 813. Orville Kimball later transferred to Westfield's G.A.R. post when he moved to that town.

44. Ibid.

45. Cemetery Records, Fairview Cemetery, Cowanesque Valley, TCHS. Orville Kimball's wife, Mary, lived until 1942, dying when she was almost ninety-seven years old.

46. Pension applications, Mar. 4, 1895, and December 1923 (no day given); physician's affidavits, Dr. Bernard B. Israel, Mar. 14 and Apr. ll, 1924; personal affidavit, Mordecai Casson, Apr. 11, 1924; attendant's affidavit, Eugene Volin, Nov. 24, 1926, NA, RG94. Drop Report–Pensioner, Jan. 12, 1927, says Casson died "about Dec 21 1926."

47. Unless otherwise noted, the biographical material about Charles Tubbs is from clippings, Personal File, Alumni Files, UC. The material includes a photocopy of Tubbs' entry in *Who's Who in Pennsylvania*, 2d ed., 571.

48. Munsell, 363–64, and Jordan, *Genealogical and Personal History*, 2: 671–73.

49. Stebbins to C.T., Mar. 6, 1862, Album.
50. Tubbs, 3–4.
51. Cemetery Records, Fairview Cemetery, Cowanesque Valley, TCHS.
52. Personal File, Alumni Files, UC. The friend who wrote the commemoration was George Merrick. He evidently was a fellow lawyer.

Appendix A

1. Self to C.T., Sept. 16, 1864, Album.
2. Leonard Kimball to C.T., Feb. 28, 1862, Album.
3. Self to C.T., June 10, 1864, Album.

Appendix B

1. The poem, "Lines," by Leonard Kimball, is affixed in the album after the last of his letters to C.T., Album. It is undated.

Notes

1. Orr to C.T., Apr. 5, 1864, Album.

Bibliography

1. Stebbins to C.T., Mar. 28, 1862, Album.

Bibliography

But good night I must close,—from an ignorant Sol-
dier on the Southern battle field, written upon old
Mother earth by the light of a camp fire to an educated
Student in the classic halls of the North,—from an
everlasting friend to a true friend,—

—*Orrin Stebbins*[1]

Manuscripts

Herrick Memorial Library, Special Collections, Alfred University, Alfred, N.Y.
   Alfred Academy and University Commencements
   Alumni Files
   General Catalogues, 1836–1900
   Organizations
   Presidential Papers
National Archives, Washington, D.C.
   Record Group 94: Records of Volunteer Union Soldiers Who Served during
      the Civil War
New York State Archives
   War Service Records
Schaffer Library, Union College, Schenectady, New York
   Alumni Files
Tioga County Historical Society, Wellsboro, Pennsylvania
   Cemetery Records, Fairview Cemetery, Cowanesque Valley
   Personal Files
   Tioga County, Pennsylvania Records
Veterans Administration, Regional Office, Washington, D.C.
   U.S. Civil War Records

Books, Articles, and Addresses

Aldrich, Lewis Cass. *History of Yates County, New York.* Syracuse: D. Mason,
   1892.

Bard, John P. "42d Regiment Infantry (Thirteenth Reserves, First Rifles)." In *Pennsylvania at Gettysburg: Ceremonies at the Dedication of the Monuments.* Harrisburg: Harrisburg Publishing, 1906.

Bates, Samuel P. *History of Pennsylvania Volunteers, 1861–5.* Vols. 1–2. Wilmington, N.C.: Broadfoot Publishing, 1993–94.

Berger, Diana S. "In the Name of Pennsylvania Charge!" *Civil War: The Magazine of the Civil War* 17 (1989): 16–21.

Bierce, Ambrose. *An Occurrence at Owl Creek Bridge and Other Stories.* London: Penguin, n.d.

Boatner, Mark Mayo, III. *The Civil War Dictionary.* New York: David McKay, 1962.

Bowman, John S. *Who Was Who in the Civil War.* Avenel, N.J.: Crescent Books, 1995.

Brock, R.A., ed. *Southern Historical Society Papers.* Richmond, Va.: Southern Historical Society, 1893.

"Bucktail Images: Keystone Riflemen in the Collection of Ronn Palm." *Military Images* 8, no. 6 (May–June 1987): 27–29.

Chapin, L.N. *A Brief History of the Thirty-Fourth Regiment N.Y.S.V.* N.p., n.d. (c. 1902).

Child, Hamilton. *Gazetteer and Business Directory of Chemung and Schuyler Counties, N.Y., for 1868–9.* Syracuse: *Journal,* 1868.

———. *Gazetteer and Business Directory of Steuben County, N.Y. for 1868–9.* Syracuse: *Journal,* 1868.

Company of Military Historians. *Military Uniforms in America.* Vol. 3, *Long Endure: The Civil War Period, 1852–1867.* Novato, Calif.: Presidio Press, 1982.

Curtin, John I. "Forty-fifth Pennsylvania Veteran Volunteers Infantry." In *Pennsylvania at Antietam: Ceremonies at the Dedication of the Monuments.* Harrisburg: Harrisburg Publishing, 1906.

Dornbusch, C. E. *Regimental Publications & Personal Narratives of the Civil War: A Checklist.* New York: New York Public Library, 1962.

Dyer, Frederick H. *A Compendium of the War of the Rebellion.* Dayton, Ohio: Morningside, 1979.

Harper, Robert S. *Ohio Handbook of the Civil War.* Columbus: Ohio Historical Society, 1961.

History of Alfred, New York. Alfred, N.Y.: Alfred Historical Society and Baker's Bridge Association, 1990.

History of the 179th Regiment NYSV. Ithaca, New York: E. D. Norton, 1900.

History of Tioga County[,] Pennsylvania. New York: W. W. Munsell, 1883.

History of Tioga County, Pennsylvania. Vols. 1–2. N.p.: R. C. Brown, 1897.

Hoffsommer, Robert D. "The Pennsylvania Bucktails." *Civil War Times Illustrated* 4 (Jan. 1966): 16–21.

Imhof, John D. "Two Roads to Gettysburg: Thomas Leiper Kane and the 13th Pennsylvania Reserves." *Gettysburg* 9 (July 1993): 53–60.

Jones, William E. *The Military History of the One Hundred & Sixty-first New-York Volunteers, Infantry, from August 15th, 1862, to October 17th, 1865.* Bath, N.Y.: Hull & Barnes, 1865.

Jordan, John W., ed. *Genealogical and Personal History of Northern Pennsylvania.* Vols. 2–3. New York: Lewis Historical Publishing, 1913.

Kimball, Orville Samuel. *History and Personal Sketches of Company I, 103 N.Y.S.V., 1862–1865.* Elmira, N.Y.: Facts Printing, 1900.

Long, E. B. *The Civil War Day by Day: An Almanac 1861–1865.* New York: Doubleday, 1971.

MacDonald, John. *Great Battles of the Civil War.* New York: Collier, 1992.

Malone, Dumas, ed. *Dictionary of American Biography,* Vol. 9. New York: Charles Scribner's Sons, 1964.

Matthews, Richard E. "The Jackson Guards: Company C, 149th Pennsylvania Infantry at Gettysburg." *Military Images* 8, no. 6 (May–June 1987): 16–25.

———. *The 149th Pennsylvania Volunteer Infantry Unit in the Civil War.* Jefferson, N.C.: McFarland, 1994.

Medical and Surgical History of the Civil War. 12 Vols. Wilmington, N.C.: Broadfoot Publishing, 1990. Originally published as *Medical and Surgical History of the War of the Rebellion (1861–1865).* Washington: Government Printing Office, 1870–1888.

Miller, William J. "The Bloody Road to Spotsylvania: Pennsylvania Bucktails, Part Two." *Civil War Regiments* 1, no. 3: 28–51.

———. "No One Doubted Colonel Charles F. Taylor's Capabilities—or His Courage under Fire." *America's Civil War* (July 1989): 10, 54–55.

Minutes of the Reunion Meetings of the Surviving Members of Company D, 149th Pennsylvania Volunteers. N.p., n.d. (c. 1905).

New York State Adjutant General's Office. *Registers of New York Regiments in the War of the Rebellion.* Vols. 7, 22, 30, 34, 40. Albany: Wynkoop, Hallenbeck, Crawford; J. B. Lyon; Oliver A. Qualyle, 1896–1904.

Norwood, John Nelson. *Fiat Lux: The Story of Alfred University.* Alfred, N.Y.: Alfred University, 1957.

Official Roster of the Soldiers of the State of Ohio in the War of the Rebellion, 1861–1866. Cincinnati: Ohio Valley Company, 1889.

Papers and Proceedings of the Tioga County Historical Society. Part 1, vol. 2. Wellsboro, Pa.: Advocate Print, 1909.

Reid, Whitelaw. *Ohio in the War: Her Statesmen[,] Generals and Soldiers.* Vol. 2, Columbus: Eclectic Publishing, 1893.

Roberts, Robert B. *Encyclopedia of Historic Forts.* New York: MacMillan, 1988.

Sandburg, Carl. *Abraham Lincoln.* 4 vols. New York: Harcourt, Brace, 1939.

Sauers, Richard A. *42nd Infantry (13th Reserves).* Advance the Colors: Pennsylvania Civil War Battle Flags. Harrisburg: Capitol Preservation Commission, 1987.

———. *45th Infantry.* Advance the Colors: Pennsylvania Civil War Battle Flags. Harrisburg: Capitol Preservation Commission, 1987.

———. *136th Infantry.* Advance the Colors: Pennsylvania Civil War Battle Flags. Harrisburg: Capitol Preservation Commission, 1991.

———. *149th Infantry.* Advance the Colors: Pennsylvania Civil War Battle Flags. Harrisburg, Capitol Preservation Commission, 1991.

Sexton, John L. *An Outline History of Tioga County, Pennsylvania.* Reprint. Wellsboro, Pa.: Tioga County Historical Society, n.d.

Sword, Wiley. "Capt. James Glenn's Sword and Pvt. J. Marshall Hill's Enfield in the Fight for the Lutheran Seminary." *Gettysburg* 8 (Jan. 1993): 9–16.

Sypher, J. R. *History of the Pennsylvania Reserve Corps.* Lancaster, Pa.: Elias Barr, 1865.

Tubbs, Charles. *Osceola in the War of the Rebellion.* Wellsboro, Pa.: Agitator Book and Job Print, 1885.

Tuttle, William H. *Names and Sketches of the Pioneer Settlers of Madison County[,] New York.* Interlaken, N.Y.: Heart of the Lakes Publishing, 1984.

Utley, Robert, and Wilcomb E. Washburn. *The American Heritage History of the Indian Wars.* New York: American Heritage, 1977.

War of the Rebellion: A Compilation of the Official Records of the Union and Confederate Armies. Washington: U.S. Government Printing Office, 1880–1901.

Index

Adams, Charles F., 109

Alabama: Bridgeport, 178; Cedar Point, 166; Fort Morgan, 166; Mobile, 66, 166, 186, 187, 190; 2nd Veteran Cavalry raiding in, 186

Alexandria (La.), 147, 151, 152

Alfred University, xvi

Amputations, 43

Anderson, Robert, 9

Anderson Life Guards, 9, 10

Andrews, Arville Raplee, 199

Andrews, Charles Tubbs, 199

Andrews, John Tuttle, 169–70, 170 (fig.); arrest for communicating with enemy, 174; on battle, 1; on Burgess' Mill battle, 174–76; children of, 199, 232n. 30; court-martial faced by, 178; death of, 200; on execution of a deserter, 172–73; in Grand Review of the Army of the Potomac, 191; joins 179th Regiment New York Volunteer Infantry, 169; lack of preparation of, 171–72; life after the war, 199–200; on Lincoln's reelection prospects, 176; marriage of, 199; mustered out of the service, 199; in New York Assembly, 199; number of letters to Tubbs, 211; rank and unit, xxi; on Tubbs as perfectionist, xvi; at Union College, 169; on Vanzile, 178; in Virginia in early 1865, 186

Andrews, Peter C., 210

Antietam, Battle of, 61, 84, 87–91

Appomattox Court House (Va.), 188

Arkansas: White River Landing, 164, 167

Armstrong, David, 31–32, 32 (fig.); asks Tubbs about eligible girls, 49, 52; on blacks, 101, 104–5; on Buell, 61; at Chickamauga, 129; children of, 199, 232n. 28; on conditions at "Camp Lu-

natic," 64; as cook for officers, 118–19, 142; death of, 199; deciding whether to reenlist, 142–43; on Emancipation Proclamation, 105; at end of 1862, 92; and Fremont, Ohio, visit, 137; on Grant, 65; on his versatility, 117; impaired health of, 195; joins 49th Regiment Ohio Volunteers, 31; life after the war, 199; on the march to Nashville, 65–66; marriage of, 199; on McCook and Rosecrans, 60; at Missionary Ridge, 129; number of letters to Tubbs, 211; ordered from the skirmish line, 141, 142–43; on the Peace Democrats, 160; rank and unit, xxi; on relationships between soldiers, 52; as semiliterate, 31–32; at Shiloh, 67, 68; at Stones River, 96–97; in Tennessee, 95–97; on Tubbs not volunteering for the war, xvii

Armstrong, Josephine Hollinger, 199, 231n. 28

Army life. *See* Military life

Army medicine. *See* Military medicine

Army of Northern Virginia: at Appomattox Court House, 188; at Bristoe Station, 132–33; at Cold Harbor, 156; in early 1865, 185; Pennsylvania invaded by, 119, 120; at the Wilderness, 155–56. *See also* Lee, Robert E.

Army of the Cumberland, 95, 119, 154, 179

Army of the Potomac: at Appomattox Court House, 188; at Bristoe Station, 132–33; Burnside becomes commander of, 92; camping on Chickahominy River, 158; at Camp Pierpont, 34; casualties at Antietam of, 90; at Chancellorsville, 117; at Cold Harbor, 156;

239

INDEX · 243

Johnson, Reverdy, 108
Johnson, Richard W., 96
Johnston, Albert Sidney, 68, 69
Johnston, Joseph E., 154, 191
Jones, Lizzie A., 200, 232n. 37
Jones, William E., 147, 149, 166, 186, 193

Kane, Thomas, 10, 22, 80, 120
Kane's Rifle Regiment. *See* 13th Pennsylvania Reserves
Kentucky: Columbus, 167; Grant's expedition to, 56; Lawrenceburg, 95; Mill Springs, 56
Kimball, Clarissa Cilley, 11
Kimball, Clark, 11, 39
Kimball, Hannah Whittemore, 39
Kimball, Harlan Page, 39, 40–41; on blacks, 103; death of, 128; discharged from the service, 118; joins 103rd Regiment New York Volunteer Infantry, 39; number of letters to Tubbs, 211; rank and unit, xxi; on southerners and the South, 75–77
Kimball, Julia, 198–99, 231n. 25
Kimball, Leonard Leverne, 14 (fig.); on camp routine, 11–13; children of, 199, 231n. 25; death of, 199, 218n. 19; discharged, 43–44; first name of, 218n. 19; in Grand Army of the Republic, 201, 232n. 42; and half-brothers Orville and Harlan, 39, 220n. 2; impaired health of, 198; joins emergency regiment for Gettysburg, 120, 123; joins 34th Regiment New York Volunteer Infantry, 11; as law student, 11, 218n. 20; life after the war, 198–99; marriage of, 198–99; number of letters to Tubbs, 211; rank and unit, xxi; reenlistment of, 185–86, 198; on Tubbs' patriotism, xvi
Kimball, Mary Cameron, 201, 232n. 45
Kimball, Orville Samuel, 39–40, 40 (fig.), 201 (fig.); administrative duties taken on by, 186; at Antietam, 88–89; on blacks, 103, 105–6, 191; boredom while on Cape Hatteras, 76; on Burnside, 60; children of, 201, 232n. 41; death of, 202; disability of, 202; in Grand Army of the Republic, 201–2, 232n. 42; at Harpers Ferry, 110–11; homesickness of, 48–49; in James Is-

land attack, 161–62; joins 103rd Regiment New York Volunteer Infantry, 39; on Harlan Kimball's health, 41; as justice of the peace, 201; life after the war, 201–2; on Lincoln's assassination, 190; Lincoln supported by, 161; marriage of, 201; mustered out of the service, 201; number of letters to Tubbs, 211; on prospects for victory in early 1865, 185; rank and unit, xxi; on Reconstruction, 191–92; reenlists, 141–42; in siege of Forts Wagner and Johnson, 127–28; in South Carolina in 1863, 132; on southerners and the South, 75–77; on view of Washington from Camp Richardson, 110
Kimball, Richard, 11
Knights of the Golden Circle, 115
Knox, John F., 232n. 38

Lawrenceburg (Ky.), 95
Leave, 64
Lee, Albert Lindley, 147, 148
Lee, Robert E.: John Brown's raid suppressed by, 110; as Commander-in-Chief, 185; at Fredericksburg, 93, 95; at Gaines' Mill, 79; and losses at Cold Harbor, 157; Pennsylvania invaded by, 119; retreat from Gettysburg, 123; Richmond saved by, 82; at South Mountain, 85; surrender at Appomattox Court House, 188. *See also* Army of Northern Virginia
Light Battalion, 119
Lincoln, Abraham: army's support for, 176, 177 (fig.); assassination of, 190, 192; black regiments curtailed by, 105; and the Copperheads, 160; and Emancipation Proclamation, 104; Grant appointed supreme commander by, 154; last call for volunteers, 185; dismisses McClellan as General-in-Chief, 66–67; New York City voting against, 160; orders federal armies to advance, 57; on the purpose of the war, 15; reelection of, 176; renomination of, 159; reviews the Bucktails, 24; Spencer at public levee of, 109; takes command during McClellan's illness, 56; at Union demonstration, 109

Natchitoches Union, 231n. 16
New Berne (N.C.), 65, 75
New Hope Church, Battle of, 155
New Iberia (La.), 136
New Orleans (La.), 30, 66, 137
New York City, 160
New York State: 85th Regiment New
  York Volunteer Infantry, 33, 69–71, 82,
  197; 145th New York, 154; 34th Regi-
  ment New York Volunteer Infantry,
  11, 13, 44, 128. *See also* 103rd Regi-
  ment New York Volunteer Infantry;
  107th Regiment New York Volunteer
  Infantry; 161st Regiment New York
  Volunteer Infantry; 179th Regiment
  New York Volunteer Infantry; 2nd
  Veteran Cavalry, New York Volunteers
Norfolk (Va.), 66
North Carolina: Burnside's expedition
  to, 56; Cape Hatteras, 75–76; New
  Berne, 65, 75; 103rd Regiment New
  York Volunteer Infantry, 75; Pamlico
  Sound, 56, 65; Roanoke Island, 65;
  Wilmington, 185

officers: arousing soldiers' ire, 60–61;
  conditions compared to those of the
  men, 16, 64; drunkenness among, 146;
  employing black servants, 102 (fig.),
  104
Ohio: 1st Light Artillery Ohio Volunteers, 145, 178–82, 186, 200; Xenia,
  133. *See also* 49th Regiment Ohio
  Volunteers
O'Laughlin, Michael, 192
103rd Regiment New York Volunteer Infantry, 39; at Antietam, 88; in Army of
  the Cumberland, 154; in Atlanta campaign, 154–55; black troops taking
  revenge on rebel prisoners of, 105–6;
  and Burnside, 60; at Harpers Ferry,
  110; illness in, 77; in James Island attack, 161–62; in North Carolina, 75;
  145th New York consolidated with,
  154; in Virginia in early 1865, 186
107th Regiment New York Volunteer Infantry: at Antietam, 87–88; at Chancellorsville, 117; at Gettysburg, 122; in
  Grand Review, 191; at Johnston's surrender, 191; losses to, 232n. 38; Orr
  joins, 45; in Tennessee in 1863, 133–35

136th Regiment Pennsylvania Volunteers: at Antietam, 88–90; at Chancellorsville, 118; in defense of Washington,
  85; at Frederick, 73; at Fredericksburg,
  230n. 8; losses of, 230n. 8; Spencer
  joins, 47
145th New York, 154
149th Regiment Pennsylvania Volunteer
  Infantry, 121
150th Regiment Pennsylvania Volunteer
  Infantry, 121
161st Regiment New York Volunteer Infantry: at Alexandria, 147, 151; to
  Baton Rouge, 47; at Bayou La Fourche, 125–26; camp life in, 53; at Cedar
  Point, 166; at Columbus, 167; dam-
  ming the Red River, 151–52; as down
  to half strength, 113; to Fort Jefferson,
  192; losses to, 167–68, 193; in Louisiana in 1863, 135–37; at Mansfield,
  147–50; to Memphis after Forrest, 167;
  at Mobile, 186, 187; Prentice joins, 45–
  46; raiding in Mississippi Valley, 167;
  returns to Elmira, 193; at Sabine Pass,
  126–27; in Shenandoah Valley, 164; in
  skirmishing following Mansfield, 150–
  51; in steamboat accident, 186–87; at
  Vicksburg, 113; watches attack on Fort
  Morgan, 166; at White River Landing,
  164, 167
179th Regiment New York Volunteer Infantry: Andrews joins, 169; at Burgess' Mill, 174–76; desertions from,
  172; as "Dunkirk Company," 171;
  losses to, 232n. 29; in Petersburg
  Campaign, 171–72
190th Pennsylvania Volunteers, 158,
  162–63, 176, 188
Orderly master clerk, 16
Orophilian Lyceum, xvi, 210
Orr, John, 45; at Antietam, 87–88; in Atlanta campaign, 154–55; on blacks,
  103–4, 105; on Chancellorsville, 117;
  children of, 200, 232n. 39; on the Copperheads, 159; death of, 200; deciding
  whether to reenlist, 143; on end of
  war, 123; at Gettysburg, 120, 122; in
  Grand Review, 191; on Grant, 155; on
  his regiment's condition, 117; joins
  107th New York Volunteer Infantry,
  45; life after the war, 200–201; Lincoln
  supported by, 159; marriage of, 45,